T0305043

REDEEMING LEADERSHIP

An Anti-Racist Feminist Intervention

Helena Liu

BRISTOL
UNIVERSITY
PRESS

First published in Great Britain in 2020 by

Bristol University Press
1-9 Old Park Hill
Bristol
BS2 8BB
UK
t: +44 (0)117 954 5940
www.bristoluniversitypress.co.uk

North America office:
c/o The University of Chicago Press
1427 East 60th Street
Chicago, IL 60637, USA
t: +1 773 702 7700
f: +1 773-702-9756
sales@press.uchicago.edu
www.press.uchicago.edu

British Library Cataloguing in Publication Data
A catalogue record for this book is available from the British Library

Library of Congress Cataloging-in-Publication Data
A catalog record for this book has been requested

ISBN 978-1-5292-0004-1 hardcover
ISBN 978-1-5292-0007-2 ePub
ISBN 978-1-5292-0005-8 ePdf

Cover design by Blu Inc
Front cover image: Library of Congress, LC-USW33-000890-ZC
(b&w film neg.)
Printed and bound in CPI Group (UK) Ltd, Croydon, CR0 4YY
Bristol University Press uses environmentally responsible
print partners

To my parents

Contents

Acknowledgements

This book was possible because of the generosity and kindness others have extended to me. I would like to express my gratitude first to my students who inspire me to be brave and give me hope that things will get better.

Thanks are also due to the industry and community partners who shared their stories and allowed me to analyse their experiences of leadership in my work. Although I cannot name them so that their anonymity may be preserved, their impact on my life has been indelible.

To BARC, my sisters in anti-racist feminist resistance, I thank you for your moral courage. Deborah Brewis, Sadhvi Dar and Angela Martinez Dy – with you I can be strong.

My dear friends, Sarrmila Balasubramaniam and Marianne Close, thank you for reading the first draft of my manuscript and generously providing your feedback. When the pain of dominator culture was too much, your friendship nourished me back to wholeness.

To Bristol University Press, especially my editor Paul Stevens and Caroline Astley-Brown, thank you for believing in this book and working tirelessly to bring it together.

I would also like to express my appreciation to my colleagues at the University of Technology Sydney for their warm collegiality and support. I'm indebted to the university for granting me a sabbatical that enabled me to travel through Malaysia and Singapore while writing this book.

My intellectual community has also offered encouragement and wisdom along the way. I thank Fahreen Alamgir, Wenjin Dai, Roshanthi Dias, Mei-fen Kuo, Lauren Gurrieri, Solange Hamrin and Anna Zueva. A writing retreat organized by Lara Owens in 2018 offered an idyllic respite where I was able to work on this book.

Thank you to my fellow members of Decolonizing Alliance and VIDA for challenging me to be a better scholar.

Finally, Benian Goh, thank you for always being by my side.

Introduction

An inhospitable world

In November 2016, the United States Republican nominee, Donald Trump, was elected to become the country's 45th President. The night that his victory was announced, former Ku Klux Klan (KKK) leader, David Duke, described the event as 'one of the most exciting nights of my life'.[1] Shortly after his inauguration, President Trump signed an executive order halting all refugee admissions and temporarily barring people from seven Muslim-majority countries from travel to the United States. Although the original order was forced to be rescinded after it met with immediate protests and severe criticism, the United States Supreme Court eventually upheld a moderated version of the ban that settled on immigration restrictions against people from Chad, Iran, Libya, Somalia, Syria and Yemen.

In the year leading up to Trump's election, Britain's vote to leave the European Union (Brexit) was steered by a campaign that relied heavily on anti-immigration rhetoric. In June 2016, Nigel Farage, the leader of the United Kingdom Independence Party (UKIP) at the time, issued a poster where 'BREAKING POINT' shrieked in red lettering across a photograph of thousands of refugees fleeing war and persecution in Slovenia in 2015, imploring voters that 'we must break free of the EU and take back control of our borders'. Although this poster, which bore a startling resemblance to an anti-Semitic Nazi campaign, was widely condemned by politicians, the message tapped

---

[1] David Duke expressed his excitement on his personal Twitter account, posting: 'This is one of the most exciting nights of my life -> make no mistake about it, our people have played a HUGE role in electing Trump! #MAGA' along with a photograph of Trump holding a thumbs up and wearing his iconic red 'Make America Great Again' cap https://twitter.com/drdavidduke/status/796249464826687488.

into an emotional undercurrent of nationalism flowing beneath this once voracious empire.

Enshrining figures like Trump and Farage in positions of power legitimized a virulent backlash to change.[2] At a white nationalist rally in August 2017, an attendee drove his car into a crowd of anti-fascist counterprotesters in Charlottesville, Virginia, fatally injuring social activist Heather Heyer. In his response, President Trump condemned what he described in his statement as 'hatred, bigotry and violence on many sides', generating the impression that he saw the white nationalists and anti-fascist counterprotesters as equally culpable in the violence.[3]

Following the Brexit vote, police statistics showed a significant increase in race-based hate crime including verbal abuse and death threats, physical assaults, arson attacks and stabbings. The targets of such attacks in the UK were primarily Eastern European migrants and Muslims.[4] Islamophobia meanwhile remains a firm feature in the United States. According to data released from the Federal Bureau of Investigation in November 2017, the number of hate crimes increased for a second consecutive year, with attacks targeting Muslim and Jewish people as well as LGBTQ people.[5]

The resurgence of far-right politics also appeared across Europe. France's right-wing nationalist party, Front National, which once touted a brazenly anti-Semitic image, received 21.3 per cent of the national vote in the first round of the country's presidential elections under its leader Marine Le Pen in April 2017, before losing the final round to centrist Emmanuel Macron in May.[6] Meanwhile, Germany's Alternative für Deutschland campaigned under anti-Islam policies,[7] as

---

[2]   CNN commentator, Van Jones, coined the term 'whitelash' following Trump's election. The exit poll data from Edison Research suggested that almost 60 per cent of all white voters chose Trump. In his live response, Jones expressed, 'this was a whitelash against a changing country, it was a whitelash against a black president in part. And that's the part where the pain comes' (see Carissimo, 2016).

[3]   Both Democratic and Republican politicians criticized Trump's refusal to explicitly rebuke white nationalists and neo-Nazis. Richard Spencer, one of the organizers of the white nationalist rally, interpreted Trump's ambiguous response in his movement's favour, tweeting 'Did Trump just denounce antifa[scists]?' while David Duke was less optimistic, tweeting that Trump should 'take a good look in the mirror & remember it was White Americans who put you in the presidency, not radical leftists'. A video of Trump's statement from 13 August 2017 can be seen on CNN (see Merica, 2017).

[4]   Burnett, 2017.

[5]   Federal Bureau of Investigation, 2017.

[6]   Schultheis, 2017.

[7]   Göpffarth, 2017.

did Austria's Freiheitliche Partei Österreichs, whose leader travelled to Trump Tower to celebrate the new US president after his election.[8] Although the other major parties have refused to work with the Sweden Democrats due to their fascist roots, the anti-immigration party rose to become the second largest at its peak in June 2017.[9] True Finns also joined the current coalition to become the second-largest party in parliament in 2015, but later split in 2017 with the election of Jussi Halla-aho, who was once fined for hate speech against Somali immigrants.[10]

Pauline Hanson first rose to Australian political prominence when she pronounced to the House of Representatives as a newly elected Member of Parliament that Australia's immigration policy needed to be reviewed and multiculturalism abolished as our country was 'in danger of being swamped by Asians'.[11] Although in the next two decades Hanson would come to represent a caricature of Australian racism, she returned as the leader of the One Nation party and later gained a seat in the Senate in 2016, proclaiming in her latest maiden speech: 'now we are in danger of being swamped by Muslims'.[12] In March 2019, an Australian man took such sentiments seriously and travelled to Christchurch, New Zealand and murdered 50 people at the Al Noor Mosque and the Linwood Islamic Centre in a brutal act of terrorism.

These examples whirling around international news are sometimes treated as aberrant expressions of extreme, far-right movements, but this backlash against a seemingly more diverse world has been building for some time. White racism has remained a legitimized and enduring feature in the United States since colonialism; a 'pervasively malignant and malicious systemic illness'.[13] The election of the country's first Black president instilled in many white Americans the fear and anger that 'their' country is leaving them behind. In countries like England and Australia, even the most conservative policies of liberal

---

[8] Mortimer, 2016.

[9] Anon, 2017a.

[10] Those who elected Jussi Halla-aho remain in the True Finns, while the former leader and ministers have started a new party called New Alternative (Milne, 2017). Halla-aho maintained a blog in 2008 that published anti-immigration and anti-Muslim pieces (Anon, 2012).

[11] Martino, 2016.

[12] Murphy, 2016.

[13] Yancy, 2018, p 1.

multiculturalism have seemed too radical for those who insist on the supreme dominance and dominion of whiteness.[14]

The romance of leadership under neoliberalism

I have recreated a picture of the current climate because leaders are not detached from their social and political contexts. Although business is ordinarily thought of as a 'neutral' activity, coolly estranged from societal debates around gender, sexuality, race, immigration and class in its impersonal pursuit for profit,[15] all evidence points to the contrary. As I will illustrate through this book, organizations and its leaders are inexorably entangled in wider systems of power and often reinforce the ideologies and practices of the status quo.

Donald Trump, Nigel Farage, Marine Le Pen and Pauline Hanson are all leaders; or at least what we would define as 'leaders' in dominant Anglo-American notions of that term. As is Harvey Weinstein, film producer and co-founder of the Weinstein Company, who was accused by over 50 women of allegations including sexual harassment, assault and rape over a span of three decades.[16] The employees at both the Weinstein Company and Weinstein's previous film studio, Miramax, recalled an abusive workplace where their leader's rampant bullying was normalized within a culture of fear.[17] The artistic director and principal conductor of London's Royal Philharmonic Orchestra, Charles Dutoit, also came under scrutiny. He was investigated after being accused by three opera singers and a classical musician of sexual assault that took place alongside rehearsals and performances on tour.[18] Meanwhile, the founding CEO of Wynn Resorts, Steve Wynn, allegedly engaged in repeated cases of sexual harassment and assault against his employees at his luxury hotels and casinos. His former employees describe an oppressive environment at work, where female employees resorted to hiding in the bathroom or back rooms when they learned he was on the premises.[19] As a personal friend of President Trump, Wynn was

---

[14] Bassel and Emejulu, 2018.

[15] Díaz García and Welter, 2011.

[16] *The New York Times* investigated Harvey Weinstein in October 2017 (Kantor and Twohey, 2017).

[17] Kirchgaessner and Ellis-Petersen, 2017.

[18] The *Associated Press* covered the story of Charles Dutoit (Gecker, 2017).

[19] *The Wall Street Journal* covered the story of Steve Wynn, seeking out interviews with over 150 current and former employees (Berzon et al, 2018).

appointed the Republican National Committee's finance chairman in January 2017.

A prevalent tendency when we hear about the cases of such leaders who perpetuate sexist or racist acts is that we think of them as deviant individuals – the so-called 'sexual predators' and 'white supremacists' who do not represent the majority of people who are 'good'. Within progressive circles, many white people hold firm to an image of themselves as respecting the values of diversity, inclusion and equality and never intentionally exerting violence on people based on their race, gender or any other aspects of their identity. The solution, therefore, is to quickly depose the malefactor and restore the unspoiled neutrality of business as usual.[20]

Leadership theorists have also been quick to defend 'leadership' against leaders. Few proponents appear to agree on what leadership is, yet many insist that it is inherently good and urgently needed. Since sociologist Max Weber articulated his concept of charismatic authority in the 1920s,[21] leadership has engaged in an enduring romance with great men who are believed to be vital to the success of organizations and societies.[22] This field of study has produced an unending series of venerations starting with the Weberian charismatic leaders before extending into 'visionary', 'transformational', 'authentic', 'spiritual' and 'wise' leaders over the last four decades. Leaders who are seen to commit gendered or racial assaults are dismissed as not 'true' leaders, thereby preserving the sacred status of leadership. Leadership, or so it seems, remains untouchable.

Such is the character of neoliberalism in our society where we disregard structures of inequality and histories of oppression, and reduce collective responsibilities onto the individual. Neoliberalism has come to define societies through market rationalities so that economic considerations take precedence over democratic values, social issues are

---

[20] This effect of over-attributing both successes and failures to leaders was first detailed in the now-classic theory on the 'romance of leadership' by management scholars James Meindl, Sanford Ehrlich and Janet Dukerich (1985). Their experiments showed that observers are prone to overestimating the control that senior managers exert over their organizations' fortunes while underplaying the external economic factors that influence organizational performance. Presciently, the authors suggested that 'the obsession with [leadership] will not easily be curtailed' (Meindl, Ehrlich and Dukerich, 1985, p 100).

[21] Weber, 1922.

[22] The association of leadership with masculinity remains an obstinate feature of our imaginary (Collinson and Hearn, 1996; Kerfoot and Knights, 1993; Lord, De Vader and Alliger, 1986; Mann, 1965; Sczesny, 2003).

translated into private matters and citizens are treated as customers.[23] Within this market-driven ethic, success is conferred onto the entrepreneurial subject; that is, those of us who learn to see ourselves as enterprise. As walking businesses, we are calculated and ambitious; we devise strategies, take risks, hide injuries and overcome weaknesses, and we resoundingly reject those who are not entrepreneurial.[24] The pursuit of change is curtailed from the societal sphere and redirected towards the self, as all social problems have become personal problems.[25] Accordingly, we treat racism and sexism as the symptoms of deviant attitudes and behaviours that are to be resolved by afflicted individuals via diversity training workshops or vigorous soul-searching.

Under neoliberalism, we have lost touch with our sociological imagination. Writing in 1959, C. Wright Mills asserted that the sociological imagination is what allows people to draw an 'intricate connection between the patterns of their own lives and the course of world history'.[26] It is a quality of mind that enables its possessor to constantly shift between the psychological and the political perspectives; drawing connections between the most intimate and most abstract areas of social life. To understand others and ourselves in the context of our social and political histories opposes neoliberal pressures to individuate and internalize social problems. An issue such as failing to go up for promotion that may have previously been seen as personal (that is, the solution would involve evaluating one's professional strengths and weaknesses, developing new skills or seeking out the advice of a mentor) can be recontextualized by considering structural issues such as how the ideal worker is understood in the organization; the opportunities that are made available (or unavailable) due to the organization's profit maximization strategies; and wider sociocultural ideas about who is more likely to be seen as having leadership potential, and who is not. Within a sociological imagination, our personal situations become indivisible from social structures.

---

[23] Giroux, 2003.

[24] Scharff, 2016.

[25] Neoliberalism gives rise to a culture of intense insecurity and fear (Giroux, 2003). As entrepreneurial subjects exhorted to see themselves as business, professionals often describe senses of heightened anxiety, overwork and competition with both themselves and others (McNay, 2009; Scharff, 2016). Meanwhile, it can also be exhilarating to imagine ourselves single-handedly realizing our professional success while accumulating material wealth and rewards. I recount my own experiences of being seduced into a neoliberal making of myself in *Organization* (Liu, 2019a).

[26] Mills, 2000, p 4.

At the same time, social structures permeate the most intimate aspects of our daily lives. Across far-right political movements is the notion that each country rightfully belongs to the white majority born (or settled) there. The installation of their representatives to power is taken by some as the affirmation that white power and its assumed set of cultural and legal protections would be restored.[27] The proponents of these movements have a tendency to construct their mission as correcting perceived historical wrongs (immigration, primarily) and now it is time to 'take their country back' or 'make their country great again'. In settler-colonial nations like my home of Australia, we invoke a convenient amnesia against the first act of illegal immigration and brandish this nativist rhetoric with disregard for the Indigenous custodians of the land.[28]

In taking a sociological view, we can see how these sentiments about rightful ownership percolate into organizations. Corporate activities around diversity management have been perceived by some workers as instruments of 'reverse discrimination', manifesting in overzealous preferential hiring practices where a woman or person of colour is said to have been chosen for a job that otherwise would have gone to a more qualified white man.[29] When understood within its sociological context, the rise of far-right politics is not the result of a few aberrant figures, but reveals instead a legacy rooted in centuries-old ideologies of race, gender and imperialism.

In the cases of Weinstein, Wynn and Dutoit, they persisted in their sexual harassment and assault for decades because their behaviours were largely normalized within a patriarchal system. Patriarchy

[27] Burnett, 2017.

[28] See *The White Possessive: Property, Power, and Indigenous Sovereignty* by Aileen Moreton-Robinson (2015).

[29] Sakile Camara and Mark Orbe's (2011) study of how individuals experience 'reverse discrimination' suggest that many people are ignorant about the foundation upon which diversity initiatives such as affirmative action are based, that is, systemic oppression and institutional racism. Both are intrinsic to the histories of white-dominated nations and have played a significant role in the oppression of non-white people. Yet many people continue to equate affirmative action with egregious acts of preferential hiring and college admissions that serve to disadvantage supposedly more deserving majority group members. Perceptions of reverse discrimination bear the assumptions that (1) all forms of discrimination are equally wrong; (2) discrimination against women and people of colour is an obsolete relic of the past; (3) neutral, meritocratic systems exist and even if structural advantage exists, the beneficiaries are innocent; and (4) sexist and racist attitudes are justifiable responses to 'reverse discrimination'. See also *Reverse Discrimination: Dismantling the Myth* by Fred Pincus (2003).

fashions women into objects for heterosexual male consumption, expects men to dominate women, and associates this domination with virility and strength. The victims repeatedly described being reluctant to make formal complaints due to a culture of fear, where professional retaliations against employees who speak out remained a very real possibility. When people overcame shame and intimidation to lodge complaints against such men, other senior members of the organizations often colluded in the protection of its leaders. The Orchestre Symphonique de Montréal, for example, admitted in January 2018 that it ignored harassment complaints against Dutoit by a number of its musicians in the 1990s.[30]

Redeeming leadership

The aim of this book is to critically interrogate leadership and reimagine how leadership may be exercised beyond domination and oppression. In this goal, the book is grounded in two fundamental tenets. The first tenet is that leadership is socially constructed. Tracing its lineage to Peter Berger and Thomas Luckman's *The Social Construction of Reality*, social constructionism focuses on how people develop shared understandings of the world that over time become reified into taken-for-granted realities.[31] Specifically, this view does not see leadership existing in any objective sense, but is concerned instead with how people characterize, negotiate and enact what they call 'leadership'. By extension, there is no core universal 'truth' of leadership to be discovered and our interest turns instead to the multiple realities that compete for legitimacy.[32] The social constructionist view of leadership is compelling because despite the preceding eight decades of research, we do not appear to be any closer to clarifying what leadership is. If anything, we have become more confused as proliferating prefixes of community-, shared-, peer-, thought- and self-leaderships have created the impression that virtually anything and everything now counts as leadership.[33]

The second tenet follows that the social construction of leadership is informed by power. The definitional vacuity of leadership means that it allows those with power to decide which interpretation of leadership

---

[30] The early complaints have been published by *Le Devoir* (Bourgault-Côté, Huss and Pineda, 2018). The Orchestre Symphonique de Montréal is conducting its own investigation. Charles Dutoit has denied all allegations against him.

[31] Berger and Luckmann, 1966.

[32] Fairhurst and Grant, 2010.

[33] Liu, 2018.

matters most. Critics have therefore argued that leadership is first and foremost a beautiful illusion created by theorists and practitioners to capture our desires and sell development programmes.[34] While leadership has indeed been profitable business, this critique could venture deeper into societal structures and histories. By interrogating the taken-for-granted ideas around what it means to be a 'leader' in our cultures, we can challenge the systems of power that underpin leadership and explore ways to resist the violences of leadership as it is defined and practised today.

And resistance against dominant power systems is already happening. On the same day Trump announced his executive order on the travel ban, thousands of protestors spontaneously gathered at airports and public spaces across the United States to appeal for the release of detained travellers.[35] Just a few days prior, on 21 January 2017, the Women's March on Washington brought together hundreds of thousands of demonstrators, all united against the new president and his political stance around issues such as immigration, civil rights, reproductive rights and climate change.[36] I gathered with a thousand people in Sydney that Sunday as a part of the 137 support marches that took place globally outside the United States. The abuses of film executives such as Harvey Weinstein prompted the revival of the #MeToo movement,[37] which leveraged social media to expose the systemic nature of sexual violence. One of the first steps out of the movement has been the formation of Time's Up, a collective of over

[34] In the last three decades, we have seen the rise of the field of Critical Leadership Studies (Collinson, 2011, 2014) to challenge the glorified constructions of leadership in our cultures (see, for example, Alvesson and Sveningsson, 2003a; Bligh, Kohles and Pillai, 2011; Boje and Rhodes, 2006; Collinson, 2005; Edwards et al, 2013; Grint, 2010a; Gronn, 2003; Jepson, 2010; Kelly, 2014; Śliwa et al, 2012; Sveningsson and Larsson, 2006; Tourish, 2013). Although critical scholars have demonstrated the positivist, individualist and psychologistic nature of existing theorizations of leadership, the field is dominated by voices from white-dominated nations in the Global North that do not always recognize the white supremacist dimensions of leadership. (For exceptions see Nkomo, 2011; Ospina and Su, 2009; Parker, 2005; Parker and ogilvie, 1996; Sinclair, 2007).

[35] Gambino et al, 2017.

[36] Hartocollis and Alcindor, 2017.

[37] The #MeToo movement of 2017 can trace its roots back to 2007 when social activist Tarana Burke used the phrase to build solidarity among survivors of sexual violence. On 15 October 2017, actor Alyssa Milano adopted the phrase as a Twitter hashtag to encourage survivors to expose and challenge the prevalence of sexual violence. The women behind the movement, including both Burke and Milano, were named as *TIME* magazine's Person of the Year in 2017 (Zacharek, Dockterman and Sweetland Edwards, 2017).

300 women working in Hollywood seeking to counter workplace sexism.[38] Time's Up looks to create legislation that will penalize organizations that tolerate persistent harassment, while funding a legal defence arm that provides working-class victims of sexual misconduct with legal assistance. The possibilities for resisting leadership are quite boundless, but they require a sociological imagination to conceptualize leadership beyond the confines of neoliberalism as well as the regimes of imperialism, white supremacy and patriarchy.

The struggles against contemporary racism and sexism flow from a global set of movements that have collectively taken many names, including multiracial feminism, decolonial feminism and women of colour feminisms.[39] These movements comprise Black, Indigenous, Latinx/Chicanx,[40] Middle Eastern and Asian feminists who speak from different positions and with different voices, they have emerged in their local contexts to interrogate the interlocking systems of racial, gender and imperial power.[41] In this book, I choose the term anti-racist feminisms,[42] which places our joint struggles against racial and gender oppression upfront. By using a collective term, I do not seek to erase the diverse interests, standpoints and intellectual traditions of specific movements or to suggest that they are somehow a homogenous collective. As anti-racist feminists do not speak with one voice, I present the ideas in this book as just one way leadership theorizing and practice could engage redemptively with difference.

Positionality and politics

These are strange times to be writing this book. Despite neoliberalism's efforts to asphyxiate sociopolitical critique in this supposedly postracial[43]

---

[38] Buckley, 2018.
[39] Baca Zinn and Thorton Dill, 1996; Lugones, 2010, 2014.
[40] The use of the 'x' suffix here is an alternative to 'Latina' and 'Chicana', which signify an identification with femaleness that not all these intellectuals share. Although some people find the 'x' inaccessible, I adopt it in order to acknowledge the contributions to Latina/o/x thought and activism by queer, gender non-conforming, and transgender people. For an essay on the use of the 'x', see 'Thinking About the "X"' by Jessica Marie Johnson (2015).
[41] Collins, 2000; hooks, 2003; Mohanty, 2003.
[42] I follow the example of Chandra Talpade Mohanty (2003; see also Mirchandani and Butler, 2006), first articulating this term in critique of critical management studies (Liu, 2017a), which inspired the proposal for this book.
[43] Postracialism refers to the idea that racism is largely a relic of the past. This sentiment was particularly prevalent in the United States, where its proponents felt that the election of the first African American president in 2009, Barack Obama, was the

and postfeminist[44] era, there has been a groundswell of grassroots efforts to dismantle the systems of power that sustain racial, gender and imperial domination. We are seeing the nature of feminist intellectualism and activism change through an ongoing 'intersectional' movement[45] that

proof that racism had ended. Where racism in the eras of slavery and Jim Crow were once extensive, the postracist argument goes that racism in our contemporary times has become episodic. So that while racism may exist, it is confined to the attitudes and behaviours of isolated individuals - 'the racists' - who can be charged and brought before the law, without really affecting the lives of people of colour. This reflects a neoliberal logic wherein social issues are individualized; not only in terms of the construction of deviant individuals, but also how a single high-profile African American will be upheld as the evidence that racism has been solved. The effect is that while racism continues to operate in more subtle, structural ways, the charges against racism are being silenced (for critiques of postracism see Ahmed, 2012; Bonilla-Silva, 2006; Lentin and Titley, 2011; Perry, 2011). One of the key manifestos of postracism is *The End of Racism* by Dinesh D'Souza (1995). D'Souza is a conservative commentator who pled guilty to campaign finance law violations in 2014, before being pardoned by Trump in May 2018. In an interview with *The New York Times*, D'Souza said of Trump that 'he said he just wanted me to be out there, to be a bigger voice than ever, defending the principles that I believe in' (Baker, 2018).

[44] Although it remains a contested term, postfeminism generally refers to an emerging gender regime that grafts feminist values such as freedom of choice, equality of opportunity and self-determination onto traditional patriarchal expectations around female sexuality, beauty and motherhood. Feminist organizational scholars Patricia Lewis, Yvonne Benschop and Ruth Simpson (2017, p 214) identified a set of recurring themes including 'an emphasis on individualism, choice and empowerment; the revival and reappearance of "natural" sexual difference; the shift from objectification to "voluntary" subjectification; the emphasis upon self-surveillance with constant monitoring and disciplining of women's bodies; the ascendancy of a make-over paradigm that not only acts on the body but also constitutes a remaking of subjectivity; the resexualisation of women's bodies; and the retreat to home as a matter of choice not obligation'. In the same way as postracialism is a backlash against antiracism, postfeminism is a backlash against feminism through rallies against the tyranny of political correctness, attributions of all women's unhappiness to feminism (such as in suppressing women's 'natural' desires to be feminine), claims that men are the real victims, or the belief that sexism has already been defeated and thus feminism is no longer needed in our new meritocratic world order (Faludi, 1991; for critiques of postfeminism see Adamson, 2017; Gill, 2014; Gill, Kelan and Scharff, 2017; Liu, 2019a; Negra, 2009; Tasker and Negra, 2007).

[45] Intersectionality broadly refers to the insight that gender, race, class (and sexuality, ethnicity, nation, dis/ability, age) operate not as fixed, unitary attributes, but as reciprocally constructing phenomena that shape social inequalities (Cho, 2013; Collins, 2015; Crenshaw, 1989). Its roots can be found in the social activism of women of colour in the 1960s and 1970s (Chun, Lipsitz and Shin, 2013; Collins, 2000, 2012; Moraga and Anzaldúa, 1983; The Combahee River Collective, 1977).

has challenged feminism to look beyond a narrow focus on gender towards the advocacy of racial, ethnic, sexual, class and disability equality. And yet perhaps because there are more open conversations about inequalities, we are seeing a backlash against diversity, inclusion and equality fuelled by fear and anxiety about a changing world.

I migrated to Australia with my parents from China in 1991 under the Hawke government, which lifted immigration restrictions following the Tiananmen Square massacre in 1989. Growing up in Sydney, I encountered daily interrogations of 'where are you from?'[46] when I wasn't hounded with cries to 'go back to where you came from' as constant reminders that I'm not a 'real' Australian. I learned that to minimize my feelings of alienation, I needed to rigorously enact an assimilationist performance. On the campus of my university where hostility against non-white foreign students was palpable, I spoke loudly with an exaggerated Australian accent and avoided speaking to, looking at or standing close to other Asian students in fear we would be mistaken for a clique. For a while when I enacted my best interpretation of Australianness, it would seem my (virtually all-white) lecturers and tutors would become less distant and hostile towards me. But it didn't take long to see that whatever benefits I gained from my attempted assimilation were fragile and fleeting. Each new classroom of each new subject in each new semester demanded an encore performance just to be seen as fully human. Although I didn't have the vocabulary for

Concerned centrally with the emancipation of women of colour, early proponents showed that oppression cannot be reduced to one axis of gender or race, but is produced through multiple, intersecting axes (Collins, 2000, 2012). The term 'intersectionality' itself was offered by legal scholar Kimberlé Crenshaw (1989, 1991) to demonstrate and challenge the limitations of the law in accounting for the intersection of racial and gender discrimination, and thus address the marginalization of women of colour.

[46] The question 'where are you from?' is now a well-documented microaggression faced by people of colour. They are typically posed to me by white Australians. If I attempt to respond with 'I'm from Australia', they frequently follow up, 'No, but where are you *really* from?' The implication here is that I'm an assumed outsider and that my racial identity is some exotic novelty that white Australians can use in a guessing game. The assumed connection between nativism and white manifests through the pervasive coding of Asian bodies as 'foreign', even for multigenerational Asian Australians who first arrived to Australia in the mid-19th century (Ang, 2003; Tan, 2006). This persistent effect of white normalization has been termed 'forever foreign'. Also see Ballinas (2017) on how this question is repeatedly posed to Mexican Americans as well as Creese (2018) for an account of African Canadians. Context, of course, matters. Sometimes this question may be asked by new migrants seeking community from a genuine place of interest and thus the question does not function as a microaggression in that context.

it then, I contorted myself into the mould of the model minority.[47] If I just worked hard without complaining, or so I believed, I would be able to overcome racism. Even my decision to become a leadership scholar first through my Honours and then my PhD was in part guided by the whiteness of the field and the delusion that in entering this field, its power and privilege would be conferred onto me. Eventually I had to confront the painful realization that accumulating and retreating into my own privilege could not alleviate the systematic dehumanization of all people of colour.[48]

Disambiguation of terms

Given the non-conventional philosophical and political traditions from which I write, I would like to clarify the use of common terms that feature in this book, particularly those that take on a different meaning to their use in everyday language.

Although we have a tendency to think of gender and race as 'natural' biological traits; like leadership, this book understands identity to be socially constructed and politically contested. We only need to look across time and place to see that what it has meant to be a 'man' and 'woman' or 'black' and 'white' have been in constant flux. Feminist

---

[47] The model minority is a controlling image used in white-dominated nations that regard Asian migrants as respectable, middle-class high achievers predisposed to academic and professional success (Chae, 2004). Although this construction may first appear complimentary, it was primarily evoked by political leaders in the United States to delegitimize Black and Hispanic social justice activists (Cho, 1997). The mythologized successes of Asian American migrants were cited by some politicians as 'proof' that racism does not exist, and in doing so, pitted different communities of colour against one another, keeping them divided (Cho, 1997; Liu, 2019b).

[48] When I later started working as a casual tutor, I would became aware of just how ingrained racism was at my institution. Once I was explicitly advised by a supervisor, 'I'm giving you assignments with surnames T–Z to mark. With all the Wing, Wang, Zhang and Zhu's, you're going to need to check extra hard for plagiarism'. Studies of student academic integrity in higher education have explored how common barriers to academic integrity such as poor understanding of plagiarism, poor academic skills and laziness/convenience (Devlin and Gray, 2007) are compounded for international students, who tend to face greater scrutiny than local students whose language styles and tones are more familiar to primarily native English-speaking staff (Baird and Dooey, 2014). However, as the highly racialized example I encountered demonstrates, students of Chinese descent often come to stand as a proxy for all that is lacking in student integrity in Australian higher education institutions, shaped by anti-immigration discourses that have long cast Chinese culture as backward, corrupt, patriarchal, difficult and inferior to the West (Kwek, 2003).

scholars have theorized the social construction of gender by showing how 'masculinity' and 'femininity' become codified in our society as we learn to regulate ourselves in line with social norms and conventions.[49] While we perform our gender identities in our everyday lives, we can adopt both 'masculine' and 'feminine' behaviours regardless of our bodily identification with a particular sex, although we can also be corrected by others when we are perceived to be behaving out of line with our assigned gender.

In the same way, race theorists have declared over a decade ago that it has been 'conclusively demonstrated that racial categories linking the physical, mental and behavioural traits of selected individuals to a hidden nature putatively shared by them as a group are without scientific basis'.[50] In that way, when I say 'whiteness', I do not mean some primordial essence imbued within white people. Like masculinity and femininity, whiteness is a complex, ever-changing set of social ideas and practices that is both inculcated in people who are defined as white and can also be adopted by those who seek to claim a sense of whiteness.[51] However, saying that gender and race are socially constructed is not to say that they are not 'real'. Despite their social construction, 'gender' and 'race' remains salient in our social reality and bears real, material consequences for people's ongoing experiences with privilege and oppression.[52]

In recognition of the sociopolitical nature of these terms, I deliberately choose certain language over others. Specifically, I will refer to white people as white rather than Caucasian.[53] The latter is

[49] Butler, 1993, 1999; Connell, 2010; West and Zimmerman, 1987, 2009.
[50] Ingram, 2005, p 243.
[51] Essed, 1991; Frankenberg, 1993; Hall, 1997; Omi and Winant, 1994; Sullivan, 2006.
[52] There is a danger in prematurely arguing that because gender and race are socially constructed, they should be abolished. For example, AnaLouise Keating (2013, p 36) warns that when we 'label people by color, gender, sexuality, religion, nationality, or any other politically charged characteristics and/or presumed embodied, psychic, political differences, we build walls between ourselves and these others. We isolate ourselves from those whom we have labeled "different". This automatic difference-based labeling process distorts our perceptions, creating arbitrary divisions and an oppositional "us-against-them" mentality that prevents us from recognising potential commonalities'. This idea assumes that the only 'difference' between identities right now are socially constructed, ignoring the very material differences that these different identities experience in terms of privileges and oppressions in contemporary organizational and social life.
[53] White as a designation of race appeared in law from the late 1600s. The term 'Caucasian' originated in the 1780s as part of the emergent European science of racial classification. After visiting the region of the Caucasus Mountains (located

an artefact of 18th century pseudo-scientific racial classifications that constructed white people as biologically superior and served to justify European colonialism. I understand that there are also geographical differences in how non-white people are collectively signified, including 'ethnic minorities' (which is popular in Australia) and 'black, Asian and minority ethnics' (or BAME, which is more common in Britain). Unless I am quoting directly from a source that uses one of these terms, I will use 'people of colour'. Although it is not a perfect label, it evokes the political struggles that have shaped this term into a tool for multiracial solidarity.[54]

White supremacy is a term in popular usage that evokes images of neo-Nazis or the Ku Klux Klan. However, when I discuss white supremacy, I am referring to the centuries-old racialized social system comprising the 'totality of the social relations and practices that reinforce white privilege'.[55] White supremacy is systemic and operates in and through everyday racism to maintain a strong positive orientation to 'white superiority, virtue, moral goodness, and action' and is ubiquitous and integral to work and social life.[56] Indeed, white supremacy is often a more poignant description of race relations than racism. Both white and non-white people who would not condone outright racial prejudice continue to support the institution of white supremacy, clutching on to a wilful ignorance of the ways white power and privilege define organizational practices.

I appreciate that the discussion of race (and gender to a lesser extent) can be uncomfortable for some people. Critical whiteness studies, as a subset of the wider field of critical race studies, is a tradition that has generally embraced frank and honest critique through its writing. The philosopher George Yancy articulates the value of this style of writing as such:

> around modern-day Georgia, Armenia and Azerbaijan), German anatomist Johann Blumenbach declared its inhabitants the most beautiful in the world, the ideal type of humans created in 'God's image', and deemed this area the likely site where humans originated. He decided that all light-skinned people from this region, along with Europeans, belonged to the same race, which he labelled Caucasian.

[54] See *Black British Academics* for a discussion of racial categorization and terminology (Gabriel, 2016). Leah Bassel and Akwugo Emejulu (2018), in contrast to my choice of terminology, explain why 'minority ethnics' is an appropriate term in the context of their study of minority women activism in England, Scotland and France.

[55] Bonilla-Silva, 2006, p 9.

[56] Feagin, 2013, p 10; see also Deitch et al, 2003; Essed, 1991; Hill, 2009; Nkomo and Al Ariss, 2014.

When it comes to race, we need forms of expressive discourse that unsettle us, that make us uncomfortable with its daring frankness that pulls us in even as it unnerves. If philosophy is to become relevant to life as lived in its messiness, then we need forms of philosophical discourse that do not lie about and obfuscate life. Instead of avoiding the funk of life, we need to communicate that funk with greater richness. The process of writing with such frankness of style, then, a style that is graphically abrasive, is an attempt on my part to mimic the world of lived pain and suffering, and to challenge styles of writing typical of so many academic philosophers, styles that I find fail to capture the nitty-gritty, vivaciousness of the everyday.[57]

Writings about white supremacy can be painful because white supremacy is painful. As people of colour, we do not have the privilege of being able to go through life ignoring race and racism. It is hurled at us through constant reminders that we do not belong, that we are not fully human. To *not* discuss white supremacy comes at a greater cost than raising such a painful topic – it requires being complicit in our own dehumanization. Although they may be confronting to read, the theorizations of white practices here are not indictments of what *all white people* do. They refer to dominant practices that, due to the hegemony of whiteness, have historically appeared normal and natural, and therefore evaded critique.[58]

The purpose of this book is not to shame men or demonize white people as the so-called 'sexists' and 'racists', although I accept that many will read my book in this way. Rather, I am interested in systems of power and the collective ideologies and practices that reinforce them. This requires recognizing the ways that we are all implicated in patriarchy and white supremacy. As women, we learn to discipline ourselves and other women into patriarchal ideals of desirability. As people of colour, we adopt tactics (like the model minority) that reproduce our own subordination in the racial order. It is frankly pointless to reduce the project of justice to the separation of 'good' and 'bad' people. Gender and racial power are so mutable, subtle and insidious that integral to our project is the need to build solidarity across gender, sexual, race and class lines.

---

[57] Yancy, 2012, p 30.
[58] Critiques against whiteness have been comprehensive and systematic. However, white power has so far sought to evade, deflect, diffuse and co-opt such critiques.

The plan of the book

Redeeming Leadership is organized in two parts. The first part of the book, 'The Violences of Leadership', illuminates the violences of leadership by arguing how its attendant myths have served to reinforce gendered and racial hierarchies. Chapter 1 explores the imperialist fantasy of white masculine dominance, strength and power. This historical image bestowed upon white men the right to command and control humanity, which translates in contemporary organizational practice to the ready association of white men with leadership. Having interrogated hegemonic white masculinity in the previous chapter, Chapter 2 presents a critique of white femininity and the rise of moderate feminisms. Entrenched in notions of beauty, delicacy and purity, the chapter examines the fraught performances of white femininity in our current age as it attempts to balance between asserting dominance and maintaining an idealized innocence. Chapter 3 offers an overview of the concept of organizational violence before examining the practitioner and academic consequences of gendered racism in the previous two chapters. Specifically, this chapter will illuminate the ways diversity management practices in organizations have been co-opted to constrain the possibilities for equality. Chapter 4 examines the varied ways that 'doing good' in organizations is underpinned by colonial narratives of white morality and patriarchal fantasies of individual heroism. Specifically, it critiques how an abiding belief in the innate goodness of whiteness has more easily enabled white people to be seen and see themselves as saviours and the ways such idealizations of leadership have contaminated efforts in philanthropy and environmental sustainability.

Having established how diverse standpoints and voices are varyingly silenced or appropriated, the second part of the book, 'Anti-Racist Feminist Redemption', turns to how we may redeem leadership. The complex, distinct and localized traditions of anti-racist feminisms will be presented in Chapter 5 to discuss how their combined wisdoms can be applied to dismantle existing structures of imperialism, white supremacy and patriarchy reproduced in leadership practice and theory. With solidarity, love and justice as guiding principles,[59] Chapter 6

---

[59] I follow from social justice activism in the use of 'solidarity' to refer to friendship and collaboration across difference (see Wadiwel, 2009 for a critical examination of solidarity). Love is a little more complex. In Sheena Vachhani's (2015, p 150) words, 'love often eludes interpretation by language, it evades logic or discursive capture'. Love here does not refer solely to romantic love, but an ethic for social transformation predicated on an affective encounter with the other (see,

explores how we may counteract the various forms of violence explored in the first part of the book through decolonizing our minds; relating with others and reimagining leadership. For white anti-racist feminists, Chapter 7 theorizes allyship as an ongoing process of struggle, rather than a fixed identification. This chapter acknowledges the shame and guilt white people experience when they engage with justice and argues for the importance of their tarrying with discomfort to redo, and even abolish, whiteness. Finally, Chapter 8 concludes by drawing together the key ideas within the book and reflecting on the real challenges of engaging in anti-racist feminist resistance. It returns to anti-racist feminisms as the hope by which we in organizations and societies with legacies of imperial, white and patriarchal domination may find solidarity, love and justice.

in particular, hooks, 2000a). Like love, justice is another nebulous concept that is typically equated with the narrow application to the law. Again, I follow the lead of social movements to understand justice as the destabilization of systems of oppression including imperialism, white supremacy, capitalism and patriarchy (see Bell, 1989; Collins, 2000; hooks, 1984). These concepts will continue to be examined throughout this book.

PART I

The Violences of Leadership

1

Dominance

In his 1996 article, 'Leaders who make a difference', organizational psychologist and leadership consultant Manfred Kets de Vries sprung to leadership's defence:

> Some organisational observers argue that the leader's role is not very significant and that the importance of leadership is highly over-rated. To them, leadership is only static in the system since an organisation is mainly influenced by the environment in which it operates. ... Granted, environmental forces do play an important role in organisational life, but underestimating the human factor makes the whole equation indecipherable. Shakespeare's *Henry V* without the character of King Henry wouldn't make any sense. The English would certainly have lost the battle of Agincourt if they had underestimated the importance of the leadership factor. Any astute observer of organisations will notice that CEOs have a considerable impact on their companies, for better or worse. And the quality of leadership is particularly relevant in situations of strategic transformation and change. A good leader has the capacity to transform strategic constraints into new challenges. Such leaders influence organisational culture and provide direction in their vital role as catalysts of change.[1]

Reading his impassioned plea for leadership in 2020 is a strange experience. The extensive promotion of leadership by scholars and practitioners in the last two decades has since lifted leadership to a

---

[1] Kets de Vries, 1996, p 486.

sacred status.[2] Leadership is now more widely assumed as a vital force for good and commonly regarded as a panacea for all manner of organizational and societal problems.[3] Ket de Vries' evocative words tapped into a neoliberal yearning for hyperagency. He encourages the reader to imagine ourselves as King Henry V commanding our army at the Battle of Agincourt. The hypnotic repetition about our power to effect 'strategic transformation and change' and 'transform strategic constraints' in our 'vital role as catalysts of change' lulls us into the seductive belief that we can and we will single-handedly change the world.

Within this romance with leadership is a love song to white masculinity. The early formation of leadership studies took shape around the values of the European Enlightenment, which instated rigid gendered and racial hierarchies.[4] At the centre of leadership stood the figure of the autonomous European man from whom leadership gloriously emanated. He represented 'orderliness, rationality and self-control' while the Others he colonized and enslaved represented 'chaos, irrationality, violence and the breakdown of self-regulation'.[5] Meanwhile, classical models of leadership were developed and disseminated for decades under the assumption of a universal subject. Although successive conceptualizations of charismatic, visionary, transformational, authentic and servant leaders were touted through universalist claims of their applicability, their proponents overwhelming theorized from a narrowly masculinist, white and North American-centric perspective. Entrenched in leadership theories are Anglo-American values such as rationality, utilitarianism, pragmatism, individualism, neoliberalism, patriarchy and whiteness presented as part of an 'objective', universal worldview.[6]

When the media reports about the lack of diversity in leadership, a sequence of statistics is usually paraded out. They might indicate that as of January 2018, just 27 of the CEOs of Fortune 500 companies, or 5.4 per cent, are women and just three, or 0.6 per cent, are Black (all of whom are male). This 'hard' evidence is often necessary to convince a sceptical audience who are quick to deny the existence of

[2] Grint, 2010a; Sinclair, 2007; Śliwa et al, 2012.
[3] For a brilliant contemporary critique of leadership's sacred status, see *Thinking Differently about Leadership: A Critical History of Leadership Studies* by Suze Wilson (2016).
[4] Kincheloe et al, 1998; Moreton-Robinson, 2000.
[5] Kincheloe et al, 1998, p.5.
[6] Liu, 2017b.

sexism and racism and accuse women and people of colour of 'playing the gender card' or the 'race card'. Yet while the figures highlight the material realities of patriarchy and white supremacy at work, they only tell part of the story that concerns individuals rather than systems of power. At the individual level, the prescription for inequality is usually to inject our organizations with more women and people of colour. This superficial 'body count' fix is very often confined to an exercise of visible minority representation without any commitment to equality and justice.[7]

Although we are indeed compelled to question how our ideas and ideals about leadership maintain the overwhelming concentration of power among elite white men, we also need to question the nature of this power itself. If commanding a Fortune 500 corporation involves subjugating employees, exploiting workers and resources in the Global South, dispossessing Indigenous peoples of their land, and contributing to the degradation of the environment, then simply having a woman or a person of colour at the helm would be unlikely to alleviate the violences of leadership. So critiquing the dominance of white masculinity is not about decrying individual white men, but rather, questioning how the underlying power systems of imperialism, white supremacy and patriarchy have come to shape the theorizing and practice of leadership as the glorification of domination and control.

In this chapter, I will first explore the association of leadership with masculinity through the vestige of Enlightenment thinking. The concept of hegemonic masculinity will be introduced to show how idealizations of leadership tend to reflect idealizations of masculinity in our society. Following this, I discuss how leadership has been further shaped by an imperialist ideology that has historically constructed whiteness as the leadership norm and exemplar. Given that white power is often subtle and invisible, I draw on critical whiteness scholarship to help bring into focus the practices of whiteness that, like masculinity, have informed what it means to be a leader. To bring these arguments to life, I illustrate with two leaders who frequently feature in media representations and popular imaginations: Richard Branson, founder of the Virgin Group, and Steve Jobs, founder of Apple. The chapter concludes with a reflection on the tolls of chasing a hegemonic masculine ideal and why it can be so difficult for some men to confront their privilege, overcome their shame and become anti-racist feminist allies.

---

[7]   Ahmed, 2009; Leong, 2012; Liu, 2017c; Van Laer and Janssens, 2011.

Creating 'great men'

The earliest theories of leadership took for granted the 'natural' association of masculinity with power. The traits venerated as signs of great leadership – individualism, assertiveness and competitiveness – were also those ascribed to men and masculinities in our cultures. That is not to say that those who identify as men *are* individualist, assertive and competitive, but that our social construction of leadership is aligned with our idealizations of masculinity.[8] Although someone identifying as a woman can demonstrate these qualities and, in doing so, attempt to persuade others that she is a legitimate leader, these qualities are more readily perceived among men so that the link between masculinity and leadership becomes strongly entwined.[9]

Max Weber's charismatic leader was sculpted from Enlightenment fantasies of heroic masculinity.[10] The leader is an independent and autonomous subject who exerts his spirit on the world through his decisive thought and energetic action. His resolve is not grounded in any dialogue or communal considerations of the interests, needs or feelings of others. Rather, he must be self-reliant, for not being so would be a sign of his lack of inner conviction and craving for authority. The ideal man renounces and repudiates such forms of weakness, leaving them to the likes of women. The mark of a ruling ideology is that it asserts itself as 'common sense'. Enlightenment gender ideals have given rise to prevailing notions that work and politics are the rightful domains of men. At work and in organizations, men are consistently regarded as more agentic, decisive and competent than women, whereas women are stereotyped as more communal, expressive and warm.[11]

Psychological research in the field of implicit leadership theory, which explore lay people's conceptions of what it means to be a leader, consistently reports masculinity as a factor in popular perceptions of

---

[8] In the cultures that dominate leadership theorizing such as the United States, this masculinity is often unacknowledged, but assumed white, cis-gender, heterosexual, elite class and able-bodied.

[9] In an early review of studies on peer perceptions, psychologist Richard Mann (1959) suggested that perceptions of leadership were correlated with masculinity. Although he found the positive association to be 'slight', Robert Lord, Christy de Vader and George Alliger's (1986) re-examination of the data found higher correlations between leadership and masculinity.

[10] For an analysis of Max Weber's social and political thinking, see *Love Or Greatness: Max Weber and Masculine Thinking* by Roslyn Bologh (1990).

[11] Eagly, 1987; Eagly and Johnson, 1990; Eagly, Wood, and Diekman, 2000; Williams and Best, 1990.

leadership.[12] In the 1970s, Virginia Schein produced an index of 92 characteristics, including intelligent, creative and emotionally stable, and presented it to male middle managers.[13] The men were required to indicate if they thought each term described (a) women in general, (b) men in general and/or (c) successful middle managers. The results of the study showed that male middle managers believed that men were more likely than women to possess the characteristics associated with managerial success. Of the 92 descriptors used, 60 were seen to be characteristic of both managers and men (for example, aggressive, objective and forceful). In contrast, only eight descriptors (for example, helpful, intuitive and aware of the feelings of others) were seen as being shared by managers and women. These results were also replicated in a follow-up study with female middle managers, which disproves a common misbelief that all people are naturally biased towards their own gender.[14] The connection between leadership attributes and male attributes led to the aphorism 'think manager–think male'.

Over the decades, continued research suggests that while the association between leadership and masculinity has weakened (especially among people who identify as women), it has not been completely abolished.[15] While both female professionals and university students tend to rate male and female managers in a more balanced way, male professionals and university students appear to hold firm to negative conceptualizations of female managers. Using Schein's index of descriptors, male participants were less likely than female participants to describe female managers as ambitious, competent, intelligent, objective and well-informed and more likely to describe them as passive, nervous, uncertain, easily influenced and having a strong need for social acceptance.[16]

The psychological research tends to treat the think manager–think male phenomenon as a collection of cognitive biases and attitudinal barriers. Although it is important that we understand the psychological processes and effects of the masculinization of leadership, psychological explanations elide the structural dimensions of gender – namely, how the association of leadership with masculinity is shaped by and in turn reinforces patriarchy. Psychology can thus be used to buttress the wider neoliberalization of our society, where solutions to gender

[12] Knights and Tullberg, 2011; Offermann, Kennedy and Wirtz, 1994; Sczesny, 2003.
[13] Schein, 1973.
[14] Schein, 1975.
[15] Brenner, Tomkiewicz and Schein, 1989; Duehr and Bono, 2006; Heilman, Block and Martell, 1995; Powell, Butterfield and Parent, 2002; Schein, 2001; Sczesny, 2003.
[16] Deal and Stevenson, 1998.

inequality in organizations become individualized.[17] For instance, organizational psychologists have cautioned that due to these gender stereotypes, 'men and women who are choosing a career track may not seek to be managers if they do not see themselves as fitting the prevailing stereotype of managers'; 'organisations may only select applicants for entry-level managerial positions whom they see as adhering to managerial stereotypes'; and 'organisations tend to exert strong pressures on their members to conform to ways acceptable to other members, particularly those in power'.[18] The sites of the struggle here are individual professionals, hiring managers and senior managers. It is up to each group to change their own self-images; recruit people with more diverse attributes and allow more diverse behaviours in organizations. In their conclusion, the researchers anticipate that as the proportion of women in management grows, masculine stereotypes about leadership will correspondingly weaken, thus supporting the 'body count' solution to gender equality.

Patriarchy, however, has no gender.[19] We are all inculcated in its ideology and embedded in its structure. I would argue that it is not solved by having more women around or, as some fear, having fewer men. Patriarchy is a fundamental system of power that institutionalizes the supremacy of men and the subordination of women. It rarely exerts this domination through any brutish imposition of totalitarian male rule that renders women powerless, but instead, weaves itself through our cultures in subtle, shifting and resilient ways.[20] One way

---

[17] Not all psychological theorizations of leadership reinforce a neoliberal worldview. Virginia Schein (2001, p 685), for example, emphasizes the way her studies can help 'lay the groundwork for corporate structural changes'. She counsels that her findings inform continued international efforts to pass equal employment opportunity legislation and develop organizational mechanisms to circumvent the negative impact of gender stereotypes.

[18] Powell, Butterfield and Parent, 2002, p 189.

[19] hooks, 2009a, p 170.

[20] Patriarchy has become the dominant ideology of many contemporary societies by constructing the idea that male dominance is universal and natural. This idea has been disseminated through Judeo-Christian narratives that ordained the woman as subordinate to the man because she was so created by god as well as evolutionary myths that sexual asymmetry is the result of men being revered hunters and women being lowly gatherers. By suggesting that male dominance is the result of a god or evolution serves to evade accountability for gender inequality. At the same time, the idea that men were historically honoured as big-game hunters has been disproven by anthropological evidence. In hunter-gatherer societies, food supply consisted mainly of what was provided through gathering and small-game hunting, in which both women and children took part. Indeed, in many of these hunter-gatherer

the patriarchal gender structure is maintained is through the inscription of gender ideals, such as those perpetuated through leadership theories. The ideal leader corresponds to what sociologist Raewyn Connell has termed 'hegemonic masculinity', which is the distinct form of masculinity that 'embodie[s] the currently most honoured way of being a man'.[21] What constitutes hegemonic masculinity varies across context. Within contemporary Western societies, the practice of hegemonic masculinities is often described as 'macho', in other words, tough, competitive, assertive, unemotional, self-reliant and heterosexual.[22] Its expression in leadership, as the previous section of this chapter explored, has taken this form in ways that mean control and conquest become taken-for-granted ways of engaging with the world.[23]

How the theory of hegemonic masculinity differs from psychological theories is that it does not equate masculinity with men. As the introduction suggested, gender is understood as a social performance. The hegemonic masculinity of leadership means that all professionals, regardless of their gender identification, are compelled to perform their identities in line with this ideal. Although white (cis-gender, heterosexual, elite-class, able-bodied) men may more closely embody hegemonic masculinity, their achievement of an elite status can never be guaranteed and requires careful, continual regulation. Indeed, the hegemonic model may not reflect the lives of any actual men; it only captures our collective desires and becomes a benchmark against which all people are measured.[24] Our reinforcement of this model not only legitimizes the domination of men over women; it also denotes the ascendency of certain men over other men.

The legacy of imperialism

Leadership, or the idea that certain individuals are more fit to influence the minds and govern the lives of others, is inextricably bound up in the European colonial project. Europe was home to the Enlightenment man, whose intellect, rationality and resolve made him not only the most suitable figure to rule over the submissive, emotional and domestic(ated) woman, but his dominion was to extend across the

societies we find evidence that all genders enjoyed relative complementarity. See Gerda Lerner's (1986) *The Creation of Patriarchy*.

[21] Connell and Messerschmidt, 2005, p 832; see also Connell, 1987, 1995.

[22] Connell, 2014; Donaldson and Tomsen, 2003; Gorman-Murray, 2013, p 138.

[23] Collinson and Hearn, 1996; Kerfoot and Knights, 1993.

[24] Connell and Messerschmidt, 2005; Liu, 2017d; Pacholok, 2009.

world. A critical mechanism of his command was through the insidious imposition of Western representations of other cultures and peoples.[25] Fundamental to European worldviews is the assumption that the primitive, savage and unruly non-West is incapable of self-definition and thus necessitates 'objective' Western scientific classification.[26] The non-West has consequently been an object of systematic scrutiny, categorization, codification and invention by the West.

The appropriation of the non-West is perhaps most prevalent in cross-cultural leadership research, where accepted frameworks define homogenizing categorizations of nationality. These frameworks are designed to provide simple, digestible overviews of non-Western countries so that corporations in the United States can accordingly formulate strategies for international expansion. A common refrain in this work is that leadership competencies and practices are inferior outside the United States. For example, we are told that the Middle East exhibits a propensity for technocratic leaders who focus on sterile considerations such as efficiency, productivity and output.[27] India and Indonesia are often characterized as deeply paternalistic, which is said to be due to the propensity for their population to accept a passive and dependent role. The Japanese are allegedly highly formal based on their feudalist traditions which would suggest a limited capacity for leadership initiative among professionals.[28] The writers who proffer these characterizations seem oblivious to their resemblance to colonial texts, where people like Lord Cromer first instructed that 'Orientals ... could not learn to walk on sidewalks, could not tell the truth, could not use logic' or a missionary who lamented that 'the Hindu is inherently untruthful and lacks moral courage'.[29]

Cross-cultural models can be tantalizingly facile, and as a student I memorized these cultural profiles with enthusiasm. However, when I found my own Chinese identity unrecognizable in the texts we read in university classrooms, I started to question the function and intent of these representations. The canonical work of social psychologist Geert Hofstede[30] on cultural dimensions gave rise to the pervasive use

---

[25] Chakrabarty, 1992; Jack and Westwood, 2009; Prasad, 2003; Westwood, 2001.

[26] Said, 1978.

[27] Western, 2012.

[28] There are a number of detailed critiques of cross-cultural management texts (see Ailon, 2008; Jack and Westwood, 2009; Kwek, 2003; McSweeney, 2002; Westwood, 2001).

[29] Said, 1994, p 151.

[30] Geert Hofstede's main contribution is his book *Culture's Consequences* (2001), first published in 1980, with which he claimed to have 'uncover[ed] the secrets of entire

of 'collectivism' as a shorthand to characterize a unitary Chinese culture. Lumped in with collectivism would frequently be Confucianism, Daoism and Buddhism in an Orientalist imagining of our ancient and arcane cultural mysteries. More virulent examples imply that Chinese culture is backward, oppressive, corrupt and difficult.[31] All these labels describe (and ascribe) a homogeneous Chinese cultural essence that perpetuates an abiding belief in difference, while ignoring the contextual and contested character of culture.[32]

Not all representations of leadership outside the Western world are so blatantly disapproving. Every few years, some theorists would excavate the far reaches of the empire for constructs like Daoist, Tribal and Ubuntu leadership in order to spice up[33] mainstream (white

national cultures' (Hofstede, 1980, p 44). He extracted data from a pre-existing database of employee attitude surveys across 66 IBM subsidiaries from around 1967 and 1973. Among those, profiles for 15 of the countries evaluated were extrapolated from fewer than 200 survey responses. However, as Hofstede assumed each country was culturally homogenous, small sample sizes were deemed irrelevant to the framework's accuracy. The statistical analysis of this data led Hofstede to develop a framework comprising four bipolar dimensions he claimed captured the essence of each nation's culture: (1) Power Distance (the extent to which the less powerful members of organizations and institutions expect and accept that power is distributed unequally); (2) Uncertainty Avoidance (intolerance for uncertainty and ambiguity); (3) Individualism versus Collectivism (the extent to which individuals are integrated into groups); and (4) Masculinity versus Femininity (assertiveness and competitiveness versus modesty and caring). Later in the 1990s, a fifth dimension was added about Long- versus Short-Term Orientation.

[31] Kwek, 2003; Liu, 2017b.

[32] According to cultural scholar Ien Ang, the term 中国人 (*zhong guo ren*, Chinese people) was not typically used within China until after the establishment of the Republic of China in 1912. Even then, people in China would more likely identify as members of certain lineages, villages, provinces, language groups or certain trades and occupations rather than a unifying nation state. 'Chinese' is thus an ambiguous and relatively new term that was mainly produced by Western categorizations of all those born within and outside China as though they are bound by a specific, essentialist sense of Chineseness (see also Wang, 2009). Other authors provide broader analyses of the social and political construction of racial and ethnic identities (see Ailon, 2008; Ailon-Souday and Kunda, 2003; Narayan, 2000; Said, 1978; Ybema and Byun, 2009).

[33] I use this phrase in reference to bell hooks' (1992a) essay, 'Eating the Other', in which she makes the observation that our culture has come to seek pleasure in the consumption of Otherness. Speaking to the commodification of racial difference, hooks (1992a, p 44) states that 'ethnicity becomes spice, seasoning that can liven up the dull dish that is mainstream white culture'. Cultural appropriation is a common form of white expansiveness, which can manifest in the dilettante adoption of other traditions, dress, language or music, usually in ways that erase or distort the cultural meaning and significance of those practices (Donaldson, 1999).

masculinist) leadership research. Such theorizations are usually not designed to point out the deficiencies of these approaches, but may come from good intentions to promote lesser known alternatives to hegemonic leadership practices in the West. However, the dilettante construction of these 'exotic' models of leadership can become a form of cultural appropriation, where theorists paint highly romantic portraits of each practice and their corresponding cultures without an intimate understanding of or respect for the underlying philosophies.

Hand in hand with the marginalization of the non-West is the marginalization of the non-white. Research within white-dominated countries like the United States has purported that African American leaders demonstrate weaker human relation and administrative skills[34] and tend to be less empowering of their subordinates.[35] Asians are thought to be uniformly passive, unassertive and lacking in leadership skills.[36] One of the most influential handbooks of leadership suggests that this perception is a result of our 'cultural background that stresses modesty'.[37] Like cross-cultural management texts, such ideas conflate race, ethnicity and culture and treat all three as deep-rooted determinants of behaviour.

As implicit leadership theory has demonstrated for masculinity, studies have found that being white is persistently perceived to be an attribute of leadership. Initially, leadership theorists following social identity theory believed that all leaders would be more readily accepted by members of their own racial group. Yet experiments of leadership attributions concluded that Asian, Hispanic and African Americans were just as likely as white Americans to evaluate white leaders as more effective.[38] Despite the persistent myth that race relations in our society is a level playing field where each equally powered racial group vies for dominance, white racial privilege acquired through centuries of colonialism and slavery cannot be so easily overcome.

Making whiteness visible

Perhaps even more so than masculinity, whiteness occupies a hegemonic status in our society that makes its power and privileges invisible.[39] In order to identify the ways in which whiteness underpins the social

[34] Richards and Jaffee, 1972.
[35] Pitts, 2005.
[36] Woo, 2000.
[37] Bass, 2008, p 968.
[38] Rosette, Leonardelli and Phillips, 2008.
[39] Dyer, 1997; Garner, 2007; MacMullan, 2009.

construction of leadership, I draw on the field of critical whiteness studies to unmask the practices of whiteness that serve to sustain its dominance. Here, I will focus on the practices of normalization, solipsism and ontological expansiveness that are implicated in the social construction of leadership.[40] Normalization refers to the ways in which whiteness 'silently imposes itself as the standard by which social difference is to be known'.[41] Normalization is seen in the way markers of race are primarily applied to non-white people in everyday discourse, while white people tend not to be racially defined. The effect is that while white people might just be referred to as the 'manager' or the 'CEO', people of colour will typically be clarified as the *Asian* manager or the *Black* CEO. In this way, normalization defines whiteness as the human 'default' that affords white people the right to speak for the commonality of humanity, when racially marked people can only speak for their race.[42] A white leader is therefore more readily perceived as representative of the whole of society and all its citizens, while people of colour are commonly seen as only narrowly serving the needs of their racial group. In my own research on Chinese managers working in Australia, many struggled to be accepted as legitimate representatives by their organizations and reported being continually suspected of being 'biased' towards their own racial group. In contrast, white people's governance, as our colonial forefathers believed, is trusted to be exercised for the 'greater good'.[43]

White solipsism refers to a way of living as though only white people exist or matter.[44] Although the literal existence of people of colour is acknowledged, white solipsism only considers white values, interests and needs as important.[45] The practice of white solipsism often results in the inability of white people to form meaningful relationships with people of colour and underpins their abdication of responsibility for

[40] I first developed this framework of whiteness in my work with Christopher Baker on Australian philanthropists (Liu and Baker, 2016).

[41] Levine-Rasky, 2013, p 45.

[42] Education scholar Peter McLaren (2000, p 150) also puts it cogently when he describes whiteness as a universalizing authority by which white subjects claim the right to speak on behalf of everyone who is non-white, while denying the agency and voice of non-white subjects. White normalization is supported by the 'refusal to acknowledge how people are implicated in certain social relations of privilege and relations of domination and subordination'. Whiteness, then, is a form of 'social amnesia' (see also Dyer, 1997).

[43] Liu, 2017c.

[44] Sullivan, 2006.

[45] Sullivan, 2006.

their effects on non-dominant groups.[46] If normalization upholds whiteness as the leadership default, solipsism encourages whiteness to be assumed as the followership default. Leadership decisions must first and foremost appeal to the desires of a white constituency.

According to philosopher Shannon Sullivan, ontological expansiveness is where 'white people tend to act and think as if all spaces – where geographical, psychical, linguistic, economic, spiritual, bodily, or otherwise – are or should be available for them to move in and out of as they wish'.[47] In practising expansion, white people assume that they can exercise total mastery over all aspects of their environment. White expansiveness resonates with leadership heroicism, where white leaders' intervention in organizational or social processes are largely treated as reflections of positive attributes such as visionary or transformational leadership and presumed to produce positive effects.[48]

Leadership legends

The expression of white, imperialist, patriarchal ideologies in leadership can be found in the stories we tell one another of great leadership. Disseminated through cultural texts, we can explore the social construction of leadership by paying attention to who graces the covers of business magazines; who is reported in the news; and who is profiled in the case studies taught in university classrooms. Studying celebrities is worthwhile because they express prevailing 'ideas of personhood' in society.[49] They stand at the nexus of many experiences and economies of contemporary life and as their trailing number of fans can attest, can have a profound effect on the self-images of their audience.[50] In this section, I explore narratives of two people who are commonly heralded as exemplary leaders: Steve Jobs and Richard Branson. In analysing their life stories as depicted in the media, I discuss what these cultural artefacts reveal about our collective fantasies of leadership.[51]

Shortly after his death, Steve Jobs' biographer introduced his 'rags to riches' life story, stating that 'his saga is the entrepreneurial creation

[46] Levine-Rasky, 2013.
[47] Sullivan, 2006, p 10.
[48] Bass, 1998; Nanus, 1995; Śliwa et al, 2012; Spoelstra and Ten Bos, 2011.
[49] Dyer, 2004, p 9.
[50] Redmond and Holmes, 2007.
[51] For a more thorough analysis of celebrity CEOs, see *Demystifying Business Celebrity* by Eric Guthey, Tim Clark and Brad Jackson (2009).

myth writ large: Steve Jobs co-founded Apple in his parents' garage in 1976, was ousted in 1985, returned to rescue it from near bankruptcy in 1997, and by the time he died, in October 2011, had built it into the world's most valuable company'.[52] Richard Branson, founder of the Virgin Group, is also introduced to us as one who rose from humble beginnings:

> the 64-year-old billionaire entrepreneur struggled with dyslexia as a child and eventually left school at 16 to launch a magazine for young people. His multinational corporate empire started in a London commune as a business selling records through mail order in the early 1970s before exploding into a behemoth that has included a record label, airlines, finance, a mobile phone network and train franchise.[53]

In relaying how the leader started out in a garage, faced bankruptcy, struggled with a learning disability, dropped out of school, the 'rags to riches' trope accentuates the sense that each of these men single-handedly built their multibillion dollar corporations from 'nothing'. The allusion to a modest background also invites the average reader to ponder the possibility that we too can acquire extraordinary wealth and power from ordinary beginnings.

These leadership case studies celebrate individualism, painting the image of an exceptionally courageous and self-reliant figure. 'Sir Richard', we are told, 'is not a man known for crumbling in the face of a challenge.'[54] Branson does not succumb to external constraints, nor is there any hint that he answers to others in steering his business. Rather, he is quoted as saying, 'my interest in life comes from setting myself huge, apparently unachievable challenges and trying to rise above them'.[55] A great leader, it seems, is entirely self-sufficient in his success. Indeed, Jobs' 'personality was integral to his way of doing business. He acted as if the normal rules didn't apply to him'.[56] In an interview with Branson, Kets de Vries portrayed him as a risk-taking renegade: 'He is still motivated by a good challenge. Having built his empire, Branson continues to lead the Virgin Group in a daring drive

[52] Isaacson, 2012, p 94.
[53] Saul, 2014.
[54] Saul, 2014.
[55] Saul, 2014.
[56] Isaacson, 2012, p 94.

for expansion, taking on one established industry after the other. He loves to shake up what he calls "fat and complacent business sectors"'.[57]

The success of Apple is likewise credited to the way Jobs ignored the needs and interests of customers and relied instead on his inner conviction:

> When Jobs took his original Macintosh team on its first retreat, one member asked whether they should do some market research to see what customers wanted. 'No,' Jobs replied, 'because customers don't know what they want until we've shown them.' He invoked Henry Ford's line 'If I'd asked customers what they wanted, they would have told me, "A faster horse!"'[58]

Ultimate success, as we are told in these representations, is to have absolute dominion over as much as possible (for example, money, people, land and properties). These media portrayals of Branson liberally apply the metaphor of 'empire' in earnest as they convey the global reach of the Virgin Group that spans 'retail operations (a chain of megastores in Australia, Britain and Ireland, continental Europe, Hong Kong, Japan, North America, and South Korea), hotels, communications (video games, book publishing, radio and television production), and an airline'.[59] Jobs is lauded for having made his mark on a panoply of industries while managing Apple: 'along the way he helped to transform seven industries: personal computing, animated movies, music, phones, tablet computing, retail stores, and digital publishing. He thus belongs in the pantheon of America's great innovators'.[60] The colonizing influence of Branson and Jobs' businesses has made them godlike in our cultural narratives, highlighting the glorification of ontological expansiveness. The mark of true power, it would seem, is not only about crossing the far reaches of the globe and transforming industries, but also penetrating hearts and minds, such as by being 'regularly cited as a role model by young people',[61] 'infus[ing] employees with an abiding passion to create groundbreaking products'[62] or 'becom[ing] a household name'.[63]

[57] Kets de Vries, 1998, p 9.
[58] Isaacson, 2012, p 97.
[59] Kets de Vries, 1998, p 9.
[60] Isaacson, 2012, p 94.
[61] Kets de Vries, 1998, p 9.
[62] Isaacson, 2012, p 100.
[63] Kets de Vries, 1998, p 9.

Colonialist myths of the European explorer appear in stories about how Jobs developed an almost supernatural self-reliance. Isaacson recounts:

> He honed his version of empathy – an intimate intuition about the desires of his customers. He developed his appreciation for intuition – feelings that are based on accumulated experiential wisdom – while he was studying Buddhism in India as a college dropout. 'The people in the Indian countryside don't use their intellect like we do; they use their intuition instead,' he recalled. 'Intuition is a very powerful thing - more powerful than intellect, in my opinion.'[64]

Jobs' time in India is framed as a spiritual hero's journey. The vagueness of this account accentuates the mystery of the narrative. That somewhere in the Indian countryside, among the exotic natives, Jobs gained access to the esoteric wisdoms of Indian Buddhism that imbued him with the abilities to intuit the inner desires of others. He now lays claim to a higher intellect that is 'more powerful' than what we can imagine here in the West. Like a superhero comic book story, people of colour are confined to marginal stereotypes like the noble savage,[65] whose main purpose is to transfer their power to the white hero so that he may go on to change/save the world.

The media not only conveys these myths of leadership via what they write, but also delivers this message through powerful visuals. I illustrate a way of looking critically at popular images circulated of these two leaders, and leaders in general, with two photographs that are broadly representative of the distinct ways Branson and Jobs are commonly portrayed in the media.

The first portrait I analyse featured in *Vanity Fair* alongside an article about the Virgin Galactic project in April 2015.[66] Branson is photographed full-length in order to show his sleek, black suit (branded with the company logo). His stance is wide in an imposing 'power pose' that takes up space and also conveys confidence and stability. He

---

[64] Isaacson, 2012, p 97.

[65] The noble savage is a romanticized construction of an uncivilized person who possesses an innate goodness that has been uncorrupted by Western civilization. For a detailed analysis of the social construction of the noble savage, including its common misbeliefs, see *The Myth of the Noble Savage* by Ter Ellingson (2001).

[66] The photograph of Richard Branson by Jonas Fredwall Karlsson can be seen online here: www.vanityfair.com/news/2015/03/what-is-it-like-to-fly-virgin-galactic

clutches another branded helmet in his left hand (the venture 'Virgin Galactic' scrawled across the front as a reminder of Branson's audacious ambitions for space travel), while his right hand is clenched in a fist. His expression is stoic, softened by a faraway gaze that appears to look past the camera, as though he can only partly engage with the audience down the lens as he is perpetually occupied with dreams of the future. A dramatic amber sunset illuminates him from behind to create a halo effect that is most prominent around his head, set against a richly saturated sky free of clouds and representing a sense of endless possibilities. Although there are three figures visible in the background, they are small, distant and silhouetted – unidentifiable ground crew who might fuss behind the scenes but will never share the limelight with the leader. A surreal effect is enhanced through the use of studio lights that illuminate Branson from the front so he appears like a glowing, godlike being, standing between earth and sky.

Figure 1: Steve Jobs.

Source: Justin Sullivan / Staff. Getty Images North America.

The portrait of Jobs, compared to the previous one of Branson, is more stripped down, but perhaps no less effective. He stands before a plain black background with only a stark white outline of the Apple logo suspended behind his shoulder in soft focus, so that the audience's gaze is drawn to Jobs himself. He seems to be in the middle of a speech, perhaps one of his infamous product presentations, raising both his hands up to accentuate a point.[67] His gaze is thrown far out to the

---

[67] Sharma and Grant provide a detailed analysis of Steve Jobs' leadership 'performances' across three keynote speeches for Apple (Sharma and Grant, 2011).

distance, like Branson, dreaming of a future vision. Jobs' iconic black turtleneck top blends into the background so that he appears in the frame almost as a floating white head and two white hands; the vital tools of his intellectual genius and technological engineering. Again, there are no other figures emphasized in this portrait. He is the perennially self-reliant hero whose potent rationality and pragmatism is more powerful than we could ever know.

The key to these media representations of leadership is that they are not merely intended to be descriptive, but prescriptive. The reader is advised to aspire to these models of leadership. Creators of these texts usually expound the philosophies, life lessons and maxims from the leaders with the unspoken assumption that we ought to follow their examples. The ascendancy of white masculinity is reinforced through these popular portrayals of leadership not merely because Branson and Jobs are white men, but because their representations promote imperialist, white supremacist and patriarchal values. The dominant idealizations of leadership compel all of us, regardless of our gender or racial identifications, to aspire to 'success' on these problematic terms.

Chasing hegemonic masculinity

One of the reasons why it can be so painful for white people and men when they hear the phrases 'white privilege' and 'male privilege' is that they experience these utterances as vicious accusations. The phrase can sound as though it implies that *all* white men are born into the lap of luxury, who need never face hardship or challenges and thus do not deserve any of their accomplishments or happiness. White privilege is, of course, not an attack on white people, but a corollary of white supremacy, as male privilege is a corollary of patriarchy.[68] These privileges are also far from monolithic, but are cross-cut by dimensions of sexuality, class, coloniality and dis/ability so that a white

---

[68] In her essay, 'White Privilege: Unpacking the Invisible Knapsack', Peggy McIntosh (1988, p 1) recounts how she 'was taught to see racism only in individual acts of meanness, not in invisible systems conferring dominance on my group'. She goes on to say: 'My schooling gave me no training in seeing myself as an oppressor, as an unfairly advantaged person, or as a participant in a damaged culture. I was taught to see myself as an individual whose moral state depended on her individual moral will. My schooling followed the pattern my colleague Elizabeth Minnich has pointed out: whites are taught to think of their lives as morally neutral, normative, and average, and also ideal, so that when we work to benefit others, this is seen as work which will allow "them" to be more like "us"'.

working-class queer man would face very different experiences at work and in society than a white elite-class straight man.

Another part of this pain I think also has to do with the difficulties of conforming to hegemonic standards. When cultural critic bell hooks[69] says 'patriarchy has no gender', she is expressing how this system of power takes its toll on all of us.[70] For men in particular, hooks poignantly observes that 'patriarchy forces fathers to act as monsters, encourages husbands and lovers to be rapists in disguise; it teaches our blood brothers to feel ashamed that they care for us, and denies all men the emotional life that would act as a humanising, self-affirming force in their lives'.[71] While many white men may reject the violent principles of hegemonic masculinity and hegemonic whiteness, these standards may still be imposed on them by others. Among all-male groups, boys and men can often be penalized with censure, ridicule or ostracism if they are seen to violate the rules of hegemonic masculinity, such as when they reveal vulnerability or try to foster emotional intimacy.[72]

As such, the book's call for anti-racist feminist resistance is not about women or people of colour storming the white masculinist citadel of leadership and seizing the kingdom with the same weapons as our oppressors. Rather, it begins with what hooks calls the 'decolonization of our minds'; recognizing then relinquishing the chains of imperialism, white supremacy and patriarchy. When we understand how we can *all* be freed from these interlocking systems of power, we may move collectively towards new practices of leadership grounded in equality and justice.

Conclusion

In the last two decades since Manfred Kets de Vries' pronouncement presented at the start of this chapter, leadership has risen to become

---

[69] hooks, 2009a, p 170. bell hooks is the pseudonym of cultural critic Gloria Jean Watkins who took her maternal great-grandmother's name in hopes of embodying her spirit as 'a sharp-tongued woman, a woman who spoke her mind, a woman who was not afraid to talk back' (hooks, 1989, p 9). Her name is not capitalized following hooks' desire to place the focus on her ideas rather than herself.

[70] Poet Rosario Morales (1983, p 93) also reflects on this idea in her prose piece published in the anthology *This Bridge Called My Back*: 'Being female doesn't stop us from being sexist we've had to choose early or late at 7 14 27 56 to think different dress different act different to struggle to organise to picket to argue to change other women's minds to change our own minds to change our feelings ours yours and mine constantly to change and change and change to fight the onslaught on our minds and bodies and feelings'.

[71] hooks, 1981, p 114.

[72] Bird, 1996.

a sacred construct. Yet built on the back of gender and colonial subjugation, leadership has been instilled from the outset with idealizations of white men's moral and intellectual superiority that granted them the birthright to govern. Both scholarly theorizations of leadership and popular representations of celebrity CEOs reinforce the ideologies of patriarchy, white supremacy and imperialism, and sustain the abiding association of leadership with white men. In critiquing the systems of power that undergird leadership, however, this chapter is not an attack on individual white men. Although white men have historically benefited the most from imperialism, white supremacy and patriarchy, their individual ascendancy in existing hierarchies is not guaranteed and, moreover, demands of them a certain identity performance that takes its toll in exchange for racial and gender privileges. As a consequence, I reject the popular 'body count' approach to leadership diversity that calls for more women and leaders of colour without critically engaging with the problematic nature of leadership itself.

That being said, the advancement of women to positions of leadership has become particularly prominent of late. Characteristic of our neoliberal moment, reports about the rise of high-profile women focus almost entirely on individuals as representing some universal female aspiration. In the next chapter, I will explore idealizations of femininity in leadership theorizing and practice, and critically interrogate the pestilent influence of patriarchy, white supremacy and imperialism even in ostensibly feminist celebrations of women leaders.

2

Purity

The master's tools will never dismantle the master's house. They may allow us temporarily to beat him at his own game, but they will never enable us to bring about genuine change.

– Audre Lorde[1]

The growing prominence of female executives in the last decade appears to portend a new era for women in leadership. The success of women like Sheryl Sandberg, whose business manual *Lean In* calls on women to 'forge a path through the obstacles, and achieve their full potential', has contributed to the idea that gender equality will be won in the free market of corporate leadership. In our postfeminist times, sexism is believed to be a relic of the past. Enlightened contemporary organizations have demolished systemic gender barriers and any odd case of discrimination is the fault of a deviant manager. With fervent conviction in their inherent meritocracy, organizations hold firm to an overriding focus on individual freedom. In this feminist utopia, female professionals are exhorted to 'lean in' and seize the myriad opportunities to become leaders.

This optimism requires turning a blind eye to systems of power and histories of oppression. Feminism, when recast in neoliberal terms, becomes an individualistic, entrepreneurial project. For example, both academic studies and practitioner handbooks have concluded with recommendations for women to cultivate an effective leadership style that strikes a balance between masculine and feminine behaviours, such as combining assertive agency with communal qualities of kindness,

[1]   Lorde, 1984, p 112.

friendliness and helpfulness.[2] As such, leadership continues to promote a hyperagentic individualist ideal, where women are told that we can single-handedly transform ourselves into valued commodities to be sold and traded as 'leaders'.[3] Meanwhile sexism becomes popularly characterized as an 'unconscious' bias that otherwise well-meaning managers can learn to overcome at half-day workshops.

The limitations of this individualism was demonstrated a few years ago when Marissa Mayer was appointed CEO of Yahoo. Six months pregnant at the time, Mayer negotiated for a nursery to be built in her office so that she could balance her caring responsibilities with her work. Although Mayer was able to utilize her wealth and position at the company to her and her family's benefit, she faced intense criticism when eight months into her appointment, she issued a ban against working from home.[4] Some of her employees who adopted flexible working arrangements to care for their own children at home pointed out how this mandate hurt those at Yahoo who did not share Mayer's power to change their work arrangements to their advantage. The point of raising this example is not to speculate whether or not Mayer made the right decision for her company to ban remote working.[5] Rather, Mayer's case shows how we have reduced collective responsibilities for gender equality to individuals. Her leadership also disrupts the simplistic narrative that female leaders will solve gender inequality. When capitalistic organizations are built on maximizing profit, performance and productivity, the gender of the individual at the helm does not alleviate the violence that their leadership brings to bear.

---

[2] Eagly and Carli, 2007; see also Kark, Waismel-Manor and Shamir, 2012; Vinkenburg et al, 2011.

[3] This transformation usually occurs through a consumeristic makeover culture that involves shopping, styling and personal grooming. For an incisive discussion of how the beauty industry has profited from a neoliberal, corporate culture that fetishizes self-confidence, see Rosalind Gill and Shani Orgad's (2015) article, 'The confidence cult(ure)'.

[4] *Business Insider* reported on the story of Yahoo's ban against working from home (Carlson, 2013).

[5] When Marissa Mayer announced her pregnancy with her first child on the same day as her appointment to Yahoo, media reports questioned her dedication to her career. Then when she revealed that she would only take two weeks of parental leave and work throughout it anyway, others questioned her dedication to her family (Cohen, 2015). It is telling that much of the media backlash against her decision levelled various criticisms against her lack of dedication to both her work and her child – criticisms rarely raised for male CEOs. By 2017, after Mayer left Yahoo, she would be named as one of the 'least likeable' CEOs of public companies in the United States (Bort, 2017).

No individualistic tactics can address the structures of patriarchal power at their root. I return again to hooks' insight that patriarchy has no gender. 'Body count' solutions where high-profile women join the ranks of leadership in organizations have so far appeared to be inadequate to transform the ideologies and practices of violence. Perhaps the most insidious effects are the ways we perpetuate racial and class domination while waving the banner for gender equality. These paradoxical power relations require more nuanced ways of identifying, analysing and challenging their consequences in work and society. In order to critically examine white femininity in this chapter, I trace how its simultaneous location of oppression (as women in patriarchy) and privilege (as white in white supremacy) manifest in practice in subtle and complex ways.

I will begin this chapter by providing a snapshot of leadership studies in the 1980s and 1990s when a brief trend towards 'feminine leadership' crossed with the rise of transformational leadership theory. Not only were the promises of feminine leadership ultimately unfulfilled but, in some cases, they shored up patriarchal power. In order to understand the failure of feminine leadership, I explore how femininity has been historically constructed through dominant ideologies of imperialism, white supremacy and patriarchy. Like masculinities, femininities are stratified along dimensions of race, sexuality and class, so that white, cis-gender, heterosexual, elite-class and able-bodied femininity stands as the feminine ideal. Female leadership, as it follows, is then modelled after the image and interests of elite women. To show this hegemonic ideal in action, I illustrate with another two high-profile leaders: Sheryl Sandberg, chief operating officer (COO) of Facebook, and Carolyn McCall, CEO of ITV (and former CEO of easyJet). I then trace the expressions of white femininity through European colonialism and show how it shaped the formation of white feminism.

A brave new female world

When overtly sexist attitudes became less socially acceptable to express, leadership studies shifted from the promotion of aggressive and competitive masculinities towards the exploration of femininity in leadership. Dominated by psychological approaches, early research sought to identify so-called 'feminine' styles of leadership that were lauded as more collaborative, nurturing and people-oriented.[6] These theories rested on the essentialist belief that women are

---

[6]   Bass, Avolio and Atwater, 1996; Druskat, 1994; Eagly and Johnson, 1990; van Engen and Willemsen, 2004; Rosener, 1990.

more collaborative, nurturing and people-oriented by nature, even though these are only some of the attributes that have historically been associated with (and demanded of) women in Anglo-American cultures. Empirical research carried out over the next decade would find little evidence for the hypothesized differences in how men and women enact leadership, thus calling into question the notion of any distinct style of 'female leadership'.[7]

This feminizing trend coincided with the rise of transformational leadership theory, which drew on the ideas of writer James MacGregor Burns to develop a model for exceptional leadership, one that 'binds leader and follower together in a mutual and continuing pursuit of a higher purpose'.[8] One review of the literature described transformational leadership as 'the single most studied and debated idea within the field of leadership studies' over the previous three decades.[9] Transformational leaders are said to communicate clear visions for the future, gain their followers' trust and empower them to achieve those goals. Specifically, Burns' influential concept was applied to organizational leaders through a framework of practices comprising idealized influence; inspirational motivation; individualized consideration and intellectual stimulation (also known as the four I's).[10] During the theory's zenith in the 1990s, some theorists noted that the qualities of transformational leadership resembled feminine styles of leadership and ventured that women were more likely than men to demonstrate these four I's of transformational leadership.[11] On this basis, some proponents were even quick to declare that women bear a leadership advantage.

Despite this enthusiasm, the female leadership advantage never materialized. Indeed, it seems that stereotypically feminine qualities such as being more kind, communal and developmental can be valued at the same time as femalehood is not. While people may expect and prefer that women behave in line with feminine stereotypes, women are not accepted as legitimate and effective leaders unless they also exhibit stereotypically masculine qualities such as being assertive, directive and tough.[12] The delicate balancing

---

[7] Vecchio, 2002.

[8] Burns, 1978, p 20.

[9] Díaz-Sáenz, 2011, p 299.

[10] Avolio, Waldman and Yammarino, 1991.

[11] Bass and Avolio, 1994; Eagly and Carli, 2007; Kark, Waismel-Manor and Shamir, 2012; Vinkenburg et al, 2011.

[12] Much of this literature assumes a cis-heterosexual default of gender identities. The dominance of essentialist treatments of gender has meant that leadership research traditionally overlooked the complex ways gender is performed by transgender,

act between these two gender stereotypes that women leaders are expected to accomplish has been referred to as the 'double bind'.[13] It is what Carly Fiorina, former CEO of Hewlett-Packard who later ran for the Republican presidential nomination in 2016, described in her memoir: 'In the chat rooms around Silicon Valley, from the time I arrived until long after I left HP, I was routinely referred to as either a "bimbo" or a "bitch" – too soft or too hard, and presumptuous, besides'.[14]

Masculinities, in contrast, appear to enjoy a certain malleability at work that femininities do not. As stereotypically feminine styles of leadership became celebrated as a refreshing additive to masculinist organizational cultures, it was predominantly (white, cis-gender, heterosexual, elite-class, able-bodied) men who carefully incorporated feminine performances who were lauded as exemplary leaders. Gender scholar Michael Messner observed that from the 1980s and 1990s, professional men began to embrace a measured softness and sensitivity. The example he offers is of President Ronald Reagan shedding a tear during a televised speech when he spoke about soldiers' sacrifices after the 1983 US invasion of Grenada.[15] Messner suggested that this signalled the changing contours of hegemonic masculinity, where men were increasingly required to balance their toughness, decisiveness and hardness with contextually appropriate moments of compassion and, sometimes, vulnerability. To avoid being seen as weak, these displays of emotion were not in response to their own failures, but restricted to areas regarding protective care, such as for children or country. Although performances of femininity can run the risk of rejection and ridicule, its payoff for an elite white man who pulls it off is to project

---

non-binary and queer leaders. See Emi Koyama's (2003) transfeminist manifesto for a disturbance of the masculine/feminine binary reproduced in theorizations of the double bind.

[13] Leadership research tends to focus on double binds narrowly in the context of gender and role expectations. Communication scholars Rebecca Curnalia and Dorian Mermer have explored the gender double bind for female politicians in the United States. They identified at least five double binds: 'women are complimented more on their bodies than brains; women have the choice to speak out and be shamed or be silent and invisible; women are subordinated, whether they define themselves as similar to or different from men; femininity is perceived as incompetence, and competence is unfeminine; and ageing women are seen as less relevant and valuable, whereas ageing men are seen as distinguished' (Curnalia and Mermer, 2014, p 27).

[14] Fiorina, 2006, p 173.

[15] Messner, 2007.

himself as a transformational leader. He is seen to masterfully blend traditional masculine capabilities of rallying followers under a stirring vision with traditional feminine capabilities that nurture and support their followers to fulfil their potential.

So the practice of feminine leadership, in the end, shores up patriarchal power. Men who adopt more nurturing and supportive approaches in their leadership tend to be perceived as innovative and special, yet women leaders who nurture and support are more likely to be dismissed as just expressing their womanly 'nature'. Early in my career, I worked at a research centre where the director cultivated a warm and affectionate approach in his leadership that was deployed to disguise his tactics of coercion and control. His ability to manipulate junior academics rested on his careful performance of feminized leadership, which ultimately allowed him to engage in rampant bullying while hiding under a cover of civility.[16] Evidently, it has been elite white men who have driven and reaped most of the rewards from these shifting gender norms.[17]

In the last two decades, transformational leadership has been subject to rigorous reassessment.[18] Despite compelling evidence of its conceptual defects, transformational leadership dominated public imaginations and shaped idealizations of leadership to an extent that we have scarcely seen before or since the height of its popularity. Transformational leadership kindled a romance for command and control that Kets de Vries also offered in the opening to the last chapter. As critical leadership scholar Dennis Tourish surmises, 'in stressing the need for leaders to "transform" others – a project which increasingly seeks to reshape their most private values, attitudes and aspirations

---

[16] I share my experiences working at this research centre in greater detail in an autoethnographic account (see Liu, 2019a).

[17] The ethnographic research of economic geographer Linda McDowell (2009) suggests that traditional macho masculinity has become detrimental for working-class men at the bottom of the capitalist system who are increasingly required to show docility and deference.

[18] Among the most authoritative evaluations is one conducted by leadership scholars Daan van Knippenberg and Sim Sitkin (2013) who comprehensively demonstrate that transformational leadership is riddled with problems. In a 60-page meta-analysis, they show how the conceptualization of the construct is flawed, with no definition of transformational leadership independent of its effects and that differentiates it from other aspects of leadership. Van Knippenberg and Sitkin argue that the vast majority of studies have taken for granted a construction of transformational leadership that is, on the terms of its own positivistic tradition, invalid.

– transformational leadership has been complicit in attempts to extend the power of formal organisational leaders in ever more intrusive directions'.[19] Eventually, the myth of transformational leadership eroded away along with the myth of the female advantage.

Transformational leadership enshrined a colonial logic via the grandiose dreams of powerful elites to not only change the world, but also change hearts and minds. The claim over this kind of control is, as Tourish demonstrated, fundamental to the practices of cults.[20] It is also how leaders like Harvey Weinstein maintain cultures of fear that empower their repeated abuses and leaders like Trump incite hatred among frightened citizens. Although the construct of transformational leadership itself may have begun to fall out of favour, the dominance of white imperialist patriarchal values holds firm. These values appear and reappear in different forms, but always carrying the same intent to command and conquer. The subtlety of this power needs to be met with equally nuanced analyses. In the following sections, I will explore what hegemonic femininity looks like in leadership practice and how it has in both the past and present been wrought in the service of white imperialist patriarchal power.

Creating 'great women'

As I outlined in the introduction to this book, I reject the tendency of psychological leadership theories to essentialize femininity; that is, to see femininity as something innate and natural to those who are assigned female at birth. What it means to be a man or a woman is instead continually produced and regulated in line with the norms and conventions of our specific social contexts. In the previous chapter, I looked at the construction of hegemonic masculinity, which has historically occupied the central, dominant position of humanity. Femininity in contrast does not have any original meaning. It is defined only *in opposition to* what is considered masculine.[21] So that if masculinity is characterized as strong, agentic and rational then femininity is weak, passive and emotional. The social construction of gender difference in and of itself is not inherently problematic, except that femininity has been traditionally deemed inferior and, as such, subordinated in patriarchal relations. The material effects of this subordination were sustained through centuries of women's

[19] Tourish, 2013, p 20.
[20] Tourish, 2013; see also Alvesson and Kärreman, 2016.
[21] Baudrillard, 1990; Butler, 1999; Cixous, 2000.

educational, political and economic disenfranchisement, and linger in contemporary organizations through the sexual objectification and assault of women employees by powerful men.

Of course, not all femininities are subordinated equally. Due to the power and privilege of whiteness, white femininity has until more recently evaded systematic analysis and critique. Theorizations of white femininity have since explored its ideological construction as well as the regulatory practices that maintain meanings about white women and their place in the social order. Of particular interest is their paradoxical location that is shaped by both the structures of gender inequality as well as the structures of white privilege. Like hegemonic masculinity, the complexity of femininity is often erased through a homogenizing white elite-class feminine ideal.[22]

As an ideological construction, white femininity is first and foremost imagined through the patriarchal values of domesticity, where white women are raised to be symbols of romantic love, marriage and motherhood.[23] Inherent to this ideal is a compulsory heterosexuality[24] as well as a compulsory homoraciality.[25] Historically and culturally, white women who choose sexual partners outside their race are reproached and threatened with the loss of white privilege.[26] At the centre of these disciplinary efforts is the idea that the bodies of white women are the rightful possessions of white men.

More leadership legends

When we look at the examples of high-profile female leaders, we can see the effects of this carefully curated femininity at work. Like their male counterparts, female leaders are overwhelmingly white, cis-gender, heterosexual, elite-class and able-bodied. They often exhibit white elite-class markers of assertiveness, self-confidence and education, but they also temper their performance with displays of softness, modesty and warmth.[27] In order to see hegemonic femininity in action, I draw on the examples of two individuals who are often heralded in the media as exceptional female leaders.

[22] Collins, 2004; Deliovsky, 2010; Markowitz, 2001.
[23] Shome, 2001, 2011.
[24] LeBlanc, 1999; Rich, 1979.
[25] Deliovsky, 2008.
[26] Stoler, 1995.
[27] This goes back to the double bind (see, for example, Curnalia and Mermer, 2014; Gherardi and Poggio, 2001; Hall and Donaghue, 2012; Jamieson, 1995; Liu, Cutcher and Grant, 2015; Oakley, 2000). Women, however, are not completely

Sheryl Sandberg rose to prominence after her now famous 2010 TED talk, Why We Have Too Few Women Leaders,[28] helped launch her female leadership handbook, *Lean In*, and a not-for-profit organization by the same name. Unlike media profiles of Richard Branson and Steve Jobs, articles about Sandberg rarely present a detailed life narrative and tend to focus instead on episodic activities that reveal her relationships with others. A magazine feature, for example, introduces Sandberg by stating: 'Many experts say that Sheryl Sandberg is responsible for Facebook's stunning success because founder Mark Zuckerburg [sic] was not good at logistics or handling other aspects of Facebook's business like HR and advertising.'[29] Another article states: 'She's the most famous number two to have ever existed. ... When other promising tech startups reach their adolescence and their young male founders need help, they often put out a public call for a Sheryl Sandberg.'[30] From the outset, Sandberg is depicted as the loyal and competent 'great woman' standing behind the 'great man'. Zuckerberg, the founding CEO of Facebook, is evoked as the socially awkward prodigy responsible for creating the social networking platform and the company, but Sandberg is constructed as the one who helped him with the people-oriented activities of the business. So although such statements are ostensibly crediting Facebook's success with Sandberg's efforts, it does so by constructing her first and foremost in relation to a man, thus underscoring that her capabilities are ultimately exercised in service of him and his company.

Sandberg's leadership is characterized squarely within a hyperfeminine stereotype. We are told that when she 'started as Facebook's COO, she went to hundreds of people's desks and interrupted their work and said: "Hi I'm Sheryl." She then asked lots of questions and listened'.[31] 'Sheryl is well known for asking many smart questions about what employees think and encouraging debate.'[32] She 'has pioneered her own approach to leadership, the hallmark of which has always been the kind

---

helpless when they get caught in a double bind. For instance, communication scholar Stephanie Schnurr (2008) has explored how women leaders can successfully reconcile their femalehood with their leadership through their use of humour.

[28] Sandberg's TED talk can be seen at www.ted.com/talks/sheryl_sandberg_why_we_have_too_few_women_leaders.html

[29] Doyle, 2017.

[30] Hempel, 2017.

[31] Doyle, 2017.

[32] Doyle, 2017.

of openness that Facebook prizes',[33] so that while 'many people think that revealing your feelings as a leader is a sign of weakness', 'Sheryl thinks it is a strength and makes employees more willing to discuss their feelings as well'.[34] An exemplary female leader, as painted through these articles, serves others. She is modest when she approaches her employees, showing a friendly cheerfulness and inviting them to address her by her first name. She humbly attends to those around her, seeking their ideas and listening to their needs. She is not driven by any self-defined mission or internal conviction; rather, we are told she consults others constantly. Unlike the emotional restraint demanded of hegemonic masculinity, Sandberg's leadership seems to be all about discussing her feelings and encouraging her employees to discuss theirs too.

The media extolls Sandberg's advocacy for gender equality. However, while male leaders tend to be able to stand as leaders in their own right, Sandberg's femalehood is persistently recentred so that we are reminded she is the *female* leader promoting *female* leadership. She is reported to have 'spoken out about the importance of teaching young girls to be leaders as early as possible in their lives' and is quoted in an interview with BBC Radio 4 saying: 'I believe everyone has inside them the ability to lead and we should let people choose that not based on their gender but on who they are and who they want to be.'[35] Sandberg's pursuit of gender equality is one that is carefully tempered. She avoids ruffling feathers by focusing on feel-good neoliberal statements that praise 'everyone' for their individual leadership essence that can be proffered to the benefit of established capitalistic structures. Her emphasis on children, in particular, allows her to further soften her image as a maternal figure who tends to the wellbeing of others.

In 2017, Sandberg's husband passed away with a sudden heart arrhythmia. In an article in *Wired* magazine, the days following when her life 'was thrust into terrifying chaos' were recounted:

> She flew home and broke the news to her two young children. … She spent seven days welcoming friends for the traditional Jewish shiva, accepting food she mostly didn't eat. Then, on the following Monday, Sandberg dropped her kids off at school, eased her SUV out of the parking lot, and headed for Facebook. Her boss – Facebook's founder Mark Zuckerberg – had encouraged her to take as much

33 Hempel, 2017.
34 Doyle, 2017.
35 Keating, 2017.

time as she needed before returning to work, but grief counsellors had advised her to get her kids back to their regular schedule. She thought it would be good to return to work while they were at school.[36]

Female leaders' personal lives are broken open and put on display in a way that is rarely seen even for the most high-profile male leaders. In this extensive account of her resilience, the article depicts Sandberg as the ideal wife and mother. In her grief, it shows us how she continues to place her children, family and friends, her boss and her work first. There are subtle hints to her own self-sacrifice, such as neglecting to eat the food she had been given, all while guarding the moral values of her family and community via the religious rituals she maintained. This story of Sandberg again suggests how rare it is for her to occupy the limelight on her own, as the mention of Zuckerberg reminds the audience of *his* exceptional leadership (exhibited in his 'feminine' show of empathy and care). Her dedication to her work, although applauded here, is also framed as following advice from grief counsellors, rather than driven by her own principles and convictions. Even the article's headline, 'Sheryl Sandberg's accidental revolution', praises her influence by asserting that it was not fuelled by any personal ambition (as that would be inappropriately masculine for a female leader), but merely the 'accidental' outcome of her self-sacrificial efforts.

In the portrait of Sandberg from 2011 included here, she is shown at a professional function. She wears a slightly stilted, self-conscious smile and her shoulders are hunched. This awkwardness suggests a certain modesty, as though she was not expecting her photograph to be taken. Like her media profiles, the image tempers her public image as a confident and successful leader (visually exemplified in her portrait on the cover of *Lean In*) and accentuates her vulnerability. At the same time, Sandberg embodies a white elite-class sensibility through her glossy brown hair, tucked behind her left ear to reveal an elegant silver earring, modest shade of nude lipstick and a shapely dress evoking an Orientalist sensuality in its design,[37] suggestively exuding through the half-unzipped collar yet still remaining respectable on a white woman's body.

---

[36] Hempel, 2017.

[37] The dress is in the style of a Chinese traditional dress known as the *qi pao* in Mandarin and *cheong sam* in Cantonese. See Rosalie Chan's (2017) essay about the history of this Chinese garment and its tradition of Western appropriation: www.racked.com/2017/4/9/15022012/qipao-traditional-chinese-new-year

Figure 2: Sheryl Sandberg.

Source: https://commons.wikimedia.org/wiki/File:Sheryl_Sandberg_Moet_
Hennessy_Financial_Times_Club_Dinner_2011.jpg

Carolyn McCall is offered to us as the 'personable, calm and friendly' leader who 'was born in Bangalore, India, and was educated in India and Singapore, followed a Catholic boarding school in the UK'.[38] When she left easyJet in 2017, an article in the *Financial Times* commended how 'in the seven years since Dame Carolyn McCall

[38] Sunderland, 2017.

became chief executive of easyJet, she has gone from being dismissed by her fiercest rivals to winning their open admiration'.[39] The article proceeds to quote two male CEOs of rival airlines: 'Michael O'Leary, the head of rival Ryanair, who once labelled the former Guardian Media Group boss a "media luvvie", said the airline industry would have been poorer without her. "I clearly underestimated her and I was proved wrong"', while 'Willie Walsh, chief executive of British Airways parent, International Airlines Group, said he was "sorry to see Carolyn leave the aviation industry. She's done a good job"'.[40] Another article quips that 'her battle against mocking male rivals, obstreperous shareholders and a sceptical establishment to become Queen of the FTSE wouldn't be a bad subject for a small-screen drama'.[41] The contributions McCall made to easyJet are recounted in how she 'took on the role with the task of boosting employee morale and focusing on customers'.[42] 'The strategy paid off, forcing others to respond. Mr O'Leary not only improved Ryanair's service, but began to speak of his own passengers in slightly more respectful tones.'[43]

Suffering is a recurrent element in the life stories of women. It is taken for granted that as a woman, McCall would be 'dismissed' by her peers and called derogatory names within gendered stereotypes of her assumed emotional and affected nature. The media rarely calls into question this aspect of systemic gender inequality, yet neither does this article produce a neoliberal narrative of how McCall may have challenged this resistance to her leadership. Instead, it gives the male leaders a platform to demonstrate their humility (another show of the 'feminine' dimensions of their leadership). Despite the article's attempt to vindicate McCall and showcase the financial success of easyJet under her leadership, McCall ends up being defined by other men who become the real protagonists of this profile. The brief mentions to her strategy not only reinforces feminine stereotypes by alluding to her propensity for customer service, but centres the Ryanair CEO to suggest how his leadership has improved (and feminized) as a result of McCall's positive gender influences on the industry.

In 2018, McCall was appointed CEO of ITV, the largest free-to-air commercial broadcaster in the United Kingdom. She is introduced in a BBC article: 'straight talking, no-nonsense, charming, effective. Those are some of the descriptions I've heard of Dame Carolyn McCall. ...

[39] Hollinger, 2017.
[40] Hollinger, 2017.
[41] Sunderland, 2017.
[42] Medland, 2017.
[43] Hollinger, 2017.

ITV's outgoing CEO Adam Crozier was considered a great success and will be a tough act to follow at ITV but tough is another word you could chuck in to describe Carolyn McCall'.[44] The article further quotes an analyst who asserts, 'she is seen as being very good with people, at building a strong management team around her and at the ability to "work the room"'. Unlike Sandberg's hyperfemininity, McCall is presented with a mix of traditional masculine and feminine qualities. She is tough, frank and direct, yet despite this, she is rarely represented as an autonomous figure in the ways that Jobs and Branson are. Instead, her leadership is framed around her dependence on others within her 'management team'. Like Sandberg in this respect, the media is careful to point out that McCall is no troublemaker when it comes to the status quo, qualifying that 'McCall would prefer not to discuss gender politics. She would like to be seen as just a boss, not a female boss'.[45]

More importantly, the media reminds us that she is the quintessential upper-class woman with an impeccable educational pedigree that traverses the British Empire and remains equally dedicated to her family as she is to her company. One article reports that McCall 'denies having planned her career, and says that after earning her degree in history and politics at Kent university, she just looked for a job to stay in the UK with friends – including her future husband Peter'.[46] Here, the media tempers McCall's ambition, and suggests her career simply happened while she invested her more appropriately feminine interests such as a heterosexual romantic relationship with her future husband. McCall also implies how being 'a mother of three teenagers – a boy and boy-girl twins' has made her a better manager: 'I have always been very organised but now I am hyper-organised as a result of having a family.'[47]

Next I analyse a photograph of McCall taken at an Easyjet event in Milan, Italy in June 2015.[48] In this portrait, McCall stands in a relaxed pose behind a railing at Malpensa airport as though she is standing on her own front porch. She exudes warmth as she leans forward as if she is about to engage in a friendly conversation with the viewer. In a similar way to Sandberg's portrait, this one of McCall softens her image as a leader, showing her to be accessible and personable. Like Sandberg, McCall's elite-class status is suggested through her polished

[44] Anon, 2017b.
[45] Sunderland, 2017.
[46] Hollinger, 2014.
[47] Sunderland, 2017.
[48] The photograph of Carolyn McCall by Chris Ratcliffe for Bloomberg can be seen online here: www.thisismoney.co.uk/money/news/article-4704610/Dame-Carolyn-McCall-wanted-boss-Britain.html

haircut, her brown hair streaked with blonde highlights, and the elegant silver and gold jewellery glittering on her throat, wrists and fingers. A shapely blue dress covers her thighs and shoulders in this shot, but a deep-plunging neckline reveals a hint of sensuality at the edge of respectability.

A tool of imperialism

Behind the stylized images of female empowerment we see in the media and leadership handbooks is a white femininity that has long been co-opted as a tool in the European colonial project. Gender played a vital role in organizing ideas of 'race' and 'civilization' and white women functioned as an important mechanism in the expansion and maintenance of the European empires.[49] When the biological sciences were used to bolster the notion of white racial superiority during the height of British imperialism, English women (of the right class and breeding) were upheld as guardians of whiteness through their reproductive role as well as the expectation that they ensured British norms and morals would be sustained in the settler colonies.[50] Where colonized women of colour were hypersexualized in colonial accounts, constructions of white women focused on their idealized purity. In the Dutch-occupied Indies, white women were described as being surrounded by servants to spare them from exerting physical labour and bathed at least twice a day to maintain their cleanliness.[51] British women travellers in Asia and Africa (usually missionaries) also

[49] See *Beyond the Pale: White Women, Racism, and History* by Vron Ware (2015). Of course, women were denied a leadership role in the empire. Historian Inderpal Grewal (1996, p 68) explains how in Britain, 'the empire was a symbol of masculinity and Englishwomen were the keepers of morals and the angels of the house; colonial matters, involving miscegenation and the darker mysteries of exotic life, were not to touch these women'. Grewal (1996, p 68) quotes a speech made by a Member of Parliament, J.A. Grant, to the House of Commons in 1913: 'in controlling a vast empire like our own, an Empire built by the mental and physical capacity of men, and maintained, as it must always be maintained, by the physical and mental capacity of masterly natures – I ask; "is there a place for women?"'

[50] Ware, 2015. Concern for the sexual activities of white women extended from as early as the 1600s. Historian Ann Stoler (1995, p 41) details how white male sexual anxiety in the Americas saw Maryland legislators accuse white women who enter into marriage with Black men as doing so 'to the satisfaction of their lascivious and lustful desires' and to the 'disgrace not only of the English but also of many other Christian nations' (see also Hodes, 1997, p 31).

[51] See *Race and the Education of Desire: Foucault's History of Sexuality and the Colonial Order of Things* by Ann Stoler (1995).

helped to depict women of colour as 'oppressed' and 'exploited' within their presumed undeveloped societies that contrasted with the freedom supposedly enjoyed by British women.[52]

After the age of high imperialism, white femininity was refashioned as a tool of white supremacy. Feminine weakness reshaped white femininity as the fragile and delicate possession that required white male protection. In the United States under Jim Crow, this construction justified lynching and other brutal forms of harm against Black men, who were regarded as dangerous threats to white women's sexual purity and innocence.[53] One of the most notorious cases of this was the murder of 14-year-old Emmett Till in 1955. Till was tortured and lynched by two white men after he was suspected of whistling at one of their wives. The woman testified in court and claimed that Till had grabbed her and threatened her, stating that she 'was just scared to death'. The all-white, all-male jury acquitted the two men, who four months later admitted their guilt to a magazine who awarded them a generous payment for their story. In 2007, at the age of 72, the woman confessed to the historian Timothy Tyson that she had fabricated the story.[54]

Integral to how white femininity supports white supremacy is a heteronormative code of aesthetics that has secured white women as epitomic objects of beauty and desire.[55] This code not only assumed Black men's predatory appetites and rationalized the violence against

---

[52] Grewal, 1996; see also Sankaran and Chng, 2004. In Anne Theriault's (2014) essay in *The Huffington Post*, she bitingly captures the modern manifestations of this colonial ideology and how it prompts white women to imagine themselves as saviours: 'Here in the West, we are frequently schooled on just how lucky we are to live the way that we do. We are often reminded of how wonderful it is to be in … a country that promotes equality between men and women. We are taught to pity the women, those *other* women, living in *other* places, who do not enjoy the same rights that we do. … We, as white feminists, are really not so different from the missionaries of several generations ago. We want to travel to far-off, dreamily exoticised lands and bring the light of the truth to the people there. Like the missionaries, we assume that we will bring wonderful, life-changing revelations to these people. We think with delight of how appreciative these women will be, how they will fall about our feet with thanks for the truth that we've brought them. We imagine how wonderful, how fulfilling it will be to know that we have *saved* these women'.

[53] Prominent scientists of the Reconstruction Era such as Lester F. Ward (who had served as the first president of the American Sociological Association) argued that Black men had a biological urge to rape white women in attempts to 'improve' their racial stock (Esposito and Romano, 2014).

[54] See *The Blood of Emmett Till* by Timothy B. Tyson (2017).

[55] Shome, 2011, 2014.

them, but constructed women of colour as aberrations to sexual norms and kept them vulnerable to sexual exploitation and assault by colonizing men.[56] For example, the hypersexualization of Black women resting on their designation with a 'wild', animalistic sexuality perpetuated the 'primitive' inferiority of Black people that was necessary to justify slavery.[57] Latina women are not only hypersexualized, but specifically cast as overproductive.[58] Images of hyperfertile Latinas are then evoked to promote anti-immigration sentiments that frame Latina bodies as being in need of state control.[59] Meanwhile, East Asian women have historically been portrayed as sexually exotic, designed for submission to heterosexual white male consumption.[60] The ongoing fetishization of women of colour is a contemporary expression of that colonial ideology.[61]

Despite the fraught history of white femininity, we tend to partake in a creative misremembering of white women's participation in colonialism, slavery and Jim Crow. Films like *The Help* depict race relations in 1960s Mississippi around the figure of a white female saviour, Eugenia 'Skeeter' Phelan (portrayed by Emma Stone), who is enshrined as a heroine for her earnest colour-blind acceptance of the black maids. Although racist villains may be depicted (seen in the nefarious Hilly Holbrook in *The Help*), they are usually two-dimensional 'straw women' designed to be reviled by a guilty audience who eagerly identify instead with the progressive female lead.[62] In films about slavery, such as *The Birth of a Nation*, white women are

---

[56] Cho, 1997; Collins, 1998; Liu, 2017a.

[57] Collins, 1998, 2004; Hammonds, 1999.

[58] Via the imposition of a heteronormative gaze (García, 2009; Vásquez, 2014).

[59] Chavez, 2003; Gutiérrez, 2008.

[60] Chou, 2012; Matthews, 2002; Tajima, 1989.

[61] Men are also sexualized in racialized ways. In order to deter miscegenation, Asian men have historically been portrayed as undersexualized – emasculated and asexual (Chan, 2001; Espiritu, 2008; Kong, 2006). Black masculinities occupied the other end of the racialized sexual spectrum where they were reduced to images of the hypersexualized savage (Bordo, 2000; hooks, 2003). Both masculinities of colour were constructed as aberrations to the Goldilocks option of white masculine sexuality (Chon-Smith, 2015; Liu, 2017d).

[62] Another tactic in these films is to depict Black people getting their revenge. In *The Help*, Minny Jackson (portrayed by Octavia Spencer) brings Hilly Holbrook a chocolate pie and watches her savour two slices before revealing to Hilly's horror that she had put her own faeces into the pie. In addition to drawing on stereotypes of Black people as primitive and uncivilized, the revenge trope can create a false impression of equal power between Black and white people, and can even infer that Black people, if they really wanted to, can overcome their oppression. I'd like to thank my friend Marianne Close for this observation.

usually represented as sympathetic bleeding heart allies who whisper gentle words to their husbands and fathers in order to spare their slaves from punishment. A notable exception is *12 Years a Slave*, which includes a gutting portrayal of white feminine cruelty in the character of Mistress Epps (portrayed by Sarah Paulson).[63] The recurring trope of the 'innocent white woman' leads us to imagine belligerent men under the hoods of the KKK, overlooking white women's past and present involvement in white nationalist movements.[64] The fantasy of white feminine innocence, perpetuated through popular culture, has led white women to believe that they are absolved from being beneficiaries of white supremacy.

In more recent decades, white femininity has garnered its own power by defining and directing feminism. Forged through in its imperial history, white femininity was accustomed to seeing itself as the vessel of morality that ought to be revered and protected, not distrusted or challenged. Due to white normalization, even white women who joined feminist activism with no intention of domination found themselves repeatedly thrust into the media limelight as assumed leaders of the movement. Some elite white women embraced this power and installed their personal concerns to represent *all* women's concerns. Rather than promote an intersectional struggle for equality, the women who colonized the movement focused on gender as the only site for change in pursuit of the power enjoyed by their fathers, brothers, husbands and sons. Blind to their racial, class, sexual and able-bodied privileges, they projected their values through universal statements that consequently constructed all women as victims of male power. This reductionistic view ignored the power that elite white women hold over non-white, queer, working-class and disabled men, while forcing non-white, queer, working-class and disabled women to align their struggles for equality with elite white women or risk invisibility and marginalization.

While white feminism has promoted for women the importance of acquiring economic and political power, they did not offer guidance about the exercise of that power. This oversight has also allowed capitalism to co-opt feminist visions for change by promoting the

---

[63] For a discussion of *The Help* and its reproduction of the white saviour narrative in our postracial neoliberal era, see Murphy and Harris (2018). Fariha Róisín (2017) has also written an excellent essay on the colonialist dictum of white saviours and how it manifests in a range of films including *Lion, Freedom Writers, The Blind Side*, and even via the male characters in *12 Years a Slave*.

[64] See *Women of the Klan: Racism and Gender in the 1920s* by Kathleen M. Blee (2009).

illusion that money brings freedom and independence.[65] Yet if the unquestioning accumulation of wealth by women supports the oppression and exploitation of working-class men and women, then it cannot be feminist.

Reproducing whiteness

In order to maintain their white privilege, white women are expected to participate in everyday 'rituals of unity and exclusion', which are mundane modes of thought and codes of speech that solidify white group membership.[66] Even in proudly multicultural societies, white people tend to socialize primarily within their own racial group.[67] By forming friendships and relationships exclusively with other white people, white social spaces are maintained in which white supremacist ideas and acts may proliferate. In these spaces, common rituals of unity include laughing along to a racist joke shared between white friends and retelling those racist jokes to others.

Rituals of exclusion include more traditional acts of racism that reinforce the marginalization of people of colour, such as by refusing to work or live with them. At the universities where I have worked, it is not uncommon for some of my white colleagues to complain about having Asian migrant students in their classrooms. Such rituals of exclusion can seem so natural and normal that university lecturers often neglect to consider how their behaviour constitutes racism. For example, they might disguise their distaste for people of colour in rationales that appear 'neutral' or even for the students' own benefit (for example, 'I'm just saying it'd be better if I could have students who can speak proper English' or 'I just feel sorry for the poor European exchange students who wanted an Australian experience but end up spending all semester stuck with Chinese people').

The marginalization of people of colour can also occur between white people, like the use of slurs to ridicule white women in interracial relationships. The work of sociologist Katerina Deliovsky has extensively explored the ways by which white women are compelled to demonstrate an allegiance to whiteness through their choice of intimate partners.[68] Grounded in her personal experience of being married to a Black man, she exposes how the anti-interracial animus directed towards white women

---

[65]   hooks, 1984.

[66]   Frye, 1992, p 150.

[67]   Bonilla-Silva, 2006.

[68]   Deliovsky, 2008, 2010.

can be carried through seeming compliments that white women are 'too beautiful to be with a Black man'.[69]

These acts of white violence exerted on, through and by white women suggest that white femininity continues to play a pivotal role in reproducing whiteness. Yet as many white women have come to understand how their own sexualization and racialization have been implicated in colonialism and white supremacy, they have also rejected and challenged established gender and racial orders. Their solidarity will be explored in the second part of this book. At the same time, American studies scholar Eva Cherniavsky suggests that white femininity is becoming less and less something that we can understand as being located in white women's bodies.[70] The next challenge for anti-racist feminist resistance is to be able to identify and critique the violences of white femininity when it is perpetuated by men and non-white women.[71]

Conclusion

While confident and competent women rise up the ranks of organizations and fill up bookshelves with their manuals for corporate success, patriarchy remains firmly in place. The resilience of patriarchy comes from its slipperiness, its malleability and its unevenness. It is not

---

[69] Deliovsky, 2010, p 109.

[70] See *Incorporations: Race, Nation, and the Body Politics of Capital* by Eva Cherniavsky (2006).

[71] There are even signs that women leaders of colour can enact white masculinity. Miki Agrawal, the co-founder and former CEO of Thinx, was accused by the former head of public relations at the company of inappropriate sexual behaviour. According to the former employee, Agrawal would frequently comment on her employees' breasts and offer graphic accounts of her own sexual exploits. She was also known to routinely change clothes in front of staff and conducted video-conference meetings while nude. Such behaviour was in many ways normalized at Thinx, which produces 'period underwear' with a self-proclaimed 'feminist' mission to destigmatize menstruation. However, the power imbalance between Agrawal and her staff meant that the leader developed a hostile working environment that made it difficult for employees to voice their discomfort or dissent. The complaint, filed with the City of New York Commission on Human Rights, also alleged that staff felt exploited by low pay and when they attempted to negotiate higher salaries, Agrawal would accuse them of being ungrateful. These accusations made of Agrawal reflect white masculinity and its normalization of domination, humiliation and the objectification of women, and show that such practices may not be essential to, or exclusively contained in, white men. The case was settled out of court and Agrawal stepped down as CEO. This story was reported in *Racked* (George-Parkin, 2017).

some monolithic structure that can be felled with a single strike by a She-E-O. Rather, patriarchy has sustained itself by appropriating its detractors. When the feminist movement challenged the concentration of power among elite white men, our culture responded with an exuberant celebration of female leaders. Indeed, some women were ushered into the media limelight, touted within neoliberal you-go-girl narratives that simultaneously functioned as an alibi against sexism. 'See how meritocratic we are!' organizations would proclaim as they publicly paraded their female leaders. Yet this practice can only be believed to advance gender equality if we think that feminism is a battle between women and men, where 'more women' equals 'more equality'.

When we look below the superficial level of body counts, we can find the problematic ways ostensibly positive narratives about female leaders shore up imperialist, white supremacist and patriarchal power. Female CEOs overwhelmingly embody a hegemonic feminine ideal that reinforces a heteronormative elite-class whiteness. High-profile women like Sheryl Sandberg and Carolyn McCall are upheld as examples of strong female leadership, but only when they are carefully packaged as respectable bourgeois ladies and devoted wives and mothers who passively stumbled into power and spend their days listening to employees and tending to others' emotional needs. This model of white femininity has not strayed very far from its colonial construction as an object of purity, beauty and innocence that required white male protection. This 'protection' while ubiquitously framed as being for white women's own good, often served as the rationale for brutal harm against men and women of colour.

Like patriarchy, whiteness is showing no inclination to concede its power. One way in which white supremacy has gathered strength in organizations in recent decades is through its infiltration of diversity management initiatives. In Chapter 3, I will explore the evolution of organizational diversity and its ironic effects in whitewashing policy and practice.

3

Destruction

Diversity seems to bear a certain ambivalence in our cultures. In some privileged contexts, it would appear that diversity has acquired a new sort of value. Organizations often claim to be enriched by diversity. They purport that attracting and maintaining a diverse workforce makes them more creative and innovative, while also allowing them to appeal to a wider customer base. Meanwhile, multicultural societies like to boast about their tolerance, inclusivity and easy access to a smorgasbord of ethnic foods. Yet lurking beneath this outer layer is a growing unease with diversity and apparent threat to white patriarchal power. On the back of the 'whitelash' that elected Trump, it appears that many people see diversity as an unwelcome incursion. More than a handful suspect that diversity is a nefarious apparatus of reverse discrimination against white people.

This contempt for diversity and its management has propelled people like James Damore to file class action lawsuits for reverse discrimination. Damore was dismissed from Google in 2017 after violating Google's code of conduct when he posted an internal memo attributing the reason fewer women than men worked in the technology industry to biological gender differences. He alleged that Google discriminated against white men while applying 'illegal hiring quotas to fill its desired percentages of women and favoured minority candidates'.[1]

Abigail Fisher sued the University of Texas after she was denied admission to the institution in 2008. She claimed that she was unfairly rejected in favour of minority applicants with poorer academic credentials.[2] However, Fisher failed to place in the top 10 per cent of

---

[1] Chuck, 2018.
[2] Mallenbaum and Jones, 2016.

her graduating class,[3] which would have guaranteed her admission to the University of Texas. Among the 47 accepted students with lower overall scores than Fisher, 42 were white, four were Latino and one was Black. Further, 168 Black and Latino students with scores identical to or higher than Fisher's were also denied admission.

Cases like Damore and Fisher provide insight into the ways white supremacy and patriarchy operate through an obstinate sense of entitlement. Google *belongs* to men. As women are biologically unsuited to a technology career, or so Damore's memo implied, they stole the jobs from more qualified men. Likewise, the University of Texas *belongs* to white students. Irrespective of actual admission scores, the fact that any Black and Latino students were accepted when a white student was not meant that they stole the places from the more deserving.

In this chapter, I will explore the destruction of difference and diversity through the theories and practices of diversity. I will begin by presenting an overview of diversity management and demonstrate how it has gradually supplanted social justice agendas through a capitalist logic. I then take the example of unconscious bias training, an increasingly prevalent solution for diversity, and critically interrogate the ways it absolves sexism and racism by normalizing them as universal cognitive functions. Considering that much of what is written about diversity centres on the figure of a white male saviour who extends inclusion to the Other, I turn to the standpoint of the Other and explore how dominant assumptions about diversity hurt those who diversity is supposed to benefit. As with all exercises of power, diversity management cannot be divorced from the ideas and practices of diversity in multicultural societies. I introduce my own nation's ambivalent relationship with diversity through its immigration policies. In this context, I pose the question 'who gets to lead?' and explore the answer through the case of an Asian Australian manager's struggles to be accepted as a leader by his subordinates.

Diversity in organizations

In 1987, the publication of a report called *Workforce 2000* drew attention to the growing demographic heterogeneity of the American workforce and its implications for the management of organizations.[4]

---

[3] Her grade point average (3.59) and SAT scores (1180 out of 1600) were solid, but not strong enough to compete against the other applicants to the university (Hannah-Jones, 2016).

[4] Johnston and Packer, 1987.

The *Workforce 2000* report predicted a shift in the makeup of employees, where the proportion of white male entrants was predicted to fall, while the numbers of women and people of colour were expected to rise. The question of how to effectively manage diversity arose among academics and practitioners in the wake of these predictions. A wide range of diversity management programmes were subsequently developed, not only across organizations in the United States, but also in other countries like Canada, Britain, Australia and New Zealand that anticipated similar demographic trends.

Despite the often self-congratulatory rhetoric, the success of organizational diversity programmes has been at best ambiguous, patchy and contested. Researchers then began to query the meaning and practice of diversity management; from its underlying ideology, assumptions and intentions to its lofty promises to enhance innovation, boost productivity and lift morale.[5] This growing field of critical diversity studies, as it came to be known, questioned the ways mainstream diversity management 'individuates difference, conceals inequalities and neutralises histories of antagonism and struggle'.[6]

The capitalistic application of diversity management has subordinated social justice in preference for economic agendas. The rationale for organizational diversity programmes overwhelmingly focuses on the commercial implications of how a diverse workforce may generate greater efficiency and effectiveness. For instance, it has been argued that a diverse workforce brings multiple perspectives to decision making, leading to creative and innovative problem solving.[7] Having diverse employees has also been said to enhance the organization's reputation in the community and reduce allegations of discrimination and costly lawsuits.[8] This managerially driven approach gained popularity because it made diversity seem 'do-able' by packaging it through case study examples and best practices that could be incorporated into the job descriptions of human resource managers.[9]

Although pragmatists may contend that diversity management has inspired managers to engage with inclusion in a way that traditional social justice arguments have not, this approach to diversity has been accepted by managers largely because it does not address

[5] Ahmed, 2007, 2012; Benschop, 2001; Kirton and Greene, 2011; Noon, 2007; Sinclair, 2006; Thomas and Ely, 2001; Zanoni et al, 2010.
[6] Ahmed and Swan, 2006, p 96.
[7] Cox and Blake, 1991.
[8] Perriton, 2009.
[9] Prasad and Mills, 1997.

fundamental structures of inequality that disadvantage segments of its workforce.[10] Yet diversity management programmes allow organizations to give the impression that they care about inclusion – often as a way to appeal to a diverse customer base – while actually doing very little.[11]

The business case rationale has further led to the instrumentalization of difference, where diversity has come to mean the 'inclusion of people who look different'.[12] With whiteness representing the organizational norm, people of colour have come to be defined in terms of the social and economic value they provide to white people and institutions.[13] Legal scholar Nancy Leong details this practice through her theory of racial capitalism, which refers to 'the process of deriving social and economic value from the racial identity of another person'.[14] In white supremacist societies like Leong's analytic context of the United States, this systemic phenomenon manifests via instances where white individuals and institutions use people of colour to acquire social and economic capital. Diversity policies and practices have provided a vehicle through which racial identity is commodified, degrading that identity into an object to be 'pursued, captured, possessed and used'.[15] Through a stated desire for Australia to become 'Asia ready', our self-declared Asian century prompted a renewed emphasis on workforce diversity, purportedly to facilitate effective economic partnerships between the regions.[16] In the privileged context of the Australian corporate sector, notions of racial diversity have in some ways become more desirable and thus (visible) non-whiteness has become a commodity for organizations to acquire and exploit.

For example, studies of corporate websites have shown that diversity is instrumentally adopted in organizations' visual branding, where

---

[10] Organization scholar Linda Perriton (2009) offers a comprehensive critique of the business case of diversity. In particular, she draws on her own background as a human resource development consultant to offer insight into how this dominant logic was so normalized that failure to communicate about diversity using the business case became interpreted as incompetence.

[11] Guerrier and Wilson, 2011.

[12] See Nirmal Puwar's (2004, p 1) excellent book, *Space Invaders: Race, Gender and Bodies Out of Place*.

[13] Ahmed, 2009; Guerrier and Wilson, 2011; Leong, 2012; Liu, 2017c; Van Laer and Janssens, 2011.

[14] Leong, 2012, p 2152.

[15] Leong, 2012, p 2155.

[16] Australian Industry Group, 2012, p 1; see also Commonwealth of Australia, 2012; O'Leary and Tilly, 2014.

companies will often overrepresent the diversity of their workforce via photographs. By displaying numerous photographs of happy people of colour, a company can use their bodies to present itself as cosmopolitan, progressive and inclusive, irrespective of its actual policies and practices.[17] It is in these ways that diversity becomes a brand.[18] Diversity has marketing appeal because it allows organizations to sell themselves as harmonious and inclusive places. This is the logic that organizations assume when they fill their websites and brochures with 'images of "colourful" happy faces'.[19] However, this gratuitous organizational pride can conceal systemic sexism and racism behind a cheerful organizational façade.

Perhaps most disturbing is the ways that diversity management has repackaged equal opportunities to make it more agreeable for white people. Generated through the civil rights movement, the first affirmative action programmes emerged in employment settings in the 1960s and were expressly designed to be reparational. Indeed, the United States Commission on Civil Rights defined affirmative action as an effort 'beyond simple termination of a discriminatory practice, adopted to correct or compensate for past or present discrimination or to prevent discrimination from recurring in the future'.[20] Affirmative action and equal opportunities understood and sought to remedy the systems of power that have historically disadvantaged certain social groups in the workplace, such as women and people of colour.

However, as our society rapidly neoliberalized and civil rights struggles faded from public memory, organizations began to replace the notion of affirmative action with diversity management. Where previous discussions of gender and race enabled more honest considerations of social inequality in organizations, the term 'diversity' expanded beyond traditional diversity axes to include identifications such as education, corporate background and personality.[21] In this

---

[17] Yvonne Guerrier and Cornelia Wilson (2011) studied 28 corporate websites in the United Kingdom, analysing the verbal and visual language of diversity. They found that (predominantly white) young women are typically used as the 'face' of the company while older white men are made less visible. The organizations in effect conveyed a superficial acceptance of visual differences.

[18] Liu, 2017c.

[19] Ahmed, 2007.

[20] Leong, 2012. The 1977 United States Commission on Civil Rights' Statement on Affirmative Action can be downloaded at: www2.law.umaryland.edu/marshall/usccr/documents/cr11054.pdf

[21] See, for example, *Beyond Race and Gender: Unleashing the Power of Your Total Workforce by Managing Diversity* by R. Roosevelt Thomas Jr. (1992).

way, we can all be seen as 'different' from one another, and therefore we are all 'diverse'. Suddenly, everyone was covered by diversity management programmes. Proponents of diversity often defend its vagueness as a strength. By not specifying gender, race or another social category, they argue that diversity can be more 'inclusive'.[22] But on whose terms is this inclusion extended? As '"diversity" does not so powerfully appeal to our sense of justice and equality',[23] it has proven to be much more attractive to many organizational elites who felt threatened by the predictions outlined in *Workforce 2000*. Diversity management supplanted (rather than supplemented) affirmative action and equal opportunity goals, depoliticizing social change into the celebration of superficial differences that ultimately leaves unequal power structures intact.

Training for tolerance

In April 2018, two black men, Rashon Nelson and Donte Robinson, were arrested at a Starbucks coffee shop in Philadelphia. Although the two men had explained that they were waiting for a friend, the store manager called law enforcement when they refused to purchase something or leave. Transcripts later released by the police showed that the 911 call was placed just two minutes after the men arrived at the store.[24] The friend showed up as the two men were handcuffed and taken away by police. In response, Starbucks CEO, Kevin Johnson,

[22] Indeed, James Damore, the employee who filed a class action lawsuit against Google for reverse discrimination against white men claimed that his lawsuit would 'really help make Google a truly inclusive place' (Chuck, 2018).

[23] Benschop, 2001, p 1166.

[24] After this news story was reported, a spate of other similar cases in the United States attracted the attention of the media in May 2018. A white woman called police to the scene when she saw Lolade Siyonbola, a Black graduate student in African studies at Yale, asleep in their dorm lounge. The white student assumed that Siyonbola was an intruder. Three black teenagers shopping at Nordstrom Rack in St Louis were trailed by employees through the store before they were met by police outside, still carrying their purchases with receipts. Three black friends checking out of an Airbnb property in Rialto were detained by police when a white neighbour called 911, suspecting them to be burglars. Another white woman called the police on a Black family having a picnic at Lake Merritt in Oakland for using a charcoal grill in the park's non-charcoal barbecue zone. These cases viscerally illustrate the ongoing trauma of being Black in America. For an analysis of Black men and the United States justice system, see *Chokehold: Policing Black Men* by Paul Butler (2017). See also Philomena Essed's (1991) classic, *Understanding Everyday Racism: An Interdisciplinary Theory*.

issued a statement of apology, avowing 'what happened, the way the incident escalated and the outcome is nothing but reprehensible'.[25] Johnson added that Starbucks will close more than 8,000 of its company-owned stores in the United States for an afternoon in order to train staff on unconscious bias.

Starbucks' response was applauded in the media for its swiftness, and Johnson in particular, who flew to Philadelphia to apologize to Nelson and Robinson in person, also attracted praise for his proactive leadership. While the response was indeed refreshing in a time where we have grown accustomed to defensiveness or denial at accusations of discrimination, the case prompted scientific debate around the effectiveness of unconscious bias training. Unconscious bias training appeared in corporations in the United States around a decade ago, although it was not until after 2013, around the time police shootings of Black people drew international attention,[26] that interest in organizational anti-bias training became more mainstream. Now approximately half of midsize companies and nearly all Fortune 500 companies have implemented it in the United States.

Unconscious or implicit bias training is founded on the idea that discriminatory attitudes on the basis of gender, race or other identifications are psychologically ingrained. Training usually involves giving workers a test to help them identify their biases, followed by a discussion around how that plays out in the workplace. As can be expected, diversity training varies considerably in practice, with some organizations developing extended face-to-face instruction with concrete ideas for taking action and others running basic self-guided computer modules.

Despite the growing prevalence of unconscious bias training, research has shown that it is not the panacea for racism and sexism that it can first appear to be. Sociologists Frank Dobbin and Alexandra Kalev

---

[25] Johnson's (2018) signed statement was published on the Starbucks website and later followed up with a video message: https://news.starbucks.com/views/a-follow-up-message-from-starbucks-ceo-in-philadelphia

[26] Cases include Trayvon Martin, an unarmed black teenager, who was fatally shot on 26 February 2012 by George Zimmerman, the neighbourhood watch coordinator for his gated community. The subsequent acquittal of Zimmerman prompted the formation of the social activist movement, Black Lives Matter. The movement helped draw attention and organize protests following two deaths in 2014: Eric Garner, who was choked to death by a police officer on 17 July 2014 in Staten Island, New York, and Michael Brown, another unarmed Black teenager, who was shot and killed on 9 August 2014 by Darren Wilson, a police officer in Ferguson, Missouri.

researched over 800 companies in the United States and found that any positive effects of training rarely lasted beyond a day or two, and in some cases they had the opposite effect and actually increased bias and hostility. Five years after implementing compulsory diversity training, the researchers found that companies saw no increase in the numbers of minority employees, while certain groups in particular (Asian Americans and African American women) actually declined. Dobbin and Kalev suggest that managers retaliate against what they see as corporate control. This tendency is said to be exacerbated in cases like Starbucks where the training may feel remedial and risks signalling to front-line employees that they are culprits of racism. 'This is what we do as human beings – we resist control', said Kalev in an interview with *The Washington Post*.[27]

The uncomfortable and unspoken truth in these claims is that bias training centres on whiteness and masculinity. They assume that managers are by default white men and, as such, take as given that managers would feel guilty, threatened and resistant to 'diversity'. Dobbin and Kalev's study spurred unfortunate headlines in the press like, 'To improve diversity, don't make people go to diversity training'.[28] In fact, this reading of their findings extends the ongoing endeavour to water down diversity policies and practices in organizations. Indeed, unconscious bias training is already a homeopathic solution with the aim of making powerful elites feel safe and comfortable. Its name avoids any hints towards 'sexism' or 'racism'.[29] More importantly, it evokes the idea that prejudice against other social groups is not only normal and natural, but a ubiquitous, universal fact of human psychology. Its very utterance absolves managers of discrimination as it reminds us that it was, after all, unconscious.[30] The failure of unconscious bias training is thus not surprising given that it was predicated on the myth that sexism and racism are not structural issues, but are psychological effects that can be easily overcome with a workshop.[31]

[27] McGregor, 2016.
[28] McGregor, 2016.
[29] 'Patriarchy' and 'white supremacy' be damned.
[30] As Mike Noon (2018, p 202) argues, 'part of the allure of the notion of unconscious bias is that it is not about blame'. He shows that a fundamental problem with unconscious bias training is its inadequate treatment of agency while making presumptions about individuals' willingness to change.
[31] Noon, 2018; Tate and Page, 2018.

Through the last two chapters of this book I have attempted to demonstrate that there is nothing unconscious about imperialism and white supremacy. The prejudicial beliefs and actions taken in organizations extend from imperialist ideologies that have for the last few centuries shaped ideas about who has the right to rule. White supremacy is not normal or natural, as it continues to uphold beliefs about the inherent criminality and danger of Black people. Theories and practices of diversity management have served to conceal white power and curtail social change and thus cannot be depended upon to cultivate inclusivity in any meaningful sense.

Internalizing racism

When scholarly articles and practitioner handbooks discuss diversity, there is often a pervasive assumption that diversity is something that white male managers do *to* women and people of colour. It is as though we think of women and people of colour as agentless forms that wander around outside organizations, waiting for a wise and benevolent white man inside the organization to throw open the doors and welcome them in. When the organization is made 'diverse', the inevitable surge in profits and performance will see the manager commended and rewarded for his 'inclusive leadership'. It would seem that the legacy of the autonomous and rational Enlightenment man is alive in the ways we so readily neglect to think of women and people of colour as capable of leadership in their own right. The second part of the book will challenge this persistent myth and explore the ways anti-racist feminist groups practise inclusion in ways that challenge rather than conceal attendant structures of inequality. For now, I will outline the consequences and effects of diversity theories and practices on those who diversity management is said to benefit.

In organizations that actively manage diversity, women and people of colour can feel exposed and hypervisible. This is because dominant notions of diversity not only treat female and non-white staff as signs of diversity, but also as responsible for it. In many cases, this logic of diversity means that female and non-white staff shoulder an additional burden of labour, where they are more likely to be called upon to help promote the organization's branding. They can also be required to become caretakers of diversity by sitting on committees responsible for solving diversity problems such as how to attract more diverse applicants or appeal to a diverse customer base. Given that diversity work is generally accorded less value in organizations than other kinds of work, getting 'stuck' in diversity work is one way of further marginalizing and disadvantaging women and people of colour.[32]

When talking about structural inequality, I find the concept of violence useful. However, it is so frequently used in everyday language that it easily loses its meaning. When I discuss violence in organizations, I am not exclusively talking about physical harm, but violence that comprises broader senses of injury against the person and psyche, including assaults on their dignity, identity and representation.[33] That is not to say that violence is to be dichotomized between the physical and the psychological, as though it could only assault the body *or* the mind. Rather, violence invariably occurs between and through flesh, and often manifests through bodily emotions such as shame, guilt, anxiety and anger and bodily signals such as flushing red and trembling.[34] Violence also tends to leave a persistent mark, imprinting itself on the body and the mind[35] and can sometimes see the victim perpetuate those violent behaviours.[36]

Violence is inherent to organizations. It can be subtle and insidious as well as dramatic.[37] Violence can also become institutionalized and sentimentalized through schemes of domination, when victims of violence come to accept the harm done to them and may even unwittingly or unwillingly be complicit in this violence.[38] When violence is supported by formal organizational structures, the guilt and responsibility for the abuse is often placed on the victim, where the violence is constructed as a necessary and inevitable part of organizational life.[39] In effect, victims are denied the right to define and therefore resist the violence.

In 2014, I saw the marks of violence on the bodies and minds of Asian Australian leaders I interviewed for a study on leadership and race. My biography informed my choice to conduct a study focusing

---

[32] Sara Ahmed and Elaine Swan (2006, p 98) articulate this idea in the introduction to their Special Issue of *Policy Futures in Education*, where they point out that staff who end up 'spending their time doing work that is undervalued and underresourced in terms of pay, power, time, financing, and commitment, and can lead to increased stress and few promotion prospects'.

[33] Hearn, 2003; Linstead, 1997; Westwood, 2003.

[34] Bourdieu, 2004; Linstead, 1997; Merleau-Ponty, 1962.

[35] Westwood, 2003.

[36] Linstead, 1997.

[37] Davidson and Langan, 2006; Hearn, 1994.

[38] Bourdieu, 2004.

[39] Linstead, 1997.

on leaders who identify as Chinese, which represents the largest subgroup of Asian Australians.[40] I sought to draw on the experiences I shared with my participants to facilitate dialogic engagement.[41] As I have detailed in my published work, I conducted interviews with 21 participants (14 identifying as men and seven as women) between April and December 2014. Sixteen held middle to senior management positions in corporations, four held positions in government and one headed a social enterprise. While each interview lasted between an hour and three hours, with a total of 29 hours and 45 minutes of formal recorded interviewing time, our time together usually involved extensive informal discussion over coffee before our interview, followed by dinner or lunch afterwards. The formal interviews began with a life history approach – 'tell me about your background, your childhood, where you went to school and your memories growing up' – and then proceeded in an informal, unstructured way, allowing the informant to choose which aspects of their life and career they wished the interview to concentrate.

With diversity marked on their bodies, the professionals described navigating a delicate balance between being expected by their companies and communities to stand for issues of diversity and multiculturalism, yet being regarded with suspicion by whose interests they represent. A former council mayor joked that journalists repeatedly asked her to comment on multiculturalism: 'The media just quotes me when there's a multicultural issue because I'm Chinese. I have interest in other issues too. Can't they ask me about my interests in education and healthcare? Why are they asking me about multiculturalism? [Laughs].' The councillor suggested that because of her visible difference, her full humanity is overlooked and denied. With her identity restricted to a racialized woman representing racial issues, the councillor also met with continual suspicion about her motivations and interests: 'Sometimes I feel that even if I help ten [white] Australians and one Chinese person, some people will still complain that I only help Chinese people.' This perception reflects

[40] Australian Bureau of Statistics, 2012. The diverse makeup of participants offered a vivid example of the plurality of those who are often homogenized with labels of not only 'Asian', but even 'Chinese', in Australia. By including everyone who self-defined as Chinese Australian, participants represented diverse backgrounds including those born and raised in mainland China, Hong Kong, Taiwan, Malaysia, Singapore, Fiji, the United States and Australia and ranging from third-generation to recent migrants. Yet common stories among the participants revealed how dominant categorizations shaped their standpoints (Ang, 2014; Tan, 2003).

[41] Clough, 1994; Denzin, 2009.

the assumption that whiteness exemplifies the human norm and thus only white people can speak for the whole of society.[42] It also reveals ongoing anxieties about multicultural Australia grounded in a persistent groupism that demarcates Australians of colour from white Australians, singling out people of colour as antagonistic and demanding their compliance with white regimes.

Another participant raised the lack of racial diversity in their organization to human resources and recalled how the white manager responded, 'Well, what do you want? Do you want a better job? Is that what it's about?' Underlying this perception is the assumption that diversity management is something white people do *to* people of colour and thus its practice *by* people of colour must represent interests fundamentally at odds with (white) Australia. This fundamental distrust of Australians of colour suspects us of caring for our own racial groups over white Australians. Diversity and its management need to be guarded by white Australians whose leadership is the only way to ensure it is exercised for the 'greater good'.[43]

Diversity in society

In Australia, a celebratory commitment to multiculturalism has been tightly woven into the discourses of our national identity since the 1970s.[44] This inclusionary national ideal was established in opposition to the exclusionary White Australia policy of the past[45] and aimed to enrich Australia by preserving its racial diversity.[46] Under this state-sponsored multicultural policy, Australians are encouraged to 'express and share their individual cultural heritage'; however, they are

[42] Dyer, 1997; Liu, 2017c.

[43] Banerjee and Linstead, 2001; Hage, 1998; Liu, 2017c; Stratton and Ang, 2013.

[44] Ang, 2003; Stratton and Ang, 2013.

[45] Following the Federation of Australia in 1901, Australia imposed an assimilationist white ideal through the White Australia policy, which limited the arrival and endorsed the deportation of non-European immigrants (Curthoys, 2003). Since the abolition of the White Australia policy in 1973, discourses of a multicultural national identity have become increasingly widespread in a landscape of post-war immigration and globalization (Jayasuriya, Walker and Gothard, 2003). In contrast to the *laissez-faire* approach of the United States, Australia is distinct in its deliberate management of ethno-cultural diversity, evidenced by its 'amalgam of policies designed to supervise incorporation and address diversity's consequences for communal relations and identity' (Walsh, 2012, p.282).

[46] Banerjee and Linstead, 2001; Hage, 1998.

cautioned that they can only do so 'within carefully defined limits' while maintaining 'an overriding and unifying commitment to Australia'.[47]

Despite the outward celebratory commitment to cultural diversity, the policies and practices are fundamentally imperialist. Race and ethnicity are ultimately defined in white terms and people of colour are seen as objects to be controlled. Multiculturalism allows lingering ideals of white supremacy to be concealed while putting sterile, commodified artefacts of difference, like ethnic restaurants and urban enclaves, on display.[48]

Whiteness remains at the core of Australian multiculturalism and in the present neoliberal capitalist landscape, people of colour are increasingly seen in terms of their economic value to a parochial and protectionist Australia.[49] In the apt words of Bobby Banerjee and Stephen Linstead, multiculturalism serves as 'an alibi against racism as well as a criterion of cultural capital through the consumption of difference without any apparent interrogation'.[50] Multiculturalism is hence not what Australia *is*, but what it *has*.[51]

In Australia, eagerness for a multicultural society resurfaced at the start of this decade within the rhetoric of an 'Asian Century'. The Asian Century signals the economic rise of Asia, a region comprising many of Australia's largest trading partners, and is concerned with how Australia can 'seize the economic opportunities that will flow and manage the strategic challenges that will arise'.[52] With the announcement of this so-called Asian Century, the disproportionately low representation of Asian Australians in positions of leadership started to feature as a topic of public interest and debate. In July 2014, the Race Discrimination Commissioner Tim Soutphommasane suggested that a 'bamboo ceiling' may exist in Australia.[53] He pointed out that although people of Asian descent comprise 12 per cent of the Australia's population,[54]

---

[47] Office of Multicultural Affairs, 1989, paras 4–5.

[48] Ang, 2003; Banerjee and Linstead, 2001; Davidson, 2003; Hage, 1998; Lo, 2006; Mak, 2003; Stratton and Ang, 2013.

[49] Liu, 2017b.

[50] Banerjee and Linstead, 2001, p 705.

[51] See *White Nation: Fantasies of White Supremacy in a Multicultural Society* by Ghassan Hage (1998).

[52] Commonwealth of Australia, 2012, p ii.

[53] Tim Soutphommasane's keynote speech 'The Asianisation of Australia?' was delivered at the Asian Studies Association of Australia Annual Conference in Perth, Australia. A transcript of the speech can be found here: www.humanrights.gov.au/news/speeches/asianisation-australia

[54] Colebatch, 2012.

they represent only 1.9 per cent of the executives in Australia's top 200 companies.[55]

Running through the discussions of the bamboo ceiling is an emphasis on how organizations may better *use* 'Asian talent' (a term that depoliticizes and individuates race into a personal capability) in the service of organizational profit and performance.[56] Even within ostensibly pro-diversity discourses that extoll the organizational benefits of racially diverse leaders, Asian people are constructed as docile bodies to be put to the service of corporate profit and performance. With leadership theories developed under the assumption of a white male default, we can sometimes fail to recognize leadership when it is practised by those who do not fit this model.

Who gets to lead?

In May 2014, one of the participants of my study allowed me to conduct a more in-depth study of his work.[57] Jeff[58] was at the time a senior manager of a large Australian information technology company. I was invited to observe a one-hour morning meeting he ran with six of his staff. The company adopts a matrix structure so Jeff was only one of four functional managers to which his staff reported. Since his appointment to the role, Jeff has scheduled weekly meetings with his staff to discuss recent organizational and client activities. In addition to interviewing Jeff four times over the next three months, I further interviewed each of his staff one-on-one about their perceptions of their manager.

First, it is important to put Jeff's identity into perspective. Jeff exhibited the hegemonic Australian masculine ideal[59] in every way but race. He identified as cis-male, heterosexual, holding a senior management position in his late 30s, married with two children, comfortably middle class, tertiary educated with an MBA, and not only able-bodied, but tall and athletic. As a '1.5 generation' Taiwanese migrant, Jeff also benefited from speaking fluent English with a broad Australian accent; making his racial Otherness only evident in

---

[55] O'Leary and Tilly, 2014, p 2.
[56] O'Leary and Tilly, 2014, p 10.
[57] I present here a condensed summary of the full analysis originally published in the *Journal of Business Ethics* (Liu, 2019b).
[58] Jeff allowed me to use his real name, but I have chosen to omit his surname and his organization.
[59] Connell, 1987, 1995; Connell and Messerschmidt, 2005.

appearance. Despite this relatively minor aspect of his intersectional identity, Jeff met considerable resistance to his leadership.

Jeff recounted his enduring commitment to a greater purpose of advocating for cultural diversity in Australian organizations. Facing personal and professional risks, he maintained the belief that fostering inclusive workplaces would ultimately strengthen his organization and bolster Australia's economy in the Asian century. Through initiatives such as the weekly meetings, Jeff leveraged his social networks to share organizational information that empowered his staff to do their jobs more effectively, while taking the opportunity to recognize and praise his team. In my view, Jeff demonstrated many of the attributes venerated in a rising construct called 'servant leadership', including humility, selflessness and compassion.[60] Originally proposed by management consultant, Robert Greenleaf, servant leaders are said to be exceptional individuals who are driven by an innate desire to be of service to others as well as their organizations and communities.[61] Consistent with my perspective outlined in the introduction to the book, I did not see servant leadership as existing in any 'real', objective sense, but I was interested in how people characterize, negotiate and practise what they called 'servant leadership'.

Jeff's staff embraced their manager as the 'servant' while questioning his claim to 'leadership'. The employees acknowledged the efforts Jeff made to empower and support his team, but instead of attributing this to leadership, they saw it as Jeff's rightful place to serve their needs. Their perceptions of Jeff were influenced by stereotypes of Asian masculinity as weak and feminized[62] – that is, seen to be inferior to the paternalistic and competitive forms of white masculinity idealized among corporate leaders. The more ambivalent employees were quick to construct Jeff as 'not tough enough' to be a *real* leader, reinforcing the individualist ideals in traditional constructs of charismatic leadership. For example, one employee recalled his first impressions of Jeff as 'very quiet initially, but he's just softly spoken that way. I guess that might be a cultural thing. ... I've seen him stressed, but not ever aggressive, necessarily. It could be a cultural thing again [laughs]'. Another employee offered, 'he's not an aggressive person by nature. He's more – he will direct where to go'. And another claimed, 'he's a very easy guy to go to work with. The only thing I find is that he's quiet, so sometimes you've

[60] Van Dierendonck, 2011; Liden et al, 2008; Reed, Vidaver-Cohen and Colwell, 2011; Russell and Stone, 2002.

[61] See *The Servant as Leader* by Robert K. Greenleaf (1970).

[62] Chan, 2001; Chen, 1999; Hirose and Pih, 2010; Liu, 2017d; Louie, 2002.

got to draw him out a little bit. Quiet as in volume-wise as well as [chuckles] "what are you trying to say exactly?"'

Even those who seemingly appreciated Jeff expounded only his technical and functional abilities within an invidious model minority stereotype, calling him 'diligent' and 'organized'.[63] One employee extolled Jeff's competence, while framing their relationship on more equal terms than that of leader and follower, describing Jeff as 'totally professional, dedicated, organized, he plans everything … he's a dream to work with so I don't mind helping him out' offered a backhanded compliment and suggested that Jeff takes on too much, saying 'he's fairly diligent in what he tries to do, there's no doubt about that. He seems to have a lot of things on his plate; he takes on ownership of a lot of things'.

My observations of Jeff suggested that sociopolitical meanings of race, gender, sexuality, age and class inform the extent to which people can be accepted or rejected as a 'leader'. As white supremacist ideologies historically constructed Asian immigrants as naturally subordinate,[64] Jeff's servant leadership behaviours were rendered 'illegible' as acts of leadership. His attempts to exercise servant leadership were more readily interpreted as his appropriate deference to white employees, rather than valiant acts of selflessness. With the exception of one employee, all others spurned their construction as 'followers', positioning themselves instead as equal or superior to their manager. These employees centred their identities as the protagonists of the organizational narrative within the assumption that white men are the rightful leaders and beneficiaries of the corporate arena.[65]

Conclusion

Despite the resistance and resentment some white people feel towards diversity, its dominant practices often work to extend white patriarchal power. Across organizations and society, diversity is reduced to superficial and sterile markers of difference. The mere presence of people who look different can then be used as an alibi for systemic inequality. 'But how can we be racist? Look at all the black and brown people we have!'

With diversity marked on their bodies, people of colour navigate a precarious balance between being expected by their organizations and

---

[63] Chae, 2004; Cho, 1997; Yeh, 2014.
[64] Kwek, 2003; Parker, 2000; Ray, 2003.
[65] Hage, 1998; Leong, 2012; Liu, 2017c.

communities to stand for issues of diversity and multiculturalism yet being regarded with suspicion about whose interests they represent. Managers of colour who advocate for increased racial diversity in their organizations would be accused of being self-interested; surreptitiously scheming for a promotion or a higher salary through their attempts at leadership. Local councillors of colour are targeted by the media to comment on issues of multiculturalism in the community, which reinforce the assumptions that people of colour are only interested in race and have no right to govern 'universal' issues like education or healthcare. In particular, business and political leaders interpret diversity through a capitalistic logic that focuses on how we may *use* people of colour to further economic agendas. People of colour are denied their agency through a dehumanizing construction that renders their leadership 'illegible' in a world still enamoured with the Enlightenment man. The 'inclusion' that diversity promises is ultimately hollow and cannot be trusted to undo white patriarchal violence.

White patriarchal power is often reinforced when leadership scholars fail to acknowledge the ways gender and race shape the production of knowledge. In the white academe that is entrenched in imperialist ideology, the act of speaking for another social group to which we do not belong and of which we have no experience is not only academically acceptable within leadership studies, but sometimes even problematically respected and rewarded.[66] I am not suggesting that there should be no theorizations from the 'outside', but when scholarship is structured through gendered and racial power as it is, it has seemed that researchers of colour who write about their own racial groups are often seen as doing self-absorbed niche research, while white scholars who write about people of colour are more likely to be seen as saviours.

The figure of the white saviour seems to be vital for concealing systemic violence and thus warrants further examination. In the next chapter – the final chapter of Part I – I will turn to this idea of the inherent benevolence of whiteness in more depth.

[66] Liu, 2017a.

4

Salvation

We are living in times beset by the seemingly constant reporting of ethical scandals and corruption. The start of this century saw the collapse of corporations including Enron,[1] HIH Insurance[2] and WorldCom[3] due to the fraudulent actions of their leaders. During the 2008 financial crisis, banking leaders were accused of hubris, greed, and even of being psychopaths.[4] As the news stories of unethical leaders multiplied, some returned to leadership to suggest that it too was the solution. Far from calling leadership into question, many scholars and practitioners counteracted the mounting examples of ethical failures with ever more glorified characterizations of leadership as quintessentially moral and good.[5] Under this prevailing logic, the antidote to bad leadership is always good leadership, where exceptional individuals are believed to be able to deliver their organizations from crises while conveying confidence, hope and optimism, and maintaining trust.[6]

---

[1] Enron was an energy trading company that collapsed after an accounting fraud scheme was revealed. The company's executives received millions of dollars from off-the-books partnerships while reporting inflated profits to shareholders. The executives sold their stocks right before reporting their loss, eventually filing for bankruptcy in 2001.

[2] HIH was the second largest insurance company in Australia when its leaders were found to have misled investors about the organization's health until its collapse in 2001.

[3] WorldCom was one of the largest telecommunications companies in the United States. In 2002, systematic accounting fraud was exposed at the company totalling $11 billion worth of misstatements that were coordinated between the co-founder, Bernard 'Bernie' Ebbers, and chief financial officer, Scott Sullivan.

[4] Boddy, 2011; Coleman and Pinder, 2010; Liu, 2015; Tett, 2009; Weitzner and Darroch, 2009.

[5] Liu, 2015.

[6] Chambers, Drysdale and Hughes, 2010; Freeman and Auster, 2011; Peus et al, 2012.

The glorified nature of leadership constrains the theorizing, development and practice of leadership. If leadership is believed to be intrinsically ethical, critical dialogues around the ways leadership perpetuates violence are silenced. Abiding fantasies about leadership can inflict harm on followers as well as leaders themselves. Particularly during times of crises or uncertainty,[7] followers can experience a sense of alienation and helplessness.[8] These feelings can also be exploited by leaders who may construct organizational or societal crises in order to foster followers' reliance on heroic figures.[9] Heroic ideals also promote leader narcissism and intensified identity work.[10] Professionals from all levels of an organization can feel pressured to strive towards 'leadership' by anxiously pursuing a self-image more in line with contemporary corporate values. However, leadership fantasies continue to be perpetuated by corporations, the media, business schools and consultancy firms that trade in the valuable commodity of 'leadership'.[11]

This chapter introduces the range of theories that have sought to articulate the moral and ethical dimensions of leadership. It will focus primarily on ethical leadership, both philosophical and social scientific strands of this theory, and critique its promotion of individual heroism. It will illustrate the limitations of an individualist approach through the examples of benevolent sexism and racism, which reveal the structural and ideological machinations of white patriarchal power. In particular, the figure of the white saviour is explored in more depth, tracing its origins back to colonial discourses and showing how it has shaped contemporary ideas of ethical leadership. Given our intense faith in benevolent leaders, how the idealization of ethical leaders plays out in practice is explored. I draw on my past empirical research to show first how the heroicization of billionaire philanthropists in Australia is underpinned by white power. I then turn to the urgent issue of environmental sustainability and, in presenting the case of a sustainability leadership development centre, show how the neoliberal self is recentred in the production of 'green leaders'.

---

[7] Bligh and Schyns, 2007; Khurana, 2011; Ruth, 2014.

[8] Gemmill and Oakley, 1992.

[9] Psychological research has shown that conservative politics typically relies on people's fear (of immigration, unemployment, terrorism, and so on) (see Ball, 2016; Westen, 2007). See also leadership scholar Keith Grint's (2010b) article about the ways people can seem to be 'addicted to command'.

[10] Alvesson and Willmott, 2002; Kets de Vries and Balazs, 2011; Sveningsson and Larsson, 2006.

[11] Liu, 2017e.

Ethical leaders

Questions about leaders' moral failings have brought ethics to the forefront of leadership theorizing in the last few decades. Ethical leadership theories are predicated on the belief that leaders play a critical role in setting the ethical tone for the organization. By nature of their role, leaders often have the power to develop strategies, articulate values and implement disciplinary and reward systems that incentivize particular behaviours.[12] Leaders also act as role models for followers, with research suggesting that employees conform to the ethical values espoused by their leaders.[13] The perception of ethical leaders has been linked to employee commitment, increased positive behaviour in the organization, and ultimately, improved organizational performance.[14]

Ethical leadership has advanced ideas for what ethical leadership is and how it ought to be practised in organizations. There are two broad orientations to scholarship, the philosophical approach and social scientific approach, that have collectively provided insights into the theory, development and practice of ethical leadership. Proponents of the philosophical approach draw on moral philosophies to offer normative models that outline a leader's duties and responsibilities. Joanne Ciulla, one of the most influential writers in this field, asserts that leaders have to be both ethical and effective.[15] She draws on virtue theory, deontology and teleology to argue that leaders need to promote eudaimonic wellbeing through ethical intentions, processes and outcomes.[16] Terry Price similarly draws on the deontological philosophy of Immanuel Kant to call for leaders to accept their duty to help others and respect all organizational members as rational agents rather than instruments to be used.[17]

Social scientific research of ethics is oriented to investigate how people perceive ethical leadership and how leaders model ethical behaviours to their followers. For instance, management scholars Michael Brown and Linda Treviño and their colleagues found that in order to be perceived as ethical, leaders need to demonstrate that

---

[12] Brown and Mitchell, 2010.
[13] Schminke et al, 2002.
[14] Kanungo, 2001; Mayer, Davis and Schoorman, 1995; Treviño, Butterfield and McCabe, 1998; Weaver, Treviño and Cochran, 1999.
[15] See *Ethics, the Heart of Leadership* by Joanne Ciulla (2004).
[16] Ciulla, 2005.
[17] Price, 2000, 2003, 2008.

they are both a strong moral person and a strong moral manager.[18] As a moral person, leaders have to be seen as honest, approachable, fair and caring. As a moral manager, leaders need to set and communicate moral standards and enforce them through reward and discipline.

Adding to the construct of 'ethical leadership' have also been kindred forms of leadership that likewise articulate an explicit moral component to the practice of leadership. Servant leadership, spiritual leadership, wise leadership and authentic leadership are just a few of the more notable models that comprise the growing list of idealized individuals who variously exhibit altruistic behaviours such as self-awareness, resilience, honesty, trustworthiness and integrity. I explored the concept of servant leadership in the previous chapter in the case of Jeff. Spiritual leaders are said to create a vision that offers leaders and followers a sense of calling, while promoting a culture grounded in values of altruistic love where leaders and followers experience membership and mutual respect.[19] The wisdom model argues that leadership ought to be exercised for the common good and a better future through the practical application of intelligence, creativity, knowledge or experience.[20] Lastly, authentic leadership, which superseded transformational leadership as the most influential model of leadership in the mid-2000s, proposed a new breed of leaders who would, by virtue of being 'true to themselves', inspire confidence, optimism and trust.[21]

Although these theories have made considerable advancements in highlighting the crucial connection between ethics and leadership, such models of moral leadership are largely treated as the preserve of exceptional individuals who possess the right traits and exhibit the right behaviours. This faith in a heroic leader to save us all underpins the perennial tendency to prescribe 'good leadership' as the remedy for 'bad leadership', while leadership itself evades critique. The following sections of this chapter will attempt to show how the theory and practice of ethical leadership reproduce the romance of leadership and elide critical interrogations of the ways in which leadership can reinforce systems of oppression.

[18] Brown, Treviño and Harrison, 2005; Brown and Mitchell, 2010; Brown and Treviño, 2006; Treviño, Brown and Hartman, 2003; Treviño, Butterfield and McCabe, 1998; Treviño, Hartman and Brown, 2000.
[19] Fry and Cohen, 2009; Reave, 2005.
[20] McKenna, Rooney and Boal, 2009; Yang, 2008, 2011.
[21] Gardner et al, 2005, 2011.

Benevolent violence

While the previous chapters have attempted to illustrate the subtle and insidious ways systems of oppression operate, organizations by and large continue to focus on overt acts of violence as the sole expression of power. They point the finger at isolated individuals – the accursed sexists and the racists – whose attitudes and behaviours are believed to be aberrations from the otherwise inclusive 'norm'. Two areas of research that have attempted to draw attention to the complexity of power has been the work on benevolent sexism and benevolent racism.

Proposed by social psychologists Peter Glick and Susan Fiske, benevolent sexism refers to an interrelated set of attitudes towards those who identify as women that may seem subjectively positive, yet nonetheless are grounded in restrictively stereotypical ideas.[22] Thus, while benevolent sexism could be expressed in seemingly affirmative ways, such as holding open the door for female employees, that behaviour is underpinned by the same patriarchal notions of women as weak and dependent and requiring male protection that inform more overtly hostile forms of sexism.

In that sense, Glick and Fiske utilize the term 'benevolent' ironically and in no way imply that benevolent sexism is a positive phenomenon, or even preferable to hostile sexism. By reinforcing women's subordinate role in patriarchy, benevolent sexism has been shown to produce in women a sense of self-doubt that negatively affects their performance at work.[23] Benevolent sexism is typically used to compensate for, or even legitimate, hostile sexism, defending their actions through rationales such as, 'I am not exploiting women; I love, protect and provide for them'.[24] Despite these attestations to altruism, both benevolent and hostile sexisms assume women to be inherently 'inferior, incompetent, and generally useless'.[25]

Organization scholars Marieke van den Brink and Yvonne Benschop exposed practices of benevolent sexism in their study of gender relations in academia.[26] In interviews with senior members of promotions committees, they found a tendency among men to presume that women (especially mothers) would struggle to balance their caring responsibilities with the demands of their careers. Often well-intentioned, the men in their study followed the misguided

---

[22] Developed under ambivalent sexism theory (Glick and Fiske, 1996).
[23] Shepherd et al, 2011.
[24] Glick and Fiske, 1996, p 492.
[25] Shepherd et al, 2011, p 2.
[26] Van den Brink and Benschop, 2012.

belief that *not* promoting women would 'protect' them from a heavy workload. Their logic was grounded in patriarchal ideas that care-taking was exclusively a female problem, therefore such concerns were never raised with male candidates.

Benevolent sexism cannot exist independently of hostile sexism.[27] But unlike hostile sexism, benevolent sexism is more socially acceptable. Benevolent sexism evades social scrutiny and critique because of our inability to form a sociological imagination; to see gender inequality as operating through everyday patriarchy as opposed to the overt actions of individual sexists.

Figure 3: 'The White Man's Burden (Apologies to Rudyard Kipling)' by Victor Gillam.

Source: *Judge*, 1 April 1899.

In 1899, Rudyard Kipling published his poem, *The White Man's Burden*.[28] In this piece, Kipling warned the United States, which

---

[27] Shepherd et al, 2011.

[28] The poem first appeared in *The New York Sun* on 10 February 1899. Later, in 1910, Alabama Baptist minister Benjamin F. Riley wrote an essay under the same title. In what historian George M. Fredrickson (1971, p 288) called a 'monument of sentimental paternalism and apparent Negrophilia', Riley (1910, p 119) claims that 'the dominant characteristic of the Negro is that of submission and tractableness. … This passive virtue has been his greatest means of conservation'.

had newly acquired many of the Spanish colonies after the Spanish American War,[29] about the 'racial responsibilities of empire-building'.[30] He exhorted the United States to look to his native Britain as a model of paternalism, following in its footsteps to foster a sense of responsibility over the colonized, whom he called 'your new-caught, sullen peoples, half devil and half child'. In other words, white Americans were urged to accept the 'burden' of looking after the inferior races they now governed.[31]

Sociologists Luigi Esposito and Victor Romano trace the practice of benevolent racism from Kipling's officious advice through the history of the United States. They highlight how Southern progressives in the late 19th and early 20th centuries rejected extreme acts of hostile racism by holding onto the belief that although Black people were biologically inferior, they 'could *also* be peaceful, docile and productive if treated with fairness and kindness'.[32] One such figure was Willis D. Weatherford, a leader in the Southern YMCA movement, who praised Black people's 'fidelity, gratitude, generosity, lack of malice, kindliness, sense of humour, and a peculiar aptitude for music and religion', even though he admitted that they were 'not the most brilliantly intellectual' and also 'lacking in self-mastery'.[33] In a speech to the Southern Sociological Congress, Weatherford claimed that his white peers were coming to recognize that Black people possessed 'those fine qualities of character displayed by the faithful slave', but that it was up to white Americans to nurture those racial traits.[34]

The cultural deficit perspective[35] is commonly invoked in benevolent racism. The perspective seeks to explain how the disadvantages faced by people of colour are due to their poor cultural values. For example,

[29] The United States ratified the Treaty of Paris that year, which allowed it to gain control over the Philippines, Guam, Puerto Rico and Cuba.
[30] Esposito and Romano, 2014, p 71.
[31] Kipling was described by George Orwell as 'morally insensitive and aesthetically disgusting'.
[32] Esposito and Romano, 2014, p 72. See also *The Black Image in the White Mind: The Debate on Afro-American Character and Destiny, 1817–1914* by George M. Fredrickson (1971).
[33] Fredrickson, 1971, pp 289–290.
[34] Fredrickson, 1971, p 290.
[35] A classic example of the cultural deficit perspective is Daniel Patrick Moynihan's 1965 report, *The Negro Family: The Case For National Action* (also known as the Moynihan Report), in which he argues that the economic and political deprivation of Black people was due to the higher rates of single-mother families in Black communities. The critique of deficit thinking is particularly sustained in education (see Solórzano and Yosso, 2001).

deficit thinking may lead to the idea that Asian people do not make good leaders because their culture socializes them to be quiet, modest and passive. Therefore, white managers are really doing Asian people a favour by not promoting them as they are probably happier being followers anyway. By blaming the marginalized individuals for their marginalization, the deficit perspective deflects any critique of structural oppression.

In contemporary organizations, we see benevolent sexism and racism in the rejection of affirmative action in favour of watered down 'diversity and inclusion' initiatives. The arguments against affirmative action in organizations are rarely presented as any blatant attempt to defend white power and privilege, but framed instead as bad policy because it supposedly implies that marginalized employees are incapable of competing with their white colleagues on equal terms. They side with 'minority employees' in their rails against affirmative action as they claim that such policies risk a sense of inferiority among minority employees themselves that will stifle their full potential and debilitate their progress in society. Practitioners of benevolent sexism and racism can therefore fortify existing structures of oppression under a guise of selfless heroism to 'empower' minority employees.

White saviours

As race, including whiteness, is a social construct, what it means to be 'white' is the product of an ongoing project of mythmaking. In critical race studies, our understandings of the fictional white self have been significantly advanced by film and television scholars who show us the limitations of imagination to 'see' ourselves and others. In their book *Screen Saviours*, Hernán Vera and Andrew Gordon call these 'sincere fictions'[36] because those who produce stereotypical images are seldom aware of the alternative possibilities.[37] When our social reality

---

[36] Borrowing from Pierre Bourdieu's (1990, p 112) idea that almost all social relations depend on 'the sincere fiction of disinterested exchange'. See also *The Gift* by Marcel Mauss (1966).

[37] During the Holocaust, social representations played a powerful role in justifying the Nazi genocide. *Der Stürmer* was a German weekly tabloid published from 1923 by Julius Streicher featuring viciously anti-Semitic stereotypes through offensive caricatures and exaggerated myths that dehumanized and demonized Jewish people. The publication became very popular and circulated at 486,000 in its peak in 1935. When Streicher was captured and tried after the war, the tribunal of judges concluded that he influenced German public imagination through *Der Stürmer* and

continues to be influenced by the ideologies of imperialism and white supremacy developed in the colonial era, racial stereotypes persist in defining who we are.

According to Vera and Gordon, the 'messianic white self is a redeemer of the weak, the great leader who saves blacks from slavery or oppression, rescues people of colour from poverty and disease, or leads Indians in the battle for their dignity and survival'.[38] Film and television became fertile ground for white writers and white directors to manifest wondrous fictions of whiteness. In the 1989 American war film *Glory*, for example, the story centres on the heroic figure of Colonel Robert Gould Shaw who took command of the first Black regiment and sacrificed his life for the cause. He is the quintessential white American hero: 'powerful, brave, cordial, kind, firm and generous – a leader'.[39] In the science fiction television series *Stargate*, Daniel Jackson is the learned scientist who applies his formidable intellect to communicate with enslaved natives and free them from their alien overlords. We see this plot arc replicated in *Indiana Jones and the Temple of Doom*, as the heroic American archaeologist helps desperate Indian villagers to retrieve a mystical stone that eventually leads to him freeing child slaves from a religious cult.

In these fantastical myths of the white saviour, there are no autonomous people of colour, only those who are led by the white protagonists. In *Glory*, the Black characters are formed by Shaw into a strong regiment, sustained by their loyalty to the noble white master. The indigenous people in *Stargate* (who are descendants of Egyptians) are portrayed as ignorant, superstitious and gullible, and would have remained forever enslaved by their alien overlords were it not for the intervention of one intelligent white American. The Indian characters in *The Temple of Doom* are split between 'loyal subjects of the British Crown or rebellious, blood-crazed Thuggee cultists'.[40] The 'good natives' who are faithful to the white protagonist are helpless to save themselves and, again, need to rely on the great (American) man to liberate them.

Although less dramatic than such films and television series, theories of leadership attempt to enhance their appeal by invoking seductive notions of white heroism. Leadership scholarship continues to paint

argued that he was as culpable as those who carried out the genocide. Streicher was sentenced to death and hung in 1946.

[38] Vera and Gordon, 2002, p 33.
[39] Vera and Gordon, 2002, p 28.
[40] Vera and Gordon, 2002, p 36.

heroic images of exceptional leaders who are adept at 'solving' moral dilemmas.[41] Our salvation is not achieved through any collaborative or consultative efforts, but, rather, we may expect a leader like Robert Gould Shaw, Daniel Jackson or Indiana Jones to liberate us by virtue of his formidable individual capabilities.[42]

Here, the Enlightenment man rears his head again in theorizations of ethical leadership. This prevailing European ideal of autonomous rationality has shaped the construction of ethical leadership as a capability inherent to individual moral agents who can wilfully relinquish personal biases in order to objectively choose 'right' over 'wrong'. Should any leader lack this capability, they may invest in training programmes that develop their competencies in 'communicating relevant values and ethical guidelines', 'modelling ethical behaviour' and 'opposing unethical practices'[43] as though these generically prescribed behaviours can universally translate into ethical conduct.

Ethical leadership theories tend to assume that leaders, via hierarchical control, rationally enact ethical behaviours, objectively enforce reward and discipline, and intentionally shape the ethical behaviour of all organizational members via a linear causal relationship. However, these assumptions are often unable to account for the complex and unpredictable ways in which social actors, from all levels of an organizational system, shape one another's perceptions and behaviours.

Despite the persistent individualism in our cultures, leadership occurs in the space between people. From this relational view, what it means to lead ethically emerges from the ongoing process of negotiated meaning-making between social actors. Rather than focus on the traits, behaviours and intentions of individual leaders (and sell development programmes to inculcate aspiring leaders with the 'right' ones), we could pay attention to the ways leadership emerges through social interactions, acts of organizing and influence and shared cultural meanings. This approach is well positioned to explore power dynamics in the processes of co-construction so that we may understand how dominant practices of leadership can be resisted and alternate practices brought into being. The second part of this book will begin to engage

---

[41] Lawler and Ashman, 2012.

[42] The psychological theories of ethical leadership offer an ever-expanding list of traits comprising high power inhibition, high moral reasoning levels, internal locus of control, low Machiavellianism, agreeableness, conscientiousness and social responsibility (Brown and Treviño, 2006; De Hoogh and Den Hartog, 2008; Walumbwa and Schaubroeck, 2009).

[43] Hassan et al, 2013, p 141.

in these radical reimaginations. For now, the next two sections of the chapter will explore how the focus on individual heroism distorts the practices of ethical leadership.

Billionaire philanthropists

One group of 'ethical leaders' that regularly enjoy media attention is those who donate portions of their wealth to charitable causes. Internationally celebrated initiatives include Melinda Gates, Bill Gates and Warren Buffett's *Giving Pledge*, which has enlisted over 200 billionaires as of 2019 to commit to donating at least half of their wealth to charity since it was announced in 2010. In the vast majority of media reports of philanthropy, philanthropists are heralded for their exemplary moral character – standing in stark contrast to the disgraced leaders embroiled in ethical scandals.

It is a widely held assumption that philanthropic giving is ethical, beneficial and desirable.[44] Philanthropy plays a significant role in the leader's enactment as a moral person. A leader's commitment to charitable giving is believed to demonstrate their altruism; a tendency towards helping others without the expectation of personal rewards. Philanthropic activities can also point to values of benevolence and integrity, where leaders are seen to possess an intrinsic concern for others and consistently hold themselves to moral principles. Yet the leaders at Enron, HIH and Worldcom also engaged in philanthropy and developed reputations as civic-minded individuals before their crimes were exposed. Such leaders are well aware of the power of impression management, the process of image building whereby leaders can employ stylistic and rhetoric techniques to bolster their images as competent, ethical and trustworthy.[45] For example, narcissistic leaders have been found to be particularly likely to make extravagant public philanthropic gestures such as donations to Ivy League universities or carrying their names through the eponymous branding of buildings, scholarships and funds.[46] This seemingly modern phenomenon mirrors the actions of wealthy industrialists of late 19th century American industrialists;

---

[44] In this context, philanthropy is conceived as the private giving of money or other assets for public purposes (Salamon, 1992). This definition excludes corporate philanthropy, which refers to the growing practice of corporations establishing their own foundations and making gifts to charitable organizations (Campbell, Moore and Metzger, 2002; Gautier and Pache, 2013).

[45] See *The Presentation of Self in Everyday Life* by Erving Goffman (1959).

[46] Spangler et al, 2012.

the so-called 'Robber Barons' such as John D. Rockefeller, Cornelius Vanderbilt and Andrew Carnegie, who turned to philanthropy in part to salvage their own reputations.[47]

Although Australia had little by way of an entrenched philanthropic tradition compared to the United States and United Kingdom, in 2013 a spate of philanthropic giving on the part of corporate leaders occurred. In a short span of two years, it seemed like Australian billionaires were in competition with one another to give away as much of their money as possible. It started with a $20 million donation from John Grill to the University of Sydney in October 2012, followed by $50 million to the Australian National University from Graham Tuckwell in February 2013, which was exceeded in October 2013 with $65 million to five universities in Western Australia from Andrew Forrest. This series of record-breaking donations combined with other smaller gifts since 2012 totalled more than $220 million, leading to proclamations of 'a new era of philanthropy in Australia'[48] and suggestions the nation was seeing 'real leadership in philanthropy'.[49]

For all the focus on these white knights, there are few reports of the outcomes of their 'aid', and even less so any perspectives from their target beneficiaries. Yet the link between philanthropy and ethical leadership is nevertheless regularly and consistently implied. This implicit association is grounded in wider glorified discourses of leadership that strengthen our confidence in the overcompetent individual and sustain the assumption that philanthropists are ethical leaders who are capable of providing solutions to social problems by virtue of their wealth.

In 2013, my colleague Christopher Baker and I analysed the media reports of 18 philanthropists in Australia over the preceding six years, from 2007 to 2013. Given the unequal distribution of wealth in our society, it is perhaps unsurprising that all these powerful figures are white. However, we did not expect to find how the media celebration of these billionaire philanthropists so powerfully echoed colonial and white supremacist ideologies that positioned white leaders as speaking for all of Australian society and representing the greater good.

The idea that white people represent the Australian norm was enhanced via their deracialization in media discourses. Not one media article on the leaders acknowledged their whiteness, treating

---

[47] Josephson, 2010.
[48] D'Angelo Fisher, 2013.
[49] Hewett, 2013.

white leaders as though they are 'unraced'. This meant that the white billionaires could assume themselves to occupy a 'neutral' position from which they could objectively decide how to improve society. This assumption was predicated on a unitary, homogenous construction of the nation grounded in historical ideals of a 'white Australia' that is presumed to share the same needs. Although explicitly describing white philanthropists' efforts as benefiting 'white causes' and the 'white community' may sound absurd, this is indeed what the media does when the philanthropist is seen to deviate from the white norm. For example, one of the Jewish philanthropists in our study was clarified as 'supporting Jewish and non-Jewish projects' as though his concern for the rest of (white) Australian society needed to be defended due to his ethnic identity.

The most troubling tropes emerged when leaders were seen to engage in 'Indigenous causes'. This was seen in the case of the media portrayal of the former CEO of Star Track Express, Greg Poche, who in 2008 donated $10 million to build a Centre for Indigenous Health. At its establishment, he is quoted as proclaiming:

> We are doing pretty well as non-indigenous people and we're living in a country where, I think, we owe something to indigenous people. There's been a feeling of frustration and helplessness at the plight of indigenous Australians. Now there's a way forward. Hopefully, people with a social conscience and the wherewithal might step up to the plate. They're certainly needed. But our generation didn't cause the problems of indigenous health and housing. It's not our fault. But that's not a practical approach to solving the problems. We have a responsibility. Non-indigenous Australians are the only people who can fix this up. Through governments, and through [initiatives like] this centre.[50]

Although whiteness here hides behind the label 'non-indigenous people', Poche is calling upon his own white peers through offering absolution to the current generation for racial inequality. He is not speaking for the significant migrant population who predominantly arrived in Australia over 150 years after British colonial settlement. Yet like the absence of acknowledgement of Indigenous values, interests and needs, the presence and perspectives of other racial groups comprising

[50] Meacham, 2008, p 31.

Australia's population are excluded from media constructions of philanthropic leadership.

Poche's proclamation is replete with white solipsism,[51] where it is white people's wellbeing, frustration and helplessness, social conscience, practical approach, responsibility and initiatives that are foregrounded throughout this excerpt. Although white people's responsibility is explicitly named, it is not treated as a reflexive awareness of the ways in which his leadership and philanthropic activities perpetuate systems of racial privilege. Instead, white Australians' responsibility towards Indigenous Australians is framed as a heroic duty where their exclusive capability ('non-indigenous Australians are the only people who can fix this up') and right ('now there's a way forward') to 'save' Indigenous Australians are constructed as given.

This portrayal of white Australian leaders in the media as the saviours of Indigenous people highlights the ways in which ostensibly ethical and inclusive attitudes white people express towards other racial groups still stem from the root of white domination.[52] While the speech delivered by Poche appears to be a far cry from colonial treatments of Indigenous Australians as racially inferior,[53] it is an act of benevolent racism that is nevertheless underpinned by the same objectifying perception of Indigenous Australians as a passive, homogenous group to be appropriated into a white leader's cause.

Sustainability leaders

> In the early phases of colonisation, the white man's burden consisted of the need to 'civilize' the non-white peoples of the world – this meant, above all, depriving them of their resources and rights. In the later phase of colonisation, the white man's burden consisted of the need to 'develop' the Third World, and this again involved depriving local communities of their resources and rights. We are now on the threshold of the third phase of colonisation, in which the white man's burden is to protect the environment ... and this, too, involves taking control of rights and resources. ... The salvation of the environment cannot be achieved through the old colonial order based on the

---

[51] Sullivan, 2006.
[52] Sullivan, 2014.
[53] Smithers, 2009.

white man's burden. The two are ethically, economically and epistemologically incongruent.[54]

In late 2013, I was urged by the director of the research centre in which I worked to attend a graduation ceremony of a development organization called the Centre for Sustainability Leadership. In our current social climate of heightened sensitivity to ecological concerns, 'sustainability leadership' has emerged as an important organizational ideal.[55] Also promoted under related labels such as environmental, ecocentric and green leadership, sustainability leadership broadly refers to the attributes and behaviours required to effect change towards environmentally sustainable practices in their organizations and communities.

The Centre for Sustainability Leadership was founded in 2005 and its programmes range from a seven-month-long series of weekly workshops and weekend retreats to an online-based training module. In Australia, the Centre played an influential role in shaping the meanings of sustainability leadership, being the sole Australian provider of leadership development programmes where sustainability is framed as the core focus before closing down in 2018. The Centre had a network of about 500 alumni, maintained relationships with major corporate partners (including Boeing, Fujitsu and ANZ Trustees) and received state government funding for its training programmes. The Centre also maintained ties with the local government, particularly representatives of the Australian Greens, who often featured as keynote speakers at its public events.

The ceremony I attended was for the graduates of a more extensive 'Future Makers Fellowship'[56] and saw around 200 attendees gather to celebrate the 50 participants who completed the programme that year. The theatre was alive with conviviality. Although the leadership development programme did not target participants of any age group, the theatre that evening appeared to be filled with people in their early to mid-twenties. The Master of Ceremonies in a powder blue tuxedo struggled to introduce the schedule of events over the din of attendees swapping stories and sharing embraces. Perhaps because I was

---

[54] Mies and Shiva, 1993, pp 264–265.
[55] Broman et al, 2014; Ferdig, 2007; Galpin and Whittington, 2012; Metcalf and Benn, 2013; Pearce, Manz and Akanno, 2013.
[56] The six-month-long Future Makers Fellowship involved workshops, 'immersive retreats' and one-on-one coaching.

an outsider, I could not help feeling a creeping sense of unease amidst the happy atmosphere. The first unavoidable observation was that the event was heavily white-dominated.[57] As the night went on and I saw graduate after graduate being introduced as they skipped on to the stage to receive their certificates, I started to wonder about the myths of leadership that were being powerfully reinforced through these kinds of rituals we perform with one another in our communities.

This sense of disquiet stayed with me for several years after that evening at the graduation ceremony. In 2017, my colleague Helena Heizmann and I conducted a study to analyse the Centre for Sustainability Leadership.[58] Specifically, we focused on the language adopted in its public websites and resources in order to investigate how it contributed to the social construction of leadership through its various programmes and activities. The full data set for our analysis consisted of 231 web-based texts created by the Centre, including 19 web articles, 55 alumni profiles, 15 videos and 142 images.

Through our analysis, we found that the Centre for Sustainability Leadership promoted a compelling identity of sustainability leaders constructed collaboratively with the participants of the development programmes. We unexpectedly found parallels between this idealized sustainability leadership identity and the enlightenment narrative of the Buddha, where the path to leadership development was depicted as a journey of spiritual enlightenment. Like the example of Steve Jobs illustrated in Chapter 1, this leadership narrative was a variation on the hero's journey, a common master plot in which the protagonist departs from their ordinary life, faces opponents and ordeals on their path, and eventually returns home with the treasures they discovered and/or conquered.[59]

In Buddhist mythology, Prince Siddhartha is depicted as an individual with exceptional talents who from an early age became attuned to the suffering of others and, unlike others in a similarly privileged position, felt a calling to alleviate it. This notion of a calling was reflected in the Centre's construction of sustainability leadership, where the Centre positioned its participants as individuals who are inherently gifted with environmental awareness and destined to become 'future makers' or 'change makers' (a trope that is frequently repeated in promotional materials). Many participants described an innate sense of leadership

---

[57] I acknowledge that some people of colour could be considered 'white-passing' and this observation should not be taken as any factual analysis or final indictment, but only the initial impression of my feeling out-of-place.

[58] Heizmann and Liu, 2018.

[59] See *The Hero with a Thousand Faces* by Joseph Campbell (1968).

("for as long as I can remember, I have felt a need to 'save the world'" and "even as a child, I have always been the kind of person who actively seeks out positive change, improvement and innovation"), mirroring Siddhartha's depiction as a special individual who is, on one level, innately concerned for and equipped to address the suffering of others, while destined to reach full enlightenment.

Parallels to Siddhartha's story also surfaced in the ways some alumni specified experiences that prompted them to renounce their previous 'ignorant' lives. In the Buddha narrative, this involved experiences such as witnessing old age, sickness and death. The identity narratives of sustainability leaders included many experiences that acted as catalysts for their personal commitment to sustainability leadership. For example, one participant described feeling "disgusted" at seeing how waste was managed, while another participant recounted seeing a memorable environmental documentary. The celebratory discourses of the Centre emphasized each participant's unique power in realizing their vision of the future.

Sustainability leaders then reached 'enlightenment' through participation in the Centre and its offerings. The Centre is said to achieve this through providing a means for the participants' self-discovery ("[the Centre] has opened up a creative side that years of academic study, wonky approach to work and words were suppressing") and by empowering participants' sense of self ("I walked away believing I can make a difference and I know what I stand for. I can make change happen"). The Centre heralded its newly empowered graduates as now possessing the capacity to make "a significant impact locally, nationally and globally in the creation of sustainable change". Specifically, this transformed self was believed to have the power to influence and inspire others and thus generate a wider followership on sustainability issues in their field. Alongside this strong sense of agency, graduates also emphasized the need to continue the journey of self-discovery and self-development by focusing on their personal wellbeing ("I'm practising 'sustainability starts with me' and taking time out for re-energizing, building resiliency and having more fun").

Finally, the graduates turned to how they may leverage their new identities as 'leaders' to build successful careers and/or businesses. Their accounts articulated future plans such as starting a consultancy firm, launching a landscaping studio and moving forward with other "innovative and collaborative projects that aim to create ripple effects for economic, environment and community development". Unlike the Buddha, the Centre rejected the notion that sustainability leaders need to give up worldly pleasures and instead suggested that its graduates would earn recognition and acclaim. Sustainability in this context is thus not a radical renunciation of the capitalist status quo, but an ethos to enhance a successful and prosperous professional career.

Arguably, leadership development organizations are constrained by the ideals of leadership and sustainability in our cultures that instil individualist fantasies of hyperagency. I do not believe that the Centre for Sustainability Leadership or its participants knowingly or willingly co-constructed their individual heroism, but like all of us, they are influenced by the hegemony of neoliberalism. With market rationalities coming to define social and environmental relations, sustainability here became commodified as a tool for career development. Neoliberalism in this sense subsumes environmental sustainability ideals in its ongoing construction as the most legitimate way to engage with the world. To compete in this marketplace, heroic and hyperagentic individualism helps developers (both literally and figuratively) sell their training programmes.

Our findings point to the tensions between the discursive claims of (sustainability) leadership developers and the neoliberal regimes they seek to transform. Heroic and spiritual framings of sustainability leadership allow the laudable but complex work of environmental sustainability to be collapsed into development programmes that celebrate and, arguably, overplay participants' capabilities to single-handedly solve environmental problems. Ironically, the foregrounding of a heroic pursuit of 'goodness' found in sustainability leadership discourse may thereby reinforce the very 'preoccupation with the self'[60] that is entrenched in neoliberal regimes and underlies our disconnection from the natural world.

Conclusion

Our various romances with leadership are intimately tied to assumptions of white masculine superiority. Constructions of leaders as charismatic, transformational and ethical are steeped in myths of white strength, innocence and benevolence that have become so powerful and pervasive that many of us recognize them to be true.

This chapter in particular explored how the assumptions that white people represent the human norm and speak for the whole of society have enhanced their association with ethical leadership. This power is rooted in colonial notions of the 'white man's burden' and reproduced

---

[60] Knights and O'Leary, 2006, p 128.

in academic and practitioner narratives of leadership. Drawing on some of my own research, the enduring heroicization of whiteness can be seen in the media reporting of billionaire philanthropists. Then through a study of the Centre for Sustainability Leadership, the aims of environmental sustainability can be co-opted into neoliberal projects of individualism.

Leadership, and its attendant myths, shore up imperialism, white supremacy and patriarchy. These ideologies form a regime that mandates ongoing violence against others and ourselves. This violence is sometimes overt, but it also often subtle, invisible and even sentimentalized as acts of benevolence. We turn that violence inwards when we contort ourselves to fit into the hegemonic models of masculinity, whiteness, able-bodiedness and cis-gender heterosexuality. We are expected to have wealth and power and we are also expected to desire it. Yet all the efforts to acquire wealth and power only seem to cleave us further to the cycle of violence.

In critically interrogating leadership, we strip it down so that we may then rebuild 'leadership' (or whatever else we may want to call it) towards a redemptive engagement with difference and diversity. To do this, we need to look to the margins, to communities that have long been seen as the led, rather than the leaders. The next chapter will enter upon the second part of the book and look towards anti-racist feminist movements that have pioneered the systemic resistance against imperialist, white supremacist and patriarchal power.

PART II

Anti-Racist Feminist Redemption

5

Anti-Racist Feminisms

In *Feminism Without Borders*, Chandra Talpade Mohanty makes the call to challenge the dominance of Western feminisms, and build autonomous feminist communities that are geographically, historically and culturally based.[1] Anti-racist feminisms represent a diverse, global set of movements that have variously sought to identify and challenge the interlocking systems of power that undergird our social and political institutions.[2] Some of the theories cited in this chapter were developed decades ago and have been deconstructed and reconstructed many times over the years. Even more so than the previous chapters, this chapter relies on footnotes to explore the nuances of more complex ideas.

Known by many names over the years including multiracial feminism,[3] decolonial feminism[4] and women of colour feminisms,[5] I choose the term 'anti-racist feminisms'[6] in this book because it places the struggle against gender and racial oppression upfront. Anti-racist feminisms acknowledge the diverse interests, standpoints and intellectual traditions of Black, Indigenous, Latinx and Chicanx, Middle Eastern and Asian feminisms, and embrace a joint political interest in '[excavating] the silences and pathological appearances of a collectivity of women assigned as the "Other"' as she is produced in Western systems of knowledge.[7] Although anti-racist feminisms

---

[1]   Mohanty's (2003, p 1) call is not a rejection of feminism, but comes from 'a deep belief in the power and significance of feminist thinking in struggles for economic and social justice'. She sees feminism as an internationalist project and commitment that is communally developed.

[2]   Collins, 2000; hooks, 2003; Mohanty, 2003.

[3]   Baca Zinn and Thorton Dill, 1996.

[4]   Lugones, 2010.

[5]   Lugones, 2014.

[6]   Mirchandani and Butler, 2006; Mohanty, 2003.

[7]   Mirza, 2009, p 3.

have pollinated diverse disciplines including legal studies, cultural studies, sociology, anthropology, history, and film and literature studies, they are scarcely known in leadership studies.

By drawing these complex, distinct and localized movements together, I do not mean to imply that they somehow can, or ought to be, reduced to a homogenous categorization. As I hope the following sections will show, I deliberately include a range of voices, some familiar and famed and others perhaps little known, expressing differing and even conflicting perspectives. For example, some of the Indigenous intellectuals I cite do not necessarily identify as feminists, preferring instead to theorize from the philosophical traditions of their own heritage.[8] Nor do scholars who may be seen as 'Black' agree with this label and the fixedness it can imply. Blackness comprises distinct and uneven global positions within Africa and throughout the African/ Black diaspora, so that women who may be incorporated into 'Black' feminism in Britain might be excluded from 'Black' feminism in the United States.[9] My intention with this chapter is to amplify the voices of those who were and continue to be misinterpreted through, if not completely erased from, the theorizing and practice of leadership, while resisting the tendency to canonize a few key figures (the 'leaders') and refusing to listen to anyone else but those select few.[10] Intellectualism, like leadership, comes from communities, not individual heroic elites. As bell hooks stated in her first book, *Ain't I A Woman*, 'all too often in our society, it is assumed that one can know all there is to know about Black people by merely hearing the life story and opinions of one Black person'.[11]

The collective politics of anti-racist feminisms are therefore spoken with many voices and characterized by contradictions and inconsistencies that reflect our different social locations. The intersectional nature of our social relations means we are embedded in various and shifting locations along these cross-cut hierarchies and at any one point in time experience different forms of both oppression and privilege. With this in mind, I maintain the plural form of anti-racist

---

[8] Lawrence and Anderson, 2005.

[9] Ifekwunigwe, 1998.

[10] Collins, 2000.

[11] hooks, 1981, p 11. As she explains in an interview on the podcast *Politically Re-Active*, hooks herself does not call herself a 'Black feminist', preferring instead to be called a 'cultural critic': www.earwolf.com/episode/speaking-with-bell-hooks-talking-daca/.

feminisms in this book and offer the ideas here as one approach within this polyvocal political project.

The scholarly and activist traditions to be discussed here emerged beyond the cultural centre where white, masculinist ideals of leadership hold court. I will thus allow anti-racist feminist knowledge to stand on their own in this chapter in a way that enables the reader to feel the impact of their possibilities in speaking against hegemonic models of leading and being. The next chapter will then explore how the principles of anti-racist feminisms may be applied to undo leadership theorizing and practice.

As anti-racist feminist theorizing de-centres white masculinity in once-held 'universal' models of humanity, it is fundamentally an act of resistance. It seeks to reassert the agency of all of us who have been subordinated in existing power structures to define ourselves as fully human. White supremacy has taught us to be suspicious of people of colour, fearing that their actions are always about shoring up power for personal gain.[12] For this reason, it is perhaps necessary to clarify that while much anti-racist feminist resistance originated from women of colour, it is not confined to serving the needs and interests of women of colour. Anti-racist feminists resoundingly express the desire for a world where everybody is free to fulfil our human potential.[13] Through the understanding that the lives and experiences of all people are inevitably products of gender, race, class and other axes of power,[14] anti-racist feminisms have the potential to redeem our theories and practices of leadership.

From the outside-within

The sustained exclusion of women of colour's voices in scholarship has historically produced solipsistic knowledge where white lives, interests and identities have been allowed to define what is considered normal and legitimate social science.[15] Sociologist Patricia Hill Collins

---

[12] I wonder if those who dominate assume that everybody strives for domination. For many right-wing politicians, it would appear that distrust towards people of colour is frequently mingled with a paranoia about an impending retribution for colonialism and racism.

[13] Woo, 1983.

[14] Baca Zinn and Thorton Dill, 1996; Collins, 2000; Crenshaw, 1991; Yuval-Davis, 2006.

[15] In her journal article, 'The emperor has no clothes', organization scholar Stella Nkomo (1992) calls out the 'naked emperor' of Western epistemic hegemony in organizational research. She cautions against this faulty generalization where the dominant white male few (along with a smattering of white women) are taken

challenged the devaluation of Black women's subjectivity in particular and drew on the rich examples of Black women's art, intellectualism, community and culture to demonstrate the processes by which Black women assert their full humanity in the face of their dehumanization in the wider society. In what came to be known as the 'outsider-within' theory,[16] Collins rejected the taken-for-granted marginalization of Black women's voices in the social sciences by putting forth the sociological rationale for studying their voices and other such forms of knowledge that are often overlooked.[17]

Such conceptualizations of women of colour may appear to conflict with the anti-essentialist stance I took in the introductory chapter of this book, where I argued that identity categories like gender and race are socially constructed and politically contested, and not biological markers reflecting inherent attributes and qualities. Indeed, some scholars are hotly critical of those who appear to reinforce gender and racial categories and labels.[18] In detailing the shared experiences

as the defining group for all social research. Furthermore, white people come to occupy the highest category and all other people end up being defined and judged in reference to them. To put it in different words, white people become the human default and people of colour are defined as variations on the norm (Bonilla-Silva, 2012; Grimes, 2001; Leonardo, 2009; Levine-Rasky, 2013; Sullivan, 2006).

[16] Patricia Hill Collins (1986) developed the landmark theory of 'outsider-within' as she reflected on the history of Black women's lives in the United States and the intimate yet marginal positions Black women have held as domestic workers in white households. She proposed that this balance between being 'insiders' of white families yet ultimately remaining 'outsiders' – the *outsider within* – offers Black women a unique standpoint from which to understand the self, family and society.

[17] While originally advanced to reclaim the epistemic authority of Black women and their intellectual activism towards social justice, the outsider-within theory has also been valuable in interpreting the experiences of other subdominant groups as well (Alimahomed, 2010; Baca Zinn, 2012; Baca Zinn and Thorton Dill, 1996; Faifua, 2010; Liu, 2018). Outsider-within identities can be found among groups of people who occupy spaces of unequal power attached to specific histories of social injustice (Collins, 1999). The theory has thus helped illuminate similar struggles for self-definition among marginalized people, while recognizing the diverse histories among outsiders-within that equip them with unique sets of oppressions and privileges. There is, however, a tendency among those who are unaware or unconcerned with the theory's conceptualization in Black feminism for the outsider-within label to be applied liberally to describe everyone and anyone who may have experienced feeling out of place.

[18] See, for example, *Transformation Now! Toward a Post-Oppositional Politics of Change* by AnaLouise Keating (2013). Although women of colour scholars like Keating make persuasive arguments against socially constructed labels and their stereotypes that close down possibilities for solidarity across identity faultlines, this argument

and wisdoms of Black womanhood, Collins can be seen in some ways as deploying what Gayatri Chakravorty Spivak termed strategic essentialism.[19] Strategic essentialism refers to the idea that social groups may philosophically reject the idea of stable, homogenous identities, but act as though they are for political purposes. Following Spivak, many feminists of colour recognize the importance of strategic essentialism that allows women of colour to find solidarity among those of us with diversity marked on our bodies. It is not only the experience of being female that unites women, but our lived experiences of structural domination and oppression. Our 'potential commonality' lies in our joint political resistance against gender, racial and class structures.[20] As Heidi Mirza contends, 'it is important to hold on to our strategic multiplicity and celebrate our "difference" within a conscious construction of "sameness"'.[21] Ultimately though, anti-racist feminisms tend to imagine a future where socially inscribed categories whether they be 'of colour' or 'white', 'female' or 'male', 'queer' or 'straight', become irrelevant in the relations we form with others. Clinging on to these labels (or, more precisely, their associated stereotypes) is unhelpful, but it is equally unhelpful to demand that they be completely abandoned right now while there continue to be material differences to the privileges and oppressions experienced by people who are assigned these labels.

In her theorizations of outsider-within theory, Collins contend that while Black feminist thought may be utilized by others, it can only be produced by Black women.[22] Few scholars have declared the same

is also readily co-opted by members of the dominant class who might entreat activists to 'stop playing the gender card' or 'stop making everything about race' in attempts to suppress the fight for social justice.

[19] Spivak first proposed strategic essentialism as a highly localized and contextually contingent tool that may be deployed to dismantle the violent use of essentialism in existing power structures. Strategic essentialism is a complex response that addresses the concerns of scholars like Mridula Nath Chakraborty (2004) who have criticized anti-essentialism as a political strategy on the part of white feminism to silence the challenges posed by feminists of colour uniting around common racial and cultural identifications. Spivak later became dismayed by the way her theory became misunderstood and misapplied, where she observed that strategic essentialism 'simply became the union ticket for essentialism' (in interview with Danius and Jonsson, 1993, p 35). By 1993, Spivak explained that she had given up on strategic essentialism as a phrase, though she remained interested in it as a project (Danius and Jonsson, 1993).

[20] Mohanty, 2003, p 49.

[21] Mirza, 2009, p 3.

[22] Collins, 1986.

about other traditions of feminism, however, I think Collins' policy is a useful and necessary safeguard against the continual misappropriation of anti-racist feminist thinking. In my field of organization studies, certain Black feminist theories have become exceedingly popular among non-Black scholars in recent years. Yet a disturbing number of scholars have colonized Black feminist thought; dismissing the theories' activist traditions and unmooring them from their social justice roots.

To clarify, the inclusion of theories from various traditions of feminisms of colour in this book is not in any way intended to be a claim of ownership, as though Anti-Racist Feminisms™ is now some pre-packaged framework that can be cited to spice up a study. These theories already exist in the world. Their creators speak for themselves and do not require a scholar from any field to 'discover' them.[23]

This chapter observes Collins' guidance to showcase anti-racist feminist thought and how its combined wisdoms may guide our resistance against the structures of power in which we are embedded. Seeing anti-racist feminisms as resistance means understanding it as a practice. One is not an anti-racist feminist, but one *does* anti-racist feminism. The proceeding sections will explore a series of interrelated ways to do anti-racist feminisms. These ideas developed by anti-racist feminist intellectuals and activists include the interlocking nature of oppressions (and its relation with intersectionality), solidarity, self-definition, love, language and reach. The ideas featured in this chapter are far from an exhaustive catalogue of the contributions anti-racist feminisms have made. Nor could every anti-racist feminist writer be included in this book.[24] There is also a regrettable skew in favour of texts that have been published in the English language, which reflect my own linguistic limitations.[25] I choose this small sample of ideas

[23] In the Christopher Columbus sense of that word. Also known as 'Columbusing': the art of discovering something that is not new (see www.npr.org/sections/codeswitch/2014/07/06/328466757/columbusing-the-art-of-discovering-something-that-is-not-new).

[24] Ana Guil-Bozal and Ruby Espejo-Lozano have been collecting a comprehensive base of Indigenous and decolonial feminist knowledge. Their work challenges the dominant narratives in which feminist liberation is constructed as a European invention. Guil-Bozal and Espejo-Lozano instead critique how patriarchal 'civilization' was imposed by colonizers on indigenous communities in which gender was not an organizing principle. As of April 2019, their research is in progress. Their project website can be found at: http://grupo.us.es/generoysocdelcto.

[25] See decolonizing scholar Sadhvi Dar's (2018) analysis of how the use of the colonizer's language (English) in the context of non-governmental organizations in India works to discipline subjects. The use of English can necessitate negotiations

from among those I have become most familiar with in this early stage of my scholarly career that, in my view, bear the most potential for disrupting the violences of leadership theorizing and practice. I will present each idea in the writers' own words as much as possible, allowing them to speak for themselves and stand on their own. I will then show how these ideas may be applied to leadership theorizing and practice in Chapter 6.

Interlocking oppressions

The premise of this book – the idea that leadership is shaped by systems of imperialist, white supremacist, capitalist and patriarchal power – is grounded in the theory of interlocking oppressions. Women activists of colour in 1960s and 1970s advanced the recognition that systems of power produce intersectional, rather than isolated, additive oppressions.[26] During this time, groups like the Combahee River Collective[27] declared:

> We are actively committed to struggling against racial, sexual, heterosexual, and class oppression, and see as our particular task the development of integrated analysis and practice based upon the fact that the major systems of oppression are interlocking. The synthesis of these oppressions creates the conditions of our lives. As Black women we see Black feminism as the logical political movement to combat the manifold and simultaneous oppressions that all women of colour face.

In the academy, it was bell hooks who crystallized the poignant phrase imperialist white supremacist capitalist patriarchy to describe the four interlocking systems of power that characterize Euro-American 'dominator culture'.[28]

between two or more cultural identities and often reproduce neocolonial structures of domination.

[26] There are a number of texts that discuss the history behind intersectionality (see, for example, Chun, Lipsitz and Shin, 2013; Collins, 2000, 2012).

[27] The Combahee River Collective (1977, p 212) was comprised of self-identified 'Black feminist lesbian activists' who operated in Boston in the United States between 1974 and 1980. Their name references the little-known military raid led by Harriet Tubman on the Combahee River in South Carolina in 1863 that freed over 750 enslaved people.

[28] hooks, 2003, 2009b. In an overview of hooks' work (Liu, 2019c), I talk about how she has expressed disappointment at audiences who laugh at her use of this

When we confine political change to one axis of power at a time, we preserve the dominator culture as a whole. In the domain of leadership, for example, white men have been willing to consider women's rights when the granting of those rights serves the interests of maintaining white supremacy. As (predominantly elite white) women began to gain economic power in the existing racial structure, many let go of their commitment to a revolutionary politics that would threaten that racial structure through which they have risen.[29] Similarly, some men of colour have held to the false promise that domination over women lends them a patriarchal power that can compensate for their lack of power in the existing racial structure.[30] Our shifting positions within interlocking systems of oppression mean that we each face different sets of privileges and oppressions (at different times, in different contexts), but a commitment to anti-racist feminist politics requires ongoing reflection of how we challenge the imperialist white supremacist capitalist patriarchy as a whole.

Although the imperialist white supremacist capitalist patriarchy is rarely cited in leadership, the kindred concept of intersectionality proposed by legal scholar Kimberlé Crenshaw[31] has risen in popularity among leadership scholars in recent years.[32] Broadly, intersectionality refers to the knowledge that identities like gender and race interact to shape the experiences of Black women.[33] The complex, multiple dimensions of Black women cannot be understood by studying sexism and racism separately.[34] Unfortunately, its application to leadership research has often been misunderstood as a superficial framework of identity categories, where studies would frequently frame their contribution along the lines of 'female leaders have been well-explored, but this study looks at older queer female leaders' or 'Black leaders have featured in many studies now, but what can we

phrase. She does not think naming these systems of power is funny and interprets the laughter of her audience as 'a weapon of patriarchal terrorism' that exposes their discomfort in being confronted with feminist disobedience (hooks, 2004, p 29). Although I do not doubt some of the laughter comes from anti-feminist and anti-Black derision, I think that in some cases laughter at the term can come from relief. When I first heard hooks so calmly and courageously name the sources of violence in my life, I was overcome with feelings of lightness and joy (Liu, 2019c).

[29] hooks, 2000b.
[30] Chen, 1999; Liu, 2017d.
[31] Crenshaw, 1989, 1991.
[32] Jean-Marie, Williams and Sherman, 2009; Richardson and Loubier, 2008; Sanchez-Hucles and Davis, 2010; Tariq and Syed, 2017; Von Wahl, 2011.
[33] Crenshaw, 1989, 1991.
[34] Crenshaw, 1989, 1991.

learn from disabled Black Muslim leaders?' These kinds of rationales reduce intersectionality to a tool for collating and commodifying difference as researchers search for ever more finite combinations of identities in attempts to 'fill a gap' in the research.[35] Through this '"flattening" of intersectionality',[36] intersectional research of leadership and organizations has remained merely descriptive and rarely engaged in structural analysis or political critique.[37] As Jasbir Puar puts it, 'much like the language of diversity, the language of intersectionality, its very invocation, it seems, largely substitutes for intersectional analysis itself'.[38] Intersectionality has become popular in part because of its depoliticization into a more palatable narrative about diversity.[39] For that reason, hooks herself rejects the construct of intersectionality[40] and maintains that the imperialist white supremacist capitalist patriarchy is more informative. Unlike intersectionality, it names the sources of violence in our culture and compels our confrontation with this truth.

As long as it is in the interests of the imperialist white supremacist capitalist patriarchy to suppress revolutionary politics, anti-racist feminisms and its attendant theories are constantly at risk of being deradicalized. The case of intersectionality shows the precariousness of anti-feminist resistance and the importance of our commitment to guard our thought and activism against the threat of co-optation and erasure. Self-declared anti-racists, anti-colonialists, anti-capitalists and feminists cannot win our fights along a single axis. We need to learn to build solidarity with those who may not share our oppressions in order to resist the interlocking forms of domination in our society.[41]

---

[35] Crenshaw remarked in a dialogic essay with other proponents of intersectionality that she originally offered the term as 'a metaphor', but has become 'amazed at how it gets over- and underused' to the extent that sometimes she 'can't even recognise it in the literature anymore' (Berger and Guidroz, 2009, p 65). Chandra Talpade Mohanty (2013, p 980) too, called into question the scholars who cite her intersectional, transnational feminist theorizing as a 'totemic symbol' while nevertheless reproducing white, imperialist power in their scholarship.

[36] Berger and Guidroz, 2009, p 70.

[37] Jordan-Zachery, 2007.

[38] Puar, 2011.

[39] Bilge, 2013; Jibrin and Salem, 2015; Rodriguez and Freeman, 2016. There are studies that have used intersectionality well (including Atewologun and Sealy, 2014; Martinez Dy, Marlow and Martin, 2017).

[40] As does Patricia Hill Collins (2004, 2015).

[41] hooks, 1984.

Solidarity

The foreword to Cherríe Moraga and Gloria Anzaldúa's now classic essay collection, *This Bridge Called My Back*, calls together those who have been marginalized:

> Blackfoot amiga Nisei hermana Down Home Up Souf Sistuh sister El Barrio suburbia Korean The Bronx Lakota Menominee Cubana Chinese Puertoriquena reservation Chicana campanera and letters testimonials poems interviews essays journal entries sharing Sisters of the yam Sisters of the rice Sisters of the corn Sisters of the plantain. ... Now that we've begun to break the silence and begun to break through the diabolically erected barriers and can hear each other and see each other, we can sit down with trust and break bread together. Rise up and break our chains as well.[42]

In anti-racist feminist movements, solidarity is both a political and ethical goal.[43] According to Mohanty, solidarity is not about assuming that we share any common oppression (as women, as people of colour, as queer, as working class), but to see ourselves as 'communities of people who have chosen to work and fight together'.[44] Moraga and Anzaldúa, along with the women of colour who contributed to their anthology, beautifully illustrate how we may 'celebrate our "difference" within a conscious construction of "sameness"'.[45] The contributors use their writings to build bridges to one another, finding interconnections in their struggles for social justice, yet without presupposing that their experiences are the same. In her foreword to the second edition, Anzaldúa reminds us that:

> We are not alone in our struggles nor separate nor autonomous but that we – white black straight queer female male – are connected and interdependent. We are each accountable for what is happening down the street, south of the border or across the sea. And those of us who have more of anything: brains, physical strength, political

---

[42] Moraga and Anzaldúa, 1983, p vi.
[43] Mohanty, 2003.
[44] Mohanty, 2003, p 7.
[45] Mirza, 2009, p 3.

power, spiritual energies, are learning to share them with those that don't have.

Solidarity entails becoming aware of our capacity to overlook the forms of domination that may not appear to immediately impact our lives, or those we believe may even serve our self-interest. Solidarity thus requires listening to voices that have been silenced in much of traditional scholarship and activism, and in some cases, fighting for causes from which you do not benefit. Speaking from the South African context, Susan Holland-Muter reflects on the way that a denial of difference within the white feminist movement has prevented South African feminists from confronting white privilege and the legacy of apartheid. Holland-Muter argues that we need to engage in 'conversations across difference' such as dialogues, debates, panels, conferences, and collaborative working and writing, but on the terms of those women who have been marginalized from the feminist movement.[46]

In my own contexts of scholarship and practice, Indigenous activists and intellectuals are repeatedly sidelined. The denial of Indigenous sovereignty is built into the leadership of societies such as Australia.[47] As a non-Indigenous Australian, I reap the rewards of colonialism, even if I can claim not to be descended from those who took active part. My own practice of anti-racist feminist resistance requires me to align my struggles with the struggles for Indigenous sovereignty, even if the actualization of this aim may mean losing my citizenship. As someone who has been cis-gender and identified as straight most of my life, I am also prone to letting the ongoing struggles of trans and queer folk fall from the forefront of my mind. But my resistance must require learning more and listening more so that I may better understand how to fight against transphobia and heterosexism, which are, after all, cornerstones of patriarchy.

Attempts to silence can also come from within our own communities. Sonja John challenges the expectations from her own community that Indigenous women ought to be loyal to their people first before their gender. She declares that as Indigenous women are the backbone of Country, attacks against Indigenous women, whether physical or political, constitute attacks against Indigenous sovereignty.[48] Within the

---

[46] She suggests Black and queer women have been particularly excluded in South Africa (Holland-Muter, 1995, p 61).

[47] See *White Possessive: Property, Power, and Indigenous Sovereignty* by Aileen Moreton-Robinson (2015).

[48] John, 2015.

diasporic Vietnamese communities, Lan Duong has written of how Vietnamese women and queer subjects are treated with suspicion for being 'deviant, unruly and nonprocreative'.[49] Through the construction of ethnically homogenous and heterosexist familial ideals, women and queer subjects are restricted and disciplined as potentially traitorous to their family, nation and diaspora.[50]

Rosario Morales, in a prose piece entitled 'We're all in the same boat', calls her readers to heed the notion that 'in the most important way we are all in the same boat'.[51] She explains this is because we are:

> all subjected to the violent pernicious ideas we have learned
> to hate that we must all struggle against them and exchange
> ways and means hints and how tos that only some of us
> are victims of sexism only some of us are victims of racism
> of the directed arrows of oppression but all of us are sexist
> racist all of us.

We may experience the violence differently, and in different contexts, but we are all embedded in the imperialist white supremacist capitalist patriarchy, and thus we all have a stake in dismantling these interlocking systems of power.

The neoliberal misapplications of diversity and intersectionality have curtailed efforts towards solidarity. By individuating diversity to everybody, we stop short of social change. Because presumably we are all 'different' from one another, there is no need to consider the similarities between our own oppression/privilege and the conditions of those with whom we seek alliance.[52] Difference then becomes a pretext for maintaining the status quo through division. Rejecting both separatism as well as assimilation into any dominant or overriding identity, Anzaldúa proposed the idea of 'new tribalism' as an affinity-based approach to alliance making and identity formation. Where conventional tribalism may rely on specific bonds of kinship, new tribalism is developed through an open-ended process of self-selection based on personal and political affinities.[53]

---

[49] Duong, 2012, p 180.
[50] See *Treacherous Subjects: Gender, Culture, and Trans-Vietnamese Feminism* by Lan P. Duong (2012).
[51] Morales, 1983, p 93.
[52] See *Power Lines: On the Subject of Feminist Alliances* by Aimee Carrillo Rowe (2008).
[53] Anzaldúa co-opts the term 'new tribalism' from a critic who accused her of naïve romanticism about her Indigenous roots, claiming that Americans should focus less on race and more on class.

At its heart, solidarity requires that, despite our differences, we recognize that we are interconnected with one another. This view rejects the ideologies that gave rise to the autonomous Enlightenment man, the heroic leader who wields absolute control over others and the environment. Rather, solidarity demands a shift towards the understanding that we are interrelated and interdependent – emotionally, socially, physically, economically, ecologically, spiritually – to all human and non-human[54] life.

Self-definition

One of the key ways in which women and people of colour are subordinated within interlocking oppressions is through the politics of representation. Historically, elite white men have been the 'knowers' when women and people of colour have been the objects to be 'known'.[55] While elite white men are typically seen as fully human, that is, complete, three-dimensional living beings with interests, goals, needs and hopes; women and people of colour are more likely to be confined within stereotypes that conform to grand narratives of imperialism, white supremacy and patriarchy. Collins calls these externally defined stereotypes 'controlling images'.[56]

The production and representation of marginalized identities in popular culture, the media and academia are about power and control. Controlling images such as the 'angry Black woman' function to denigrate Black women's assertiveness and suppress the ways they may threaten the status quo.[57] One of the most enduring controlling images of (primarily East) Asian women is that of the submissive 'lotus blossom'. Extending traditional Orientalist representations of the exotic East,[58] Asian women are framed as weak, passive, docile, servile and

---

[54] See the beautiful work of feminist scholar Janet G. Sayers (2017) for an example of how being-in-the-world with non-human animals can be foundational to not only organizational and social life, but thought itself.

[55] Moreton-Robinson, 2004.

[56] Collins, 2000.

[57] In the book chapter, 'Mammies, matriarchs, and other controlling images', Collins (2000) details the ways Black women have been portrayed via a number of negative images. While she examines mammies, matriarchs and welfare recipients, other Black feminists have critiqued images like Jezebel and Sapphire (see, for example, West, 2012). Controlling images are designed to disguise social relations, '[making] racism, sexism, poverty, and other forms of social injustice appear to be natural, normal, and inevitable parts of everyday life' (Collins, 2000, p 69).

[58] See the classic text *Orientalism* by Edward Said (1978).

quiet.[59] For Yen Le Espiritu, these images are 'ideological assaults' that condense 'multiple differences into one-dimensional caricatures – construct a reality in which racial, class, and gender oppression are defensible'.[60] As Orientalism originated in representations of the Middle East, Arabs and Islam,[61] Middle Eastern women, particularly Muslim women, are similarly framed as the long-suffering, forcibly veiled victims who crave Western liberation from an oppressive culture. Following the events of 9/11, the exoticization of Orientalism shifted further to the 'Far East', and few of us would need to be told that the Middle East and the Arab World are now overwhelming portrayed as breeding grounds for fundamentalist terrorism.[62] Latinos/as are constructed as *cholos* and hot-tempered harlots,[63] while Mexicans in particular have been historically portrayed in old Hollywood films as the treacherous *bandido*.[64] A defining pattern among controlling images is that they construct women and people of colour as 'problems' that require white male saviours to fix.

Anti-racist feminisms reject the reality of our oppressors and assert the right for women and people of colour to develop self-definitions of our own identities as well as our own standards for evaluating ourselves beyond sexist and racist stereotypes.[65] It may appear that controlling images are simply a mild nuisance and that people of colour who 'know better' can just ignore stereotypical representations of themselves in our cultures. Yet as patriarchy has no gender, white supremacy also has no race. People of colour immersed in white supremacy develop what W.E.B. DuBois theorized as a 'double consciousness', where they come

---

[59] The 'lotus blossom' stereotype is also known by the names 'china doll' and 'geisha' (Tajima, 1989; Uchida, 1998). As Karen Pyke and Denise Johnson (2003, p 36) explain, 'by casting Black women as not feminine enough and Asian women as too feminine, white forms of gender are racialized as normal and superior'.

[60] Espiritu, 2008, p 15.

[61] Said, 1978.

[62] See the documentary *Reel Bad Arabs: How Hollywood Vilifies a People* (Jhally, 2006). For a rhetorical analysis of terrorism, see *Communicating Terror: The Rhetorical Dimensions of Terrorism* by Joseph S. Tuman (2010). The racialization of terrorism has meant that countries like the United States remain uninformed and unequipped to deal with the significant proportion of domestic terrorist attacks perpetrated by white terrorists (Williams, 2017).

[63] Yosso and García, 2010.

[64] Pérez Huber and Solórzano, 2015; see also the work of Clara E. Rodríguez, 1997; 2004.

[65] Lugones, 2006.

to see themselves through the dominator's gaze.[66] The manifestations of double consciousness include a sense of one's own inferiority that can be seen in the Black-on-Black violence of both traditional colonies and modern ghettos.[67] It can also see individuals endorse ideologies or policies that are repressive to one's group, as DuBois observed among his Black contemporaries, like Booker T. Washington, who argued for the Black population to receive only industrial training and be confined to manual labour.[68] Part and parcel of being a person of colour is about negotiating our double consciousness.

Emerance Baker proposes that Native women reject the controlling images of Native women as 'captured, civilised and venerated' through examples such as Pocahontas and Demasduit (renamed Mary March), and find self-definition through their storytelling.[69] Native peoples have been telling stories for generations, but the storytelling that Baker envisions is a deliberate strategy of cultural imagination. Their writings are 'expressions of a loving gaze' on what it means to be Indian.[70] However, the ongoing struggle for emancipation and sovereignty means that historically marginalized people must also 'control how our stories are told and who does the telling'.[71] For Indigenous peoples in particular, this means resisting 'the silencing of our [Native] voices and the ghettoisation of our words' as the 'quaint customs of an archaic culture', but centring the 'telling and retelling our stories for ourselves in our own ways'.[72] Baker maintains that, as storytellers, Native writers have the power to develop alternate ways of being in the world that will make their communities whole again.

---

[66] In his classic book, *The Souls of Black Folk*, originally published in 1903, W.E.B. DuBois (2005, p 9) conceptualized double consciousness as 'a peculiar sensation ... of always looking at one's self through the eyes of others, of measuring one's soul by the tape of a world that looks on in amused contempt and pity'. For DuBois, Black identity is defined by this contradictory standpoint of seeing oneself through the white gaze where Black subjectivity is denied and Black people are objectified. Within the double consciousness, Black people internalize white ideologies so that they constantly feel dislocated from themselves while trying to keep from being 'torn asunder'.

[67] Fanon, 1994; Sung, 2015; Wasserman, Clair and Platt, 2012.

[68] For a history of Black political conservativism in the United States, see *Saviors or Sellouts: The Promise and Peril of Black Conservatism, from Booker T. Washington to Condoleezza Rice* by Christopher A. Bracey (2008).

[69] Baker, 2005, p 111.

[70] Baker, 2005, p 111.

[71] Baker, 2005, p 113.

[72] Baker, 2005, p 113.

The point of self-definition then is to nurture self-love. This 'self' suffix here is not a neoliberal capital 's' Self who imagines themself as central, autonomous and heroic, standing above and beyond others, communities, society, land and nature, but a radically relational small 's' self. By loving ourselves, we may come to love femaleness, queerness, Blackness,[73] Indianness[74] and all the other dimensions of identity that have been marginalized in dominator culture. And in choosing to love the Other, we can begin to take down the imperialist white supremacist capitalist patriarchy.

Love

The answer, under dominator culture, is to make love the foundation of our resistance. For hooks, 'the moment we choose to love we begin to move against domination, against oppression. The moment we choose to love we begin to move towards freedom, to act in ways that liberate ourselves and others'.[75]

But what is love? Love in dominator culture has been manipulated into a form of control. In heteropatriarchal bonds, it was assumed women, being the nurturing, caring partner, would give love, while powerful men in return would provide and protect.[76] Norma Alarcón reflects on the slipperiness between devotion and obedience in her own Indo-Hispanic culture and how women who share her background have been more vulnerable to fall prey to subjugation disguised as love.[77] Likewise in white societies, the colonized Others are expected to adore and admire their more civilized colonizers who believed they were bringing the rest of the world into modernity.[78]

The sexual fetishization of women of colour has also perverted what it means for us to love and be loved, where stereotypes about our

---

[73] In bell hooks' (1992b) essay, 'Loving blackness as political resistance', she argues that blackness is the quintessential signifier of what oppression means in the United States. Citing the Black theologian James Cone, hooks urges all of us, Black people, white people and all people of colour, to stand against white supremacy by choosing to value, and indeed to love, blackness.

[74] Baker, 2005.

[75] hooks, 1994, p 298.

[76] hooks, 2000c. See also *Love, Power, and Knowledge: Towards a Feminist Transformation of the Sciences* by Hilary Rose (1994).

[77] Alarcón, 1983.

[78] See chapter 5, 'Colonial love in Fanon and Moffatt', in *Philosophy and Love: From Plato to Popular Culture* by Linnell Secomb (2007) as well as *White Love and Other Events in Filipino History* by Vicente L. Rafael (2000).

sexual availability for white heterosexual men continue to objectify and dehumanize. In her examination of Asian American sexual politics, Rosalind Chou wonders whether women of colour with increased racial consciousness can ever be sure that romantic interest from non-Asian partners is free from racial stereotyping.[79]

In another way, white nationalists who have been granted platforms under the Trump presidency pervert the language of love; claiming their actions are fuelled by their love of self, love of the white race and love of country. Such illusory forms of love are dangerous and because they can be confused with resistance. Resistance is complex and precarious and requires careful vigilance.

Anti-racist feminisms can help us to find love beyond the bonds of domination.[80] It defines a love 'rooted in recognition and acceptance' and that 'combines acknowledgment, care, responsibility, commitment and knowledge'.[81] Love within anti-racist feminisms has ethical and political dimensions that are activated to enable social transformation. This ethic of love is grounded in the need to change the systems of power that support gender, sexual, racial and class domination towards more egalitarian forms of social and community relations.

As the personal is the political, and the political the personal; the decolonization of our world must go hand in hand with the decolonization of our minds. Decolonizing our minds encompasses new ways of seeing ourselves and our identities beyond the controlling images that wound us. It also means imagining alternate 'democratic' ways of relating through love. The power of hegemony is that ruling ideologies close our minds to possibilities beyond what appears normal and natural to us. Love, within an anti-racist feminist politics, opens up the possibilities for us to think, be and live differently as interconnected subjects in communities making a conscious choice to reject violence.

Language

Language is another site of struggle. The invisible dominance of whiteness is continually reinforced when it remains unnamed in our research, so that while racialized subjects are singled out as *Asian* managers and *Black* managers, white managers get to be just 'managers'.[82] Our racial

---

[79] See *Asian American Sexual Politics: The Construction of Race, Gender, and Sexuality* by Rosalind S. Chou (2012).

[80] hooks, 2000a.

[81] hooks, 2000c, p 104.

[82] Dyer, 1997; Grimes, 2001; Liu and Baker, 2016; Nkomo, 1992.

grammar[83] may register the explicit designation of hegemonic identity categories as awkward or unnecessarily cumbersome. An example I often cite is that it may be more accurate and informative to state, 'this is a study of how white middle-class able-bodied self-identified heterosexual cis-male managers demonstrate inclusivity towards white middle-class able-bodied self-identified heterosexual cis-female employees' than it is to describe such research as, 'this study explores how managers practise gender inclusivity'. The universality (and indeed grandiosity) of the latter is diminished when the racial, class, dis/ability and sexual blindness is redressed; highlighting the power of multiple privileges in leadership theorizing.

Other anti-racist feminist thinkers like myself have questioned our positions writing against the violences of Western thought and practice with the very language of Western thought and practice in a location for knowledge production circumscribed by the West (academia). Peruvemba Jaya, for example, questions the ways she 'support[s] the hegemony of the coloniser by embodying the elitist possession of knowledge of a certain language', going on to ask, 'why, in order to be heard, must this critique come from within the dominant metropolitan location and be voiced in the language of the Western majority?'[84] As an academic, I have been trained to speak and write in a very specific style that has legitimacy in dominator culture. It is a language that embodies a colonial legacy, wielding words that convey a scientific objectivity and bourgeois civility. When I stop embodying this voice and speak as the 中国移民, I can quickly become inaudible, illegible and incomprehensible. For Jaya, we need to learn to express different 'voices' from different 'locations'. María Lugones is one example of an intellectual who has practised disobedience to the monolingualism, monoculturalism and monologicalism institutionalized through British and US imperialism.[85] She describes how translation, when it is an opportunity for understanding, is an ethical, political and, indeed, *loving* act.[86]

---

[83] I use this wonderful term by sociologist Eduardo Bonilla-Silva (2012), who explains that racial domination is enabled by a racial grammar that normalizes the standards of white supremacy as the standards for all sorts of everyday events and transactions.

[84] Jaya, 2001, p 228.

[85] Lugones, 2014.

[86] I simplify the processes and politics of translation here to imagine an egalitarian bridging across linguistic differences to build solidarity. Translation is, of course, complicated and ambivalent. In her 1989 experimental documentary film *Surname Viet Given Name Nam*, Trinh T. Minh-ha challenges the Western desire for certain

Language is not always to be operationalized towards straightforward comprehensibility. Anti-racist feminist writing and speech can involve creative ways of 'disrupting dominant ways of perceiving, understanding and experiencing the world' and inventing new ways to be in the world that 'affirm life in all its expressions and manifestations'.[87] One such example is Trinh T. Minh-ha's use of what she calls 'headless and bottomless' storytelling, which 'never stops beginning or ending'.[88] This style of storytelling subverts the expectations in Western stories to have a beginning, a middle and an end. It also denies the construction of a unitary subject that is so common in tales of heroic leaders.

Reach

hooks notes that while visionary feminist thinking is perhaps most accepted and embraced in academic circles, it has become increasingly produced through exclusionary language comprehensible only by people who are highly literate, well-educated and, more often than not, materially privileged. Many anti-racist feminists urge scholars to express a radical politics that reaches a broader audience. As Trinh T. Minh-ha puts it, 'knowledge for knowledge's sake is sickness'.[89] Anti-racist feminist movements have typically been born from communities at the grassroots and possess the power to speak to practitioners as well as scholars. Corporate professionals who are deepest within the belly of the imperialist white supremacist capitalist patriarchy are rarely thrown the lifeline of anti-racist feminisms. They are left instead to contend with reductionistic management handbooks like *Lean In*, *#GIRLBOSS* and *The Confidence Code* that promote a neoliberal fantasy of gender parity while leaving imperialist white supremacist capitalist, and even patriarchal, practices intact.

For Sheena Vachhani, the anti-racist feminist turn to love can be developed through writing.[90] Feminist writing has the potential to reconstruct how the feminine is co-opted in the service of organizations and to reclaim organizational spaces with the voices of gendered, racialized, classed and queer subjects who have been traditionally marginalized. Like hooks, Vachhani rallies visionary feminists to

---

knowledge by deliberately making the women's accented speech inaudible and featuring subtitles that do not elucidate the speeches (Duong, 2009).

[87] Rodriguez, 2017, p 176.

[88] Trinh, 1989, p 2.

[89] Trinh, 1989, p 2.

[90] Vachhani, 2015; see also Steyaert, 2015.

resist confining our writing to theoretically impenetrable expressions enclaved within academic journals and instead to activate our writing by disseminating it more widely.

Peruvemba Jaya reminds us that, as educators, we have the power to disseminate knowledge through the classroom. Our Business Schools frequently proclaim that we are the providers of 'world-class education' and yet, as Jaya notes, our curricula rarely embrace multiple worldviews, knowledges, histories and philosophies.[91] The typical Business School degree reinforces imperialist, white supremacist, capitalist and patriarchal ideologies, equipping graduates with the hegemonic values that they then identify and reproduce in their everyday lives at work and beyond. In 2014, student movements around the world across multiple disciplines challenged the hegemony, posing the question to their universities: 'Why is my curriculum white?' as a response to the lack of diversity found in their course content and reading lists. This question spurred a transnational initiative to critically interrogate the curriculum in higher education and the ways in which it reinforces white power and privilege. One important concern that this initiative highlights is the need to integrate non-Western perspectives and values into higher education curricula in a meaningful way, rather than in a dilettante or tokenistic fashion where a few famous non-Western figures are dropped into the lecture slides to 'spice up' a course.

Conclusion

This chapter elucidated a unifying collection of anti-racist feminist wisdoms that bear the potential to reimagine leadership theorizing and practice. First, our ongoing resistance means recognizing the interlocking nature of oppression. In most countries in the West, the four dominant power systems that undergird our cultures are imperialism, white supremacy, capitalism and patriarchy. Other cultures

---

[91] Jaya (2001) proposes that we decolonize management education by subverting the hegemony of Western thought. Speaking from her own pedagogical interventions, she expands the history of management to include 'classics' from countries and cultures beyond Europe and the United States such as Sun Tzu, Kautilya and Ibn Khaldun. She also explains the constructed nature of representations, showing students how the media, for example, produce and disseminate controlling images of the Arab world that cannot be taken for granted as 'reality'. When we teach leadership, examples cannot be confined to the high-profile CEOs of Western corporations, but Jaya (2001, p 230) says 'we need to tell stories of leaders such as Anwar Sadat, Nasser, Mahatma Gandhi, Rani Jhansi, Desmond Tutu, Nelson Mandela, alongside these other tales that we tell'. Later in Chapter 6, I will also critique the ways figures such as Mahatma Gandhi are misremembered in white imaginations.

will have contextual variations of the oppressions they face, such as alternate racial, ethnic and caste hierarchies. In Singapore, for instance, writer Sangeetha Thanapal has observed the prevalence of Chinese privilege, wherein institutionalized racism enables the Chinese ethnic population to acquire the most social, economic and political power.[92] This holistic awareness of interlocking oppressions allows us to identify the more subtle exercises of power that prevail in contemporary social life, where seeming progress in one area, such as gender equality, may reinforce colonial, racial and economic inequality.

An anti-feminist politics recognizes our fundamental interconnectedness to one another and thus seeks solidarity by building bridges across our differences. This solidarity neither necessitates assimilation to any homogenizing identity category (for example, 'women' or 'people of colour') nor cuts itself short at an individualistic notion that 'we are all different' as an excuse against affinity-making. Anti-racist feminist solidarity means seeking alliances with others in our joint struggles against the imperialist white supremacist capitalist patriarchy, especially with those who have been silenced in society at large as well as within our own communities.

Anti-racist feminisms transcend what hegemony leads us to believe to be possible. The processes of transcendence include challenging the controlling images that serve to fix non-dominant groups into stereotypes, allowing all people to reclaim themselves as fully human. It also includes developing new ways of being in the world and relating to one another – human and non-human life and the natural environment – from a basis of love rather of domination. As we advance our struggles towards social justice, we need to speak from, to and with the people of our community who live and work at the coalface of oppression. This requires us to speak with many voices across multiple languages and from many different locations in order to develop social transformation from the grassroots.

Solidarity, love and justice are not easy. A commitment to anti-racist feminisms inevitably involves struggle where we will all probably grapple with feelings of anger, frustration and despair alongside inadequacy, guilt and shame. It requires collaborating with others who are positioned beyond our social and political membership groups and, indeed, may require rethinking those group memberships

[92] See Thanapal in conversation with Adeline Koh explaining the concept of Chinese privilege in Singapore at: www.boundary2.org/2015/03/chinese-privilege-gender-and-intersectionality-in-singapore-a-conversation-between-adeline-koh-and-sangeetha-thanapal/.

through potentially painful sacrifices of belonging.[93] This may mean questioning our romantic ideals around heterosexual love and the ways it has historically been perverted in patriarchal bonds as domination in disguise.[94] It could also mean deconstructing ideas of the 'family' and its associated myths and mechanisms that can be applied to subjugate women and queer subjects.[95]

The theories and practices that may be described as anti-racist feminist are complex, varied, at times even conflicting, and born from and specific to particular local contexts. When we choose anti-racist feminisms, we adopt it as a practice – one that involves an ongoing struggle towards the decolonization of our world and our minds. In the next chapter, I will apply the combined wisdoms of this chapter to the theorizing and practice of leadership, exploring how leadership may be reimagined and possibly redeemed.

[93] Duong, 2012.
[94] Alarcón, 1983; hooks, 2000c.
[95] Duong, 2012.

6

Undoing Leadership

Leadership has been a blank canvas on which we paint the fantasies of imperialism, white supremacy, capitalism and patriarchy. Its romanticization through charismatic, transformational, authentic, servant, ethical and sustainable leaderships[1] has been vulnerable to corruption. Even when leaders convince others and themselves that they are benevolent and inclusive, they can nevertheless enact colonial, racial, economic and gendered violence. Leadership may not, and perhaps should not, be redeemed.

Speaking within just the Anglophonic world, we have at our disposal language that more precisely and accurately captures the activities that so-called 'leaders' do. Administration, coordination, collaboration, communication, supervision, team-building and decision-making may be more useful descriptors for the day-to-day practices of people whose work involves responsibility to others. Relinquishing broad-brush illusions of leadership may also allow us to name the activities conducted in governments, organizations and communities that may have been obfuscated by the romance with leadership, including domination, discrimination and exclusion.

While we may imagine leadership to be exemplified in the gripping speeches delivered by charismatic CEOs or the bold decisions handed down in the executive boardroom, these activities only occasionally feature in the mundane reality of managerial work.[2] What makes business and organizations function is the work that happens in the space between people; the unglamorous processes of coordination, collaboration and communication that knit the various and varied

---

[1]   Earlier in the morning before writing this, I read a manuscript in which the authors attempted to propose 'compassionate leadership' as the next aspirational model for theorizing, development and practice.

[2]   Alvesson and Sveningsson, 2003b.

activities of workers together. Anti-racist feminist thinking would also remind us that what makes the seemingly heroic work of leadership possible is the oft-invisible labour that is disproportionately performed by women and people of colour as carers in the organizational and domestic spheres. Leadership and organizations are reliant on the work that happens at home, including the people who cook, clean and care for workers and their families that enable them to continue working. To celebrate individual leaders in our societies is to fixate on a narrow and relatively insignificant part of humanity. It overlooks life's rich interconnectedness in favour of a romance that serves only to bolster the status of our society's elites.

Leadership is too powerful and profitable for developers, consultants and leaders themselves to accept critique. It is also career-making for academics, not just those who venerate leadership, but also those like me who critique it. So if leadership continues to grow and spread, then it is necessary to cut it at the roots. Following from the collective wisdoms of anti-racist feminisms, I will discuss ways we may rethink our engagement with leadership through a recognition of interlocking oppressions, experimenting with language and reach, and struggling towards solidarity, self-definition and love. In particular, I will look at three layers of how we may 'do' leadership theorizing and practice differently: decolonizing our minds; relating with others and reimagining leadership. These are not discreet domains of activity, but interconnected processes of social transformation; so that in relating with others, we can collaboratively reimagine leadership, and by reimagining dominant constructions of leadership, it will more readily enable us to decolonize our minds.

Decolonizing our minds

Anti-racist feminisms have argued for the importance for all people to free ourselves from the dominator's gaze, reclaim our self-definitions beyond controlling images,[3] and begin healing from a lifetime of self-denial and self-negation.[4] This process of self-love is what hooks calls 'decolonizing our minds'. Growing up continually assaulted with controlling images about ourselves and other marginalized people develops in us a double consciousness[5] that can make it difficult to relinquish the contemptuous white masculinist gaze. Relinquishing the

---

[3]   Collins, 2000.
[4]   Gabriel, 2007.
[5]   DuBois, 2005.

dominator's gaze means confronting the taken-for-granted hegemony of white masculinist power and rejecting its hierarchies that position blackness as inferior to whiteness, femininity as subordinate to masculinity, queer as deviant from cis-gender, heterosexual normality, disability as a defective form of able-bodiedness and the economically deprived as inherently lesser than the wealthy. Only when we break these binaries can we begin to reconfigure our social relations towards love.

When we set off on this journey of decolonization, our psyches can become safe spaces free from the dehumanizing gaze of the dominator.[6] For many of us, this could be the first safe space, or perhaps the only safe space, which we have in a world that imposes its controlling images on our bodies. It is from this space that we may begin to construct independent self-definitions and recognize the self-definitions of other marginalized peoples with whom we relate. According to Collins, 'a changed consciousness encourages people to change the conditions of their lives'.[7]

In learning to love ourselves, essentialism becomes a dangerous trap. That is, when we think we are reclaiming a love for aspects of our identity, but we are in fact recycling the very controlling images that have been constructed of these identities. This trap is all the more treacherous when controlling images such as the noble savage or model minority may appear from the outset to be somewhat positive. In postfeminist discourses, this can be seen in the ways women are framed as reclaiming some natural feminine essence. In these discourses, structural inequality is explained away by claiming that 'normal' women *want* to return to traditional gendered roles and be 'girly', domestic and sexually desirable to men, while neglecting to consider the ways that this highly white, heteronormative, patriarchal and middle-class vision of femininity is in itself a controlling image.[8]

In our organizations and societies, leadership is overwhelmingly accorded to white, cis-gender, heterosexual, elite-class and able-bodied men. Leadership then often remains out of reach for those who do not embody these gendered, sexualized and racialized ideals. When I sought participants for my study on leadership among Asian Australians, the professionals I spoke to frequently protested that they were 'not really leaders'. When I asked them to clarify what they meant, many

---

[6] Collins, 2000.

[7] Collins, 2000, p 117.

[8] See *What a Girl Wants? Fantasizing the Reclamation of Self in Postfeminism* by Diane Negra (2009).

struggled to provide an answer. Some wondered if they were not senior enough, seeing only the executive level as qualifying for 'leadership', even if they possessed decades of people-management experience. The ones who did claim the mantle of 'leadership' understood that doing so was a political act, yet almost everyone I spoke to saw leadership as something cold and distant that belonged to white Australians and could, at best, only be tenuously grasped.[9]

The confluence of imperialist, white supremacist, capitalist and patriarchal values is reflected in idealizations of a neoliberal professional subject who treats themself as an enterprise and it is such individuals who are deemed to have 'leadership' potential. Decolonizing our minds will include disidentifying from neoliberal constructions of the ideal worker/leader, especially when those idealizations reproduce harm onto others and ourselves. A recent study of predominantly white, European executive women by management scholars Darren Baker and Elisabeth Kelan revealed the ways that the women were psychologically and emotionally invested in the neoliberal fantasies of a fair, meritocratic workplace.[10] Rather than recognizing instances of gender discrimination for what they were (for example, when male colleagues were promoted before them or received higher pay and bonuses), executive women rationalized and individualized experiences as outcomes of their own making. The executive women also blamed less successful women for playing the victim and failing to embody the neoliberal ideal. In internalizing the reality of the oppressor, even highly privileged European women could not escape the violence of self-blame, while further reinforcing white, capitalist and patriarchal power and its ongoing subordination of less privileged others.

For some, it can be a depressing idea to think that structural inequality cannot be solved at the individual level. Leadership handbooks and popular media tout the idea that we can overcome any barrier through assertiveness, self-confidence, power-posing, resilience, gratitude, a makeover or the power of attraction. We are told that we can achieve anything if we only acted as though we believed that inequality and injustice do not exist. Yet they clearly do exist and are

---

[9]   The idea of leadership as a white possession became apparent once I began writing up my findings for submission to academic journals. Although I wrote up the manuscripts as studies of Asian Australian *leaders* and *leadership*, three out of the four articles I wrote were queried by reviewers as 'not really being about leaders'. Leadership, despite its social constructedness, seems to remain illegible on the bodies of non-white people.

[10] Baker and Kelan, 2018.

evidently reinforced in more subtle and insidious ways. Changing our consciousness is thus an important starting point towards emancipation, but it is not adequate in and of itself to dismantle the imperialist white supremacist capitalist patriarchy. For that, those of us committed to decolonization need to come together, develop ways to build coalitions across differences and collectively reimagine leadership beyond the terms set by dominator culture.

Relating with others

Capitalist and patriarchal norms have dictated the terms of relationships to be built on competition and control. Instead, we can develop ways to relate to others 'in the same boat' both within and outside organizations. As academics, conferences, workshops, research teams and reading/writing groups are all ways we can carve out a time and space in which we could explore alternate ways of relating to one another. In our increasingly neoliberal universities, care has become imperative in order to survive the violence of deteriorating workplace conditions.[11] When I used to work at a university characterized by intense performance metrics, surveillance and rampant bullying, I found solace in a critical theory reading group that met once a month to share food and discuss the writings of Marcia Langton, María Lugones and Jack/Judith Halberstam. Through dialogue and debate, my fellow participants of the reading group challenged and delighted me through mutual learning and love.

A marketing manager I spoke to for my study of Asian Australian leaders described to me the pleasure of meeting periodically with a women's reading group at her bank. Their set reading when we met was Sheryl Sandberg's *Lean In*, but Lynn (a pseudonym) noted that their discussions were more about thoughtful critique than eager agreement. At the coalface of corporate practice, professional women like Lynn know best of the limitations of postfeminism and its lofty promises.

---

[11] As I write this, I am saddened by the news of Malcolm Anderson, a lecturer in accounting at Cardiff University, who took his own life in February 2018 after he had been struggling with a heavy workload (Pells, 2018). The deteriorating conditions of neoliberal organizations have been well documented. In the academy, issues of wellness have recently been explored in a special issue of *The Canadian Geographer/Le Géographe Canadien*, Volume 60, Issue 2: https://onlinelibrary. wiley.com/toc/15410064/2016/60/2. The toll on women academics of colour in particular can be seen in anthologies such as *Inside the Ivory Tower: Narratives of Women of Colour Surviving and Thriving in British Academia* by Deborah Gabriel and Shirley Anne Tate (2017).

While popular management handbooks such as *Lean In* may be more easily accessible outside academia, there are opportunities once such groups are established to introduce more radical ideas for discussion even in more conservative organizations. The books of bell hooks and Gloria Anzaldúa are written in ways that are accessible to non-academic audiences, while a number of scholars like Richard Fung and Trinh T. Minh-ha produce films as part and parcel of their intellectual activism. A growing number of podcasts and YouTube channels are also dedicated to accessible discussions of anti-racist feminisms.[12]

Through these grassroots efforts to build caring and loving relationships, we can disrupt the hegemony of traditional relational practices based on individualism, hierarchy and control. As communities for 'consciousness raising', participants may collectively learn to identify and name previously invisible power dynamics. For instance, we may become adept at incorporating new language into our racial grammar, calling out the ways our organizations valorize *white* values, *white* perspectives, *white* needs and interests, *white* people and *white* leadership. Such interventions may at first seem trivial, yet such spaces in organizations and societies where participants can find respite from dominator culture are often desperately and urgently needed in their local contexts. As these spaces begin to expand the boundaries of what is possible, and model relations of solidarity, love, care, collaboration and a joint commitment to justice, they dismantle the normative status of violence.

Through our narratives of great leaders we valorize the capability of individuals like Richard Branson and Steve Jobs to master their environments, transform their industries and penetrate followers' hearts and minds. In my study of Asian Australian leaders, I met a banking manager, Jay, whose articulation of the importance of 'sensuality'

---

[12] *Popaganda* produced by Bitch Media discusses pop culture news, film and television as well as issues relating to organizations and work such as freelancing, sexual harassment and the imposter syndrome through an anti-racist feminist perspective: www.bitchmedia.org/feminist-podcasts. *Politically Re-Active*, produced by First Look Media and Panoply, is hosted by comedians W. Kamau Bell and Hari Kondabolu, who discuss politics and democracy in the United States. It ran for two seasons from 2016 to 2017. The episodes can be found at www.politicallyreactive.com/. An interview with bell hooks is featured in Season 2 in the episode 'Speaking with bell hooks & talking DACA'. Scene On Radio produced a 14-part, Peabody-nominated podcast series, *Seeing White*, which explores what it means to be white in the United States: www.sceneonradio.org/seeing-white/. Decoded is a video series on YouTube produced by MTV News that discusses race and popular culture primarily for a teen audience: www.mtv.com/shows/decoded.

to his relationships inspired a whole paper on Asian masculinities.[13] He described how this profoundly relational approach informs the management of his staff in ways that transgressed hegemonic norms of imperialist white masculinity:

> Sensuality to me is a more luxurious idea. The concept is more luxurious. It's more about tenderness, about loving, about empathy with someone. For me, that's what sensuality is. ... If someone's sensual, it kind of means that they're doing something that gives another person an explosive pleasure to their senses. In order to do that you have to understand what this person would enjoy, how can I make them feel good? That's the empathy part of it. Sexuality can be formulaic ... sensuality's more about trying to put yourself in their shoes and try to understand where they're coming from. [At work] empathy's important, regardless of who you're dealing with. Empathy allows you to understand where another person is coming from and when you understand ... you feel for them and that shapes how to manage or work with others in a more positive way.

Jay's leadership practice in the organization eschews the kind of competitive individualism inherent in masculinist renderings of leadership.[14] He does not chase outputs and outcomes, nor does he seek control. Unlike mainstream leadership practice, the 'point' of his management is not to persuade his staff to submit to his will; to work harder and faster or be more committed to organizational goals. Jay speaks more about melding with others as opposed to a unilateral penetration; grounded in connection and reciprocity so that while he 'enters another's shoes', he does so in a way that allows them to touch him back and enables him to 'feel for them'. His approach to relating with others lingers in the moment where both he and the other are mutually recognized as fully human.

Those of us who find ourselves privileged enough to serve in leadership roles, like Jay, have the opportunity to reject the existing system of domination that undergirds leadership. Even while this

---

[13] My paper, 'Sensuality as subversion: Doing masculinity with Chinese Australian professionals', was published in *Gender, Work and Organization* (Liu, 2017d) and I draw on here again a particularly memorable example that inspired the entire framing of the article.

[14] Collinson and Hearn, 1996; Kerfoot and Knights, 1993.

system may have conferred on us our power, we can exercise this power to change the dominator's rules. As Jeff's example demonstrated in Chapter 3, our attempts to do leadership differently may not necessarily be accepted by employees and the organization as legitimate. Others may challenge our claim to leadership and reframe the narratives to maintain the imperialist, white supremacist, patriarchal status quo. Changing the ways we relate to others therefore will probably be insufficient on its own to undo leadership and needs to be practised in concert with ongoing efforts to transform social meanings of leadership and decolonize our minds.

Too often we think of redemptive race relations as happening between the binary of 'white' and 'black', where Black followers convince white leaders to treat them with dignity. White people do indeed have a significant role to play in developing a more hospitable world, as I will explore in the next chapter, but the previous chapter demonstrated the diversity *within* umbrella labels like 'Black', 'Indigenous' and 'feminist'. Solidarity can therefore start within the margins by recognizing our differences yet finding meeting points in our struggles against the imperialist white supremacist capitalist patriarchy. For example, this could mean that Black employees may challenge discrimination against queer folks, queer staff may raise concerns about the inclusion of disabled employees, and disabled employees could remain aware of those who become marginalized due to their class background. Subversively, this kind of solidarity across intersecting racial, gender, sexual and class lines has the potential to evade pervasive suspicions in white institutions that see the leadership of marginalized people in service of their communities as self-serving. Building allyship across seemingly separate, but actually overlapping, groups decentres domination, so that we may first find recognition and redemption in the peripheries of organizations and society before we unsettle the centre.

Reimagining leadership

The myths and legends of leadership we currently tell are defined in white masculinist terms that glorify imperialist ideals of conquest and control. Following from anti-racist feminist resistance towards self-definition, we can redefine what it means to lead. As educators, we can change the stories and exemplars of leaders we feature in our curricula. Rather than focus on high-profile executives and politicians through case studies that extol their self-sufficiency, we can broaden the definitional boundaries of leadership to include community organizers who work in more egalitarian teams alongside members of the community and those they seek to serve. These examples may be used to highlight the ways that leadership is not something that is unilaterally imposed by a leader onto their followers, but something that occurs in the space between people. The outcomes then of this leadership might be collaboratively produced through sharing voice, ongoing dialogue, perhaps even struggle and debate, as well as mutual respect and love.

We might also locate leadership in the resistance against the status quo. A caveat is that while many popular leadership narratives invoke the tropes of rebellion, they rarely involve any real stakes. Instead, the stories simply reproduce the valorization of masculinity in portrayals of leaders as individualistic, self-reliant and brave. An Australian university launched a marketing campaign and placed a billboard near the campus where a young, white, male astronomer was featured alongside the tagline: 'We must be there for the curious, the disruptors and the unsure.' This billboard conveyed what the university sought in its new brand: the conquest of the unknown; the courage to effect change; the conviction to secure certainty, all while positioning the university as the protector – or indeed, the leader – who will usher in the future through its tireless pursuit of knowledge. However, few organizations welcome resistance and rebellion in anything beyond their branding, for doing so would mean unsettling the very values of individualism, masculinity, conquest and control that such organizations embody.[15]

Stories of leadership that challenge the interlocking systems of oppression in their contexts may include activist groups and movements, rather than for-profit organizations. The contributions of the Combahee River Collective to intersectional understandings of resistance have already been discussed. Between 1974 and 1980 the Boston-based group comprised of self-identifying 'Black feminist lesbian activists' established an array of services attending to issues of domestic violence, reproductive rights and food access in poor communities.

In Britain, the East London Federation of the Suffragettes was a radical group that formed in 1914 to fight for working women's

---

[15] A queer scholar parodied this billboard on social media, publishing the photograph with an amendment to the quote so that it read, 'We must be there for the *bi*-curious, the disruptors and the unsure'. Her small act of humour highlights for me the creative ways employees find ways to resist corporate ideology, while making an important critique about the heteronormative culture of our campus.

rights throughout the First World War.[16] The Federation included working-class women and women of colour whose contributions to the women's liberation movement have historically been sidelined. Unlike other suffragette groups, the Federation advocated for universal suffrage. As factories closed and food prices rose, the members of the Federation led community action to support those affected by the war. Their initiatives included opening a volunteer-run children's health clinic, distributing milk to starving infants and running canteens that served nutritious food at cost price. The Federation even recruited a small 'People's Army' of supporters who defended the members against police brutality.

Over the years, my own scholarship has travelled closer to the community through my work with Building the Anti-Racist Classroom (BARC), a collective I co-founded with Sadhvi Dar, Angela Martinez Dy and Deborah Brewis[17] to challenge the institutionalized racism of Business Schools in the white academe.[18] We came together in the wake of a wider movement in our discipline known as the Decolonizing Alliance[19] that emerged through various encounters and exchanges at the 2017 International Critical Management Studies Conference. Our work seeks to centre the concerns of students of colour, leveraging our own power, privilege and platforms in academia to amplify their protests against white supremacy[20] and apply multidisciplinary tools to build community with people of colour in our sector and develop our collective capacities for resistance.

Among and between ourselves, we have grown to incorporate alternate forms of leadership. We are non-hierarchical. We begin every meeting with a 'check-in', where each participant shares what is happening in their lives. Every voice is heard so that each of our full selves may be recognized by our sisters before we start collaboration. When disagreements arise, we raise issues through a

---

[16] This project was developed by The Women's Hall in collaboration with Four Corners, Tower Hamlets Local History Library & Archives, East End Women's Museum and Women's History Month in East London. It ran at the East End Women's Museum from March to December 2018. Information about the project can be found at: https://eastendwomensmuseum.org/the-womens-hall. Thanks are due to Elaine Swan for bringing this brilliant project to my attention.

[17] Another founding member, Afroz Zain Algiers, stepped down from active organizing but remains an artist in residence with the collective. Udeni Salmon also worked with us for a period after our establishment.

[18] Dar, 2019; Gabriel and Tate, 2017.

[19] https://decolonizingalliance.wordpress.com/

[20] Dar and Salmon, 2019; Sisters of Resistance, 2019.

reflexive acknowledgement of our own limitations and failings that contributed to any misunderstandings and missteps. We celebrate one another's strengths and prioritize the love we have for each other in the face of interpersonal conflict.

Such practices of 'leadership' shift the focus from individuals to the bonds of criticality, togetherness and joy that are developed between people committed to social justice and transformation. Not only are these examples instructive of the ways we could relate with others differently in our leadership, but they also offer alternative narratives for what constitute leadership in our culture. Activist groups can subvert dominant assumptions that to be a leader necessitates ascendancy within a hierarchy of power and exerting command and control over those who occupy the lower ranks. These collectives shift narratives of leadership to what is happening in the space between people who work cooperatively with one another towards social justice. They expand the definitions of what is possible, where leadership no longer has to be located within heroic individuals. These examples acknowledge that leadership can be exercised from marginalized communities of working-class women or women of colour without, and sometimes in spite of, the influence of an authority figure.

Other more infamous examples of resistive leaders such as Martin Luther King Jr and Mohandas Karamchand Gandhi made vital contributions to the struggles during their lifetimes, but their cases highlight a problematic tendency to appropriate these figures into tame, neoliberal narratives after their deaths. Their examples can be shared as illustrations of how resistance can be co-opted into dominant notions of leadership that reinforce some of the structures of power that these leaders fought in (and with) their lives. For instance, Martin Luther King Jr holds sway in our public imagination as a 'kindly and powerful orator who led the successful non-violent movement for civil rights', but few white accounts acknowledge his radical calls for social change.[21] Throughout his public life, King challenged three forces that he saw as moral threats to the world: militarism; materialism and racism, which can be seen to correlate with hooks' systems of imperialist, capitalist and white supremacist oppression. In our public memory, we rarely remember King as a vocal opponent of the Vietnam War or recall how he expressed dismay at white people's 'racial ignorance'.[22] King

---

[21] See *Misremembering Dr. King: Revisiting the Legacy of Martin Luther King Jr* by Jennifer J. Yanco (2014).
[22] Yanco, 2014, p 73.

is almost ubiquitously heralded as a hero, but this celebrated image is one that has largely been distorted and domesticated by white voices.[23]

Mohandas Karamchand Gandhi, later canonized as Mahatma Gandhi, takes on an almost mystical role in public imaginations in the West as a peaceful figure who advocated non-violent resistance against British colonial rule. What remain less well known are his critiques of imperialism as an ever-expanding capitalist enterprise that both exploited colonies for their resources and saw them as potential consumers. His resistance to imperialism was not thought to end at driving out the British. Rather, his articulation of non-violent resistance (*satyagraha*) was a democratic and collective undertaking of self-discipline in the face of danger. This form of resistance demonstrated to the international audience the moral inferiority of the colonial rulers as they carried out militarized suppression of unarmed resisters.[24] Gandhi also supported the caste system, which reflected the views on race he developed in his time living in South Africa, where he successfully petitioned the Durban Post Office in 1895 to install a third entrance after one for Black people and one for white people so that Indians did not need to share the Black entrance.[25] Radical anti-imperialist contemporaries of Gandhi such as Bhimrao Ramji Ambedkar, an intellectual born into an 'Untouchable' family, are much less prominent in the West.[26]

In excavating celebrated figures from the past, we can imagine that their struggles were successful in order to avoid confronting how the power systems they challenged persist in the present day. In that way, we can appropriate their examples to suggest that King and the civil rights movement abolished racism and now we live in happy racial unity or that Gandhi stood up against the British Empire and now imperialism is a relic of the past. At the same time, the heroicization of historical figures can preclude their critique and prevent us from engaging in thoughtful dialogue about how we may better advance our resistance.

Finally, those of us who are privileged to engage in creative work or operate in cultural industries have the power to challenge controlling

---

[23] See also the edited collection by historian Lewis V. Baldwin and theologian Rufus Burrow (2013), *The Domestication of Martin Luther King Jr.: Clarence B. Jones, Right-Wing Conservatism, and the Manipulation of the King Legacy*.

[24] Childs and Williams, 2013.

[25] Roy, 2014.

[26] See the republished text of Bhimrao Ramji Ambedkar's speech (originally written in 1936), *Annihilation of Caste*, with an essay by Arundhati Roy (2014) entitled 'The doctor and the saint' (Ambedkar, 2014).

images. In my research, I have had the opportunity to meet Jason, a former actor turned film producer.[27] His experiences working as an Asian actor in Australia allowed him to develop an acute awareness of how representations of Asian people on screen can act as a vehicle of gender and racial oppression (or resistance). He recalled the ways as an actor he was continually expected to be complicit in stereotypical portrayals of Asian men in popular media as illiterate criminals. At auditions he would be frequently asked to speak in broken English, confined to roles playing thieves, burglars and drug addicts. These roles imitate controlling images of the 'yellow peril' that proliferated during the White Australia era.[28] Jason's frustration with the mainstream Australian film and television industry later led him to start his own film production company in Singapore, which enabled him to engage more directly in the politics of Asian representation:

> One of the reasons I decided to start a production company and to write and direct was that at least I can choose the people that are going to be in my stories. I still want to act, but as an actor, I really had no control over casting and over the story; the ultimate outcome of your character and how you're portrayed. And I just got sick of it – the stereotypes. To be honest, even in Asia, stereotypes abound. Singapore is just full of actors who are very happy to play stereotypical Asian character that many people find funny, but not particularly good for the image of the Asian male. … So my mission after that was really just to keep pursuing the destruction of the stereotype of the ways Asians are portrayed in the media, and in some ways do the opposite, which is to not create stereotypes; to just play ordinary characters and aspirational characters in the media. … The change has to come from people who are most aware of

[27] I first shared Jason's story in *Gender, Work and Organization* (Liu, 2017d), although I did not have the opportunity then to include the following excerpt from his interview in the original article.

[28] Following the Federation of Australia in 1901, Australia legislated a racial hierarchy through the White Australia policy, which limited the arrival and endorsed the deportation of non-European immigrants (Curthoys, 2003; Liu, 2019b). In response to the growing number of Chinese migrants who began arriving to Australia from the Pearl Delta region of South China from the mid-1800s (Ang, 2003; Tan, 2006), stereotypes of Chinese immigrants as smugglers, gangsters and licentious opium smokers were propagated by white Australians in order to construct the Chinese as a menace to an otherwise moral white society (Kuo, 2013; Liu, 2019b).

it because we hired an Indian-Malaysian man, as a kind of romantic lead in a love triangle. [The actor] said to us, "No one has ever, ever hired me as a romantic lead because I'm Indian".

Jason utilizes his position of leadership in the creative industries to advance self-defined representations of Asian people, particularly Asian men. It is, of course, not necessary for all of us to establish film companies. Both formal and informal organizations abound with opportunities for storytelling.

Conclusion

If leadership is to be redeemed, its current definition in imperialist, white supremacist, capitalist and patriarchal terms needs to be undone. Rejecting leadership as we know it is difficult because leadership has not only been socially constructed, but romanticized, through these interlocking systems of power. We have thus come to understand leadership via the beautiful illusions of a white knight who alone possesses the power to solve all organizational and societal problems. Even when the violent realities of leaders and their leadership are exposed, they are often quickly disregarded as not *real* leaders. Leadership appears to occupy a sacred status with which it continually evades critique.

Traditionally, white knights have come to us in the form of white, cis-gender, heterosexual, elite-class, able-bodied men, and while we are beginning to see increasingly diverse bodies take on the mantle of leadership in white-dominated societies, it seems that leaders of all genders and races are still expected to conform to prevailing white patriarchal norms. It is therefore insufficient to argue that the problems of leadership will correct themselves when we have more women leaders or leaders of colour. To paraphrase the words of Audre Lorde, we may temporarily beat the imperialist, white supremacist, capitalist patriarchy at its own game, but we will never be able to bring about genuine change.[29]

Through this book, I have tried to show that leadership itself is the problem. To undo leadership as we know it so that we have the hope to redeem it via the values of justice, solidarity and love, we need to decolonize our minds, find new ways to relate to one another and

[29] Lorde, 1984.

reimagine our social meanings of leadership. This chapter has provided some hints for how these interrelated paths for resistance may begin. Specifically, we might learn to love the aspects of ourselves and others that have been marginalized in dominator culture. We can develop ways to recognize the value of our knowledge and practices, even if they have been rejected in mainstream ideas of what constitutes 'leadership'. Rejecting these norms then allows us to find ways to do leadership differently. Eschewing the leadership ideals around heroic individualism, control and conquest, we might find ways to relate to others through solidarity and love. Anti-racist feminist movements provide a wealth of inspiration for consciousness-raising collectives where simple acts of breaking bread and sharing space are often profoundly powerful. Finally, undoing leadership also involves working together to change the stories we tell of leaders and leadership so that the social meanings of leadership may grow to encompass the invisible and forgotten acts of resistance by marginalized people and communities.

7

White Allyship

In the wake of the Brexit vote in June 2016, *The Guardian* reported that white people in Britain had started wearing safety pins in a public show of solidarity with immigrants.[1] The symbol of the safety pin conveyed the idea that immigrants had nothing to fear from them – that they are 'safe'. In the aftermath of Trump's election, white Americans also wore safety pins in order to show support to those made most vulnerable by the new president's rise to power, such as people of colour, especially Muslims, members of the LGBTQ community, and undocumented migrants and their families.[2] Although the intentions behind this gesture may have been genuine,[3] some people were seen to be sporting the safety pin as an identity statement. 'Look at me! I'm a *good* white person!' Yet there was no action or strategy behind what then became an empty emblem of white guilt. In fact, the hollow gesture was easily co-opted by white nationalists, who wore safety pins in attempts to trick those distraught by the election outcome.[4] The safety pin trend highlighted that allyship had become appropriated by some white people into a desirable social status that was denuded of all its commitment to change.

---

[1]   Anon, 2016.

[2]   Safronova, 2016.

[3]   I know of some academics in the United States who wore safety pins after Trump's election and spent time with students who approached them to discuss their concerns one-on-one. It can be argued that it was not the safety pin itself that prompted trust, but usually the academics' history of empathy and care they had demonstrated over time that designated them as allies.

[4]   The safety pin symbol was also co-opted by jewellery makers who produced, marketed and sold safety pin necklaces made with precious metals and gems (Lindsay, 2016).

A safety pin, on its own, is insufficient to protect marginalized people. Allyship demands civic engagement, strategy and action.[5] Perhaps the most poignant distinction is that being an ally is not a status that white people can designate themselves. It can only be assigned by those marginalized who recognize the ally's struggles towards solidarity.

> In a society in which the machinations of racism are everywhere, white people are *the* problem. Said differently, racism is a *white* problem. People who were white created white supremacy and people who are white sustain it. Our actions, attitudes, and ways of being subvert justice, cross-racial solidarity, and reconciliation. More insidiously, we benefit profusely from the prevalence of racial injustice, even as we are spiritually, psychologically, and morally malformed by it.[6]

These words of theologian Jennifer Harvey capture why it is so vital that white people take responsibility for white supremacy. Despite the ways white people are personally (albeit often unwittingly) implicated in the everyday reproduction of white supremacy, there is still a considerable number who refuse to believe that they should be held accountable to dismantle it.

White allyship describes the ongoing processes of responsibility assumed by people who present as white to operate in solidarity with people of colour to dismantle white supremacy. White allyship is difficult. It is a constant struggle with oneself, with others and with the relations of domination embedded in an imperialist, white supremacist world. As a consequence, white allies are rare, rarer than good white people who profess to be non-racist. Being an ally is more than simply not wanting to be seen as a racist. It requires active, deliberate, ongoing engagement with critique and reflexivity.

The next section will discuss the concept of white fragility and how its persistence under neoliberalism has left white allyship so elusive. This chapter will then turn to explore to approaches to white allyship: redoing whiteness and abolishing whiteness. Redoing

---

[5] As allyship has become increasingly misunderstood as a socially desirable identity label, some activists, such as #BlackLivesMatter co-founder Alicia Garza, are calling for the term 'allies' to be abandoned in favour of 'co-conspirators', which highlights the radical action inherent in this political practice. See Garza's interview on *Politically Re-Active* in the episode entitled 'What did we learn? With Alicia Garza and Wyatt Cenac': www.politicallyreactive.com/.

[6] Harvey, 2007, p 7.

whiteness focuses on how people who identify as white may work to subvert the dominant ways of 'doing whiteness' including normalization, solipsism and ontological expansiveness. Abolishing whiteness seeks a more radical rethinking of the nature of whiteness. It questions if whiteness is at all possible beyond violence and calls on white people to become 'race traitors' and relinquish their identification with this oppressive group.

As with diversity in organizations, many white people believe that they are unraced and thus racism does not affect them. When I present anti-racist feminisms to predominantly white audiences, an attendee will usually implore at the end of my talk, 'So tell me what I should *do!*' If my answer is not to their liking (perhaps they consider it too complicated, too hard or just not phrased gently and unthreateningly enough), they can blame me for their lack of action in promoting racial equality. They see it as the role of people of colour to 'solve the problem' of race for them, yet only on their terms. Neither redoing nor abolishing whiteness are quick fixes. Ultimately, this chapter challenges would-be white allies to conduct their own reading and research and work out for themselves what would be most meaningful for them to do in the context of their allyship.

> We need to be clear that there is no such thing as giving up one's privilege to be 'outside' the system. One is always *in* the system. The only question is whether one is part of the system in a way that challenges or strengthens the status quo. Privilege is not something I *take* and which therefore have the option of *not* taking. It is something that society *gives* me, and unless I change the institutions which give it to me, they will continue to give it, and I will continue to *have* it, however noble and egalitarian my intentions.[7]

Shame and guilt

Privilege, particularly white or male privilege, can be difficult to see and painful to accept for those who benefit. As discussed in Chapter 1, this very word can conjure up intense feelings of anger. Its utterance is taken by some as an accusation, insinuating that the 'privileged' one was born into the lap of luxury and has never experienced hardship in their life. It may bear repeating that white privilege is not an attack

---

[7]   Brod, 1989, p 280.

on white people, but a corollary of white supremacy, just as male privilege is a corollary of patriarchy. Privileges are granted prenatally so the recipient cannot choose to refuse them, nor can they give them away. These privileges are also far from monolithic, but are cross-cut by dimensions of sexuality, class, coloniality and dis/ability.

As sociologist Harry Brod's opening quote to this section attests, privilege has little to do with whether or not we are 'good' people. Privileges are bestowed on people by institutions solely on the basis of favoured identifications like whiteness, maleness, heterosexuality, able-bodiedness or belonging to the elite classes. Through our varied histories of imperialism, countries like the United States, Britain, Canada, Australia and New Zealand have been marked by white power-holders who purposefully shaped structures on behalf of their race to benefit white people and withhold benefits from people of colour. These decisions included declarations of 'terra nullius',[8] which, like the notion of manifest destiny,[9] asserted white ownership over lands through the murder and forcible removal of native people. It also involved enshrining laws that constructed Black people as slaves (as property owned by whites) and laws that restricted immigration of people of colour.

When white supremacy is built into the law, it no longer becomes a choice that white people can actively make to disobey such practices. As individuals, white people tend to go along with the law. Whether intentionally or not, white people participate in the system of power that inflates the value of their race while deflating the value of others. One of the many privileges of whiteness is not having to acknowledge one's privilege and maintain the belief that organizations and societies are meritocratic. Under neoliberalism, we often struggle to see the complete picture,[10] and we form instead a mythic worldview where

---

[8] When invading British settlers arrived in Australia in 1788, they claimed that the land was *terra nullius* – land belonging to no one – which was thus free for them to take. For Aileen Moreton-Robinson (2015), the non-Indigenous sense of belonging is tied to this original theft, the lie of *terra nullius* that has enabled colonizers to claim the right to live on Indigenous lands.

[9] 'Manifest destiny' was first coined by journalist John Louis O'Sullivan in 1845. O'Sullivan used this phrase to justify the annexation of Texas and expansion into the Oregon territory against British claims. The superiority of the American claim to these areas was said to be 'by the right of our manifest destiny to overspread and to possess the whole of the continent which Providence has given us for the development of the great experiment of liberty and federated self-government entrusted to us' (from the *New York Morning News*, 27 December 1845, cited in Radford Ruether, 2007, p 70). See *America, Amerikkka: Elect Nation and Imperial Violence* by Rosemary Radford Ruether (2007).

[10] Or in other words, having a sociological imagination (Mills, 2000).

individuals are believed to be wholly responsible for their destinies. Within this logic, the privileges of whiteness, maleness, heterosexuality, able-bodiedness or the elite classes can be seen to be self-earned and completely deserved. On the other side of the coin, the structural disadvantages faced by non-dominant groups can also be blamed on the individuals themselves who are castigated for 'bringing up race/ gender/sexuality/and so on' and not working hard enough to achieve success for themselves. Maintaining this neoliberal myth allows white people in particular to disconnect themselves from the painful realities of racism. Even for those with the best intentions, the privilege to be removed from racism can render white people unable to form an understanding of others' lives or develop the motivation for social change.

Part of the discomfort white people experience is the shame and guilt that can arise when they realize that white supremacy is a system from which they benefit. White guilt is said to be problematic when it becomes a barrier to further engagement; for example, when the pain drives white people to avoid reminders of race and racism (which usually involves avoiding people of colour altogether).[11] White guilt can also generate feelings of resentment towards those who challenge their racism or to feel paralysed with an overwhelming sense of helplessness or hopelessness.[12] In psychological theorizing, guilt is disentangled from the related concept of shame. Shame is described as an emotion in which 'the entire self feels exposed, inferior and degraded'.[13] Experiences of shame typically feel more intense and acute than guilt as the subject becomes preoccupied with others' opinions of them.[14] Guilt is said to be less devastating as the primary concern is not with the self, but with the behaviour. For that reason, guilt is often associated with a greater concern for others' feelings and linked to an empathetic attempt towards reparation. As such, guilt is considered the more moral of the two emotions, although both can be experienced at the same time.[15]

Taking psychological theories into account, perhaps what is commonly referred to as 'white guilt' in the critical whiteness studies literature is better understood as white shame. This shame fixates

[11] Aal, 2001; DiAngelo, 2012.
[12] DiAngelo, 2012.
[13] Eisenberg, 2000, p 667.
[14] Eisenberg, 2000.
[15] Eisenberg, 2000.

on the self and how one thinks one is being negatively perceived by society at large.[16] It is ultimately solipsistic. Guilt, at least according to psychological theorizing, may have the greater potential for moral growth. The unease generated through guilt when nurtured with critical and reflexive awareness for the structural nature of white supremacy may transcend a preoccupation with the self towards meaningful allyship.

Fragility

Discomfort may indeed bear the possibility of individual and social transformation.[17] In her theorizations of discomfort, education scholar Barbara Applebaum reflected on the tendency of teachers to soothe white emotions through her personal experience of delivering a guest lecture for a colleague on white denials of racism. When white students in her classroom reacted with anger and agitation to such critical discussions of race and racism, she was reproached by her colleague for being too 'hard' on the white students. In an elegant analysis, Applebaum considers the problematic pedagogy of 'comfor*ting* (as a verb) white students' discomfort' and theorizes how we may support white people without valorizing white power and privilege and serving white fragility.[18]

White fragility is a term proposed by anti-racist educator Robin DiAngelo.[19] It refers to:

> a state in which even a minimum amount of racial stress becomes intolerable, triggering a range of defensive moves. These moves include the outward display of emotions such as anger, fear, and guilt, and behaviours such as

---

[16] A common binary that white people assume is what DiAngelo (2012, p 12) refers to as 'racist = bad / not racist = good'. The intersectional politics among white people means that the notion one is racist can also insinuate that the wrongdoer is ignorant, uneducated or lower-class 'white trash'. This reductionistic binary ignores the structural nature of racial power that implicates everyone in white supremacy. One can lose touch with anti-racist resistance in the eager attempt to simply present oneself as a *good* white. See also *Good White People: The Problem With Middle-Class White Anti-Racism* by Shannon Sullivan (2014).

[17] Applebaum, 2017. See also *Being White, Being Good: White Complicity, White Moral Responsibility, and Social Justice Pedagogy* by Barbara Applebaum (2010).

[18] Applebaum, 2017, p 864.

[19] See *White Fragility: Why It's So Hard for White People to Talk About Racism* by Robin DiAngelo (2018).

argumentation, silence, and leaving the stress-inducing situation.[20]

It is important to note here that white fragility does not simply mean that white people have a lower threshold for discomfort as though it is a passive sense of being. For Applebaum, white fragility is an active form of 'doing' whiteness.[21] It is a performance that reiterates what it means to be white and is complicit in upholding white power and privilege.

White fragility is grounded in the entitlement most white people believe they have to racial comfort. She observes how when white people engage in critical conversations about racism with people of colour, many attest that they 'don't feel safe'. DiAngelo in turn interprets this confession as meaning they do not feel *comfortable*. As white people have predominantly been shielded from the realities of their racial power and privilege, they can be discomforted when they are forced to acknowledge historical (and current) brutalities towards people of colour. When such racial discomfort arises, most white people will insist that something is 'wrong' and typically blame the person or event who triggered the discomfort (often a person of colour). This resistance to discomfort – a discomfort that people of colour cope with every day in white supremacist societies – is what arguably leads many white people to self-segregation. Research on interracial friendship suggests that in the 'multicultural' United States, less than 10 per cent of white people have Black friends.[22]

[20] DiAngelo, 2011, p 54.

[21] Applebaum (2017) follows Judith Butler's (1999, p 33) theorizations of gender where gender is understood as 'performatively produced and compelled by the regulatory practices of gender coherence'. According to Butler, there is no real, essential truth behind what it means to be a man or a woman. Rather, gender identity is *constituted* by the very expressions that are then ascribed to gender. See *Gender Trouble: Feminism and the Subversion of Identity* by Judith Butler (1999).

[22] I cite here Eduardo Bonilla-Silva's (2006, p 108) review of existing research (see also DiAngelo, 2012). It is interesting to note that a much larger proportion of white Americans claim they have Black friends than they do in reality. Bonilla-Silva suggests that, when surveyed, around 20 per cent of white Americans would say they have Black friends. Many respondents would 'promote' the Black people in their lives to the status of 'good friends' or even 'best friends', yet when white respondents are further probed in interviews, most will admit that the Black people they had in mind are not really friends at all, but may be acquaintances or colleagues with whom they may have only had modest interactions in the past (Bonilla-Silva, 2006). DiAngelo believes that the rising African American influence on popular culture and the growing number of high-profile Black celebrities enhance for white people the sense that they have Black people in their lives even when that is not the case.

When we refuse to engage in vulnerability through open and honest discussions of power, we are in fact reproducing imperialist and patriarchal values of control and mastery. *In*vulnerability as a position allows us to ignore the aspects of social life that are 'inconvenient, disadvantageous or uncomfortable for us', such as the prevalence of racism and the persistence of white supremacy.[23]

Invulnerability can in fact take on the mask of vulnerability. For example, a well-documented strategy of white feminine fragility is the way white women burst into tears when people of colour challenge their racism. In deploying tears, white women play to the myth of white feminine innocence, preserving their self-image as moral people while deflecting attention away from the concerns of people of colour.[24] Nolan Cabrera's research on white male undergraduate students in the United States has suggested that they too have a tendency to fall back on victimization.[25] They confuse the erosion of their privileges with oppression and when they respond with anger, they come to believe that they are actually under attack.[26] It follows then that the practice of white fragility recentres white people's emotions, disregards the needs and interests of people of colour and exerts the violence that people of colour already continually endure.

Applebaum argues that white people need to tarry with discomfort rather than flee from it. A space of comfort for white students, she suggests, is often a space of violence for students of colour. When white people feel uncomfortable, it may indeed be a sign that the white supremacist status quo is being challenged. In the words of education scholar Megan Boler, a pedagogy of discomfort is how 'we invite one another to risk "living at the edge of our skin", where we find the greatest hope of revisioning ourselves'.[27] For white allies willing to relinquish fragility and risk discomfort in the hope of self and social transformation, it requires a willingness and capacity to be vulnerable. I will proceed to discuss two approaches for white people to challenge white supremacy: redoing whiteness and abolishing whiteness.

Although these approaches are conceptually contradictory (one cannot redo whiteness if one seeks to abolish it), I think they illuminate the multidimensional strategies needed to challenge white supremacy

[23] Applebaum here draws on philosopher Erinn Gilson's (2014, p 76) work on the ethics of vulnerability.

[24] Srivastava, 2006.

[25] Cabrera, 2014a.

[26] Cabrera, 2014b; see also Carroll, 2011.

[27] Boler, 1999, p 200.

in practice. Abolition offers a fundamental disidentification with whiteness that critically stands against its historical and contemporary brutalities. As vital as this form of resistance is, it requires a determined congregation of people to make its impact felt. Meanwhile, the practices of redoing whiteness provide more concrete actions white allies can take in the present to subvert white domination towards the ultimate aim of dismantling white supremacist systems.

Redoing whiteness

Redoing whiteness requires us to reflexively interrogate the practices of whiteness and reinvent ways of doing whiteness differently.[28] This process involves subverting normalization, solipsism and ontological expansiveness. Whiteness imparts an invisible advantage to white men and women, yet few white leaders are called to question their whiteness or asked to justify their dominance in leadership positions.[29] We can challenge white normalization by exposing and raising awareness about the mechanisms by which white power and privilege are kept in place yet hidden from view.[30] The first step is to name whiteness where it exists. If we agree that race matters in social life, then it needs to be called out in all cases of social practice and research.

When challenging white normalization, we need to be cautious that naming white power and privilege does not simply become about recentring whiteness.[31] Calling out white power and privilege should expose and disrupt racism, not fetishize whiteness. Australian Indigenous scholar Aileen Moreton-Robinson observed how white feminists who write about their white privilege have a tendency to then recentre whiteness in their following work.[32] Their one-off acknowledgement of white privilege then serves as an alibi against future racism. This ability to choose to disengage from race is an example of the racial privilege exercised by white scholars. To redo white normalization, white people (especially white scholars) need to question 'how they come to, and what allows them to produce and write knowledge as deracialised subject/knowers'.[33]

[28] The concept of redoing whiteness is grounded in parallel arguments about redoing gender, as theorized by Candace West and Don Zimmerman (2009) as well as the aforementioned work of Judith Butler (1999).
[29] Blackmore, 2010; McIntosh, 1988.
[30] Grimes, 2002.
[31] Blackmore, 2010.
[32] Moreton-Robinson, 2000.
[33] Moreton-Robinson, 2000, p 351.

With rapidly proliferating research, art, literature, music, film and television, and theatre created by people of colour, there is a growing body of self-defined narratives from which we can understand the experiences of non-dominant peoples in their own words. Cultivating the interest to hear these voices in the first place disrupts white solipsism. Although mainstream popular culture is generally fixed to modest deviations from the white masculinist norm, and consuming their tokenistic examples is unlikely to provide a nuanced appreciation of marginalized perspectives, a diverse range of voices can be heard through community-based shows and new media.

To take an analogous example in leadership studies, well-established academic journals deemed 'prestigious' by peak bodies tend to be more conservative and getting published in those outlets usually, though not always, requires tempering our writing to conform to the standards of Western positivistic science. To find theorizing of race that reflects what George Yancy calls the 'nitty-gritty, vivaciousness of the everyday',[34] we need to be prepared to read widely, transcending the inner circles of the academic elite and traversing disciplinary borders where marginalized people are telling their truths in ways that resist being 'swallowed up by the Eurocentric will to dominate'.[35] As critical leadership scholars, we can lay the groundwork for wide-scale scholarly resistance – epistemic disobedience[36] – against white supremacist ways of knowing.[37] Rather than indulge in comparative research where non-white subjects are examined in relation to their deviation from the white norm, non-white subjects need to be understood through their self-definitions. Empirical studies could take deep dives into the social practices of little-known groups, honouring the voices of their members, affirming their narratives and illuminating the nuances of their cultures.[38]

The habit of ontological expansiveness, however, means that even in racially progressive practice, white leaders assumed it would be their rightful place to showcase marginalized groups and lead the efforts of their inclusion.[39] Although white allies have an important role to play in the ongoing project of racial equality, the magnetic pull back towards domination has been strengthened through histories of imperialism

[34]   Yancy, 2012, p 30.
[35]   Taliaferro Baszile, 2015, p 240.
[36]   Mignolo, 2009, p 162.
[37]   Bell, 1995.
[38]   Denzin, 2009.
[39]   Sullivan, 2014.

and racism. Redoing expansiveness means practising contraction; being smaller, softer and quieter.[40]

White privilege enables people who identify as white to decide whether or not they will listen to or hear others. Elaine Swan offers listening as a practice white people can cultivate to undo ontological expansiveness.[41] Following communication scholar Tanja Dreher,[42] a politics of listening in relation to inequalities means learning to listen receptively; seeking ongoing permission to listen and shifting to the margins of discussions when that permission is granted. White people also need to learn to let go and be absent when their listening is not welcome.[43] Political listening is not about imposing one's need for empathy, therapy or friendship onto non-white people as though it is a feel-good panacea for white guilt.[44] Listening can in fact be risky, painful and discomforting, but indeed necessary for consciousness-raising to understand one's world from the point of view of those who have been harmed by it.[45] Listening as a form of radical white praxis is the opposite of expansiveness, requiring white people to learn how to be unobtrusive and unimportant.[46]

Practising listening and other forms of white contraction would mean resisting the temptation to speak for the Other within a colonialist white saviour fantasy.[47] Even white scholars who feel themselves genuinely inspired by philosophies and practices outside their cultures need to critically interrogate when it may not be their place to be cultural carriers. I attended a conference where a white Australian woman presented on her study of African migrants in Australia. A particular participant in her study expressed frustration with both her own African identity and the attempts of her African migrant peers to build community with her. The researcher did not disclose why or how she came to be researching African migrants. Instead, she appeared to be amused by this participant's anti-Black sentiments and repeatedly proclaimed that the participant wanted her story told. The

---

[40] When I've presented this idea at seminars, white audience members have wondered how then their 'contraction' would be noticed and make an impact. It's interesting to me that there's such a persistent assumption that white people ought to lead change.

[41] Swan (2017) explores progressive white praxis.

[42] Dreher, 2009.

[43] Dreher, 2009.

[44] Swan, 2017; see also Ahmed, 2008.

[45] Swan, 2017.

[46] Dreher, 2009.

[47] Blackmore, 2010; Haggis and Schech, 2000.

white researcher was unfamiliar with anti-racist thought and was thus unable to make sense of her participant's internalized white supremacy.[48] From her white gaze, the participant's story was interpreted through a more damaging narrative that took her anti-Blackness at face value as the normal and natural way to feel about African identity.[49]

In a panel on Indigenous research ethics, a white audience member confessed to the room that she was having mixed feelings about being invited to join an all-white research team to study Aboriginal communities. When the Aboriginal and Māori scholars in the room challenged her to decline the invitation, she became flustered and protested that the research project was not her idea, but she did not want to appear rude by withdrawing from the project either. Surrounded by Indigenous peers, the audience member sought to showcase her allyship by voluntarily sharing her sense of shame over the all-white research team, but when her continued complicity with the project was challenged by the Indigenous scholars, she was forced to admit that she struggled to disrupt the white racial comfort afforded in self-segregated groups,[50] as well as perhaps, give up the professional privileges of being named as an investigator on a large-scale funded project.

While some white scholars may come from a place of good intent to raise the profile of people of colour, not all stories may be for them to tell. For the white women in the previous two examples, the notion of white innocence clung to their self-concepts, with both researchers attributing the agency outward – 'my Black participant *made* me write this' or 'my other white colleagues *made* me join the research team'. Their examples highlight the considerable, though often unspoken rewards white scholars enjoy when they perpetuate white supremacy in research, including prestigious projects, publications and funding.

Within extant white supremacist structures, in some cases having white scholars on research teams is the only way anti-racist projects receive visibility and legitimacy and attract grant funding. In those cases, allies lend their white names and bodies to the cause of anti-racism with

[48] From W.E.B. DuBois' (2005) *The Souls of Black Folk* to Frantz Fanon's (1994) *Black Skin, White Masks*, Black intellectuals have reflected on and critiqued the 'pieces of the oppressor which are planted deeply within each of us' (Lorde, 2009, p 26).

[49] It is not uncommon at academic journals for such work to be handled by all-white editors and peer reviewers who may fail to identify let alone critique racist representations of participants of colour. Were she to publish her work, it would reinforce the dominance and legitimacy of white supremacist knowledge that will potentially proliferate through future theorizing and teaching.

[50] DiAngelo, 2012.

the view that the politics furthered in such projects will in the long term erode the white supremacist basis that empowers white scholars to lend validity to science and scholarship.[51] Such allies conscious of the power and privilege that their actions reproduce may deliberately refuse the rewards of white supremacy. For instance, an allied colleague of mine volunteers her time and energy to support and develop anti-racist research, but explicitly refuses co-authorship from her colleagues of colour. Her generosity stands in stark contrast to the careerism that characterizes many of us in the academy who seek to be an ally only when it is professionally and politically advantageous.

Anti-racist methodologies can also be applied to do whiteness differently through the implementation of empirical research. Cultural scholar Norman Denzin has articulated through his work a set of criteria to evaluate scholarship that strives towards racial justice. For Denzin, anti-racist scholarship:

> (a) interrogates existing cultural, sexist, and racial stereotypes, especially those connected to family, femininity, masculinity, marriage, and intimacy; (b) gives primacy to concrete lived experience; (c) uses dialogue and an ethics of personal responsibility, values beauty, spirituality, and a love of others; (d) implements an emancipatory agenda committed to equality, freedom, and social justice and participatory democratic practices; (e) emphasises community, collective action, solidarity, and group empowerment.[52]

Abolishing whiteness

Alongside theorizations for the *redoing* of whiteness beyond an ideology of domination, radical interrogators of white supremacy have also proposed a manifesto for *abolishing* whiteness. The provocations of New Abolitionism come from self-proclaimed 'race traitors' who seek to 'study whiteness in order to abolish it'.[53] From the point of

[51] Although racially ignorant blunders still appear from time to time, such as when all-white teams are marshalled to speak to advance 'diversity' research, my sense (and my hope) is that this dimension of white privilege is dissipating. In Australia, for example, government funding for Indigenous organizations now mandate that the research programmes are led by an Indigenous Australian researcher.

[52] Denzin, 2009, p 141.

[53] The core tenets of this radical political project has been articulated by Noel Ignatiev (1997). His own work on the history of Irish immigration in the United States, published in *How the Irish Became White* (1995), argues that the embracing of white

view of this project, whiteness without the habits of normalization, solipsism and ontological expansiveness would cease to be whiteness at all. As one of its earliest proponents, American studies scholar David Roediger, puts it, 'it is not merely that whiteness is oppressive and false; it is that whiteness is *nothing but* oppressive and false'.[54] According to the abolitionists, whiteness itself has no biology or culture.[55] It is instead as Frankenberg's definition of whiteness contends, defined by its position of social dominance and sustained through its ongoing practice of racial oppression.[56] In the words of writer James Baldwin, 'as long as you think that you are white, there is no hope for you'.[57] Without the privileges attached to whiteness, the white race would no longer exist.

Despite the recent rise of safety pin allies, white people have traditionally reserved solidarity for fellow whites. White racial bonding is predicated on the unspoken agreement between white people to keep each other comfortable and not challenge one another's racism in order to maintain the existing racial hierarchy and the power and privilege it affords.[58] This bonding does not necessarily require white people to enthusiastically engage in racist speech or action in every context. Indeed, silence is often sufficient for complicity. Silence is support – it escapes the need to hold fellow whites accountable and challenge white supremacy.

The New Abolitionists believe that when those aligned with being white defect from this identification, they become free to realize themselves as other things: as workers, youth, women or any other self-definitions they wish to explore. Would-be defectors need to 'break the laws of whiteness so flagrantly as to destroy the myth of white unanimity'.[59] This would mean challenging every manifestation of white supremacy: for example, by responding to an anti-Black

supremacy among Irish Americans (as primarily exercised through violence against African Americans) underpinned Irish Americans' so-called 'success' in the white republic.
[54] Roediger, 1994, p 13, emphasis original.
[55] Ignatiev, 1997.
[56] Ignatiev, 1997.
[57] Baldwin's quote comes from the film, *The Price of the Ticket* (1994). He reflects that while this quote may seem more poetic than political for those who have struggled to even persuade white people to disarm racism, let alone abolish whiteness, a highly poetic politics may be what is exactly required to disrupt white resistance against anti-racism.
[58] DiAngelo, 2012; see also Sleeter, 1996.
[59] Ignatiev, 1997, p 5.

remark with the defiant retort, 'What makes you think I'm white?'[60] By refusing to remain silent in these situations, defectors disrupt white racial bonding and shatter white solidarity. White allies like Robin DiAngelo have written about how their resistance is met with rejection from their peers.[61] The various ways that white abolitionists are punished for their resistance against white power and privilege remind us that allyship is difficult because it bears a cost. It rarely feels like the triumphant act of heroism we might experience when we don a safety pin, 'tweet' a selfie at a protest or add a banner to our Facebook profile picture. Allyship is painful, resistance can hurt, and that is why so few people are really willing to engage in it.

According to abolitionists, we only need a determined congregation of people to disrupt whiteness through their visible rejection of its membership.[62] Although white people cannot completely relinquish their privileges, at least initially, by strenuously jeopardizing their own abilities to draw on white privilege, a critical mass of race traitors has the potential to fracture the white race, 'and former whites, born again, will be able to take part, together with others, in building a new human community'.[63] Abolishing whiteness circumvents the tendency to venerate white saviours as good white anti-racists and instead calls for white people to become traitors to the white race.

Conclusion

While white allyship has become a popular identity within progressive circles in an era of Brexit and Trump, its appropriation into empty emblems has sparked an important debate on the possibility of cross-racial solidarity. Allyship, however, cannot be achieved through quick fixes. It requires ongoing critical self-reflection and analysis to resist the ideologies of imperialism, white supremacy and patriarchy that we have internalized. Because allyship is often difficult and painful, many white people succumb to feelings of anger, shame and guilt. As

---

[60] Ignatiev, 1997, p 5. Katya Pechenkina, a white-passing Russian co-author of mine, has written about her experiences of being 'tested' by white Australians for her loyalty to whiteness in our joint article (Liu and Pechenkina, 2016). She recounted how a racist joke would be made in her presence and her reaction closely monitored. When she challenged the racism, she became marked as the Other and rejected by the group as 'too foreign' to understand the normalized practices of Australian whiteness.

[61] DiAngelo, 2012.

[62] Ignatiev, 1997.

[63] Ignatiev, 1997, p 6.

such, they may choose to enact white fragility and set off a range of defensive moves in order to preserve their racially ignorant comfort. According to anti-racist educators, being a white ally requires that we tarry with racial discomfort than attempt to flee from it. It is when we risk 'living at the edge of our skin',[64] critically interrogating assumptions and developing new understandings, that we may find the greatest hope towards both social and self-transformation.

Invulnerability, in many ways, is glorified within the ideal leader. Exceptional leaders are believed to be confident, decisive and self-sufficient. In the context of white power and privilege, such idealizations make racial comfort a necessary condition for leadership. Leaders cannot afford to be seen to tarry with discomfort as they engage with non-dominant groups and marginalized voices. They need to operate within a protected chamber in which their vision, values, beliefs and assumptions will be taken as universal. This may in part explain why diversity is varyingly hotly resisted or savagely co-opted in organizations as maintaining white segregation also preserves white racial comfort. Under these conditions, there would be even less incentive for white leaders to relinquish white fragility as doing so would only open themselves up to be challenged and changed.

This chapter offered two approaches to challenging the whiteness inherent not just in leadership, but in everyday social life. Redoing whiteness offers practices that subvert the dominant approaches of whiteness including normalization, solipsism and ontological expansiveness. In a way, redoing whiteness calls on those who identify as white to resist their attribution as leaders within the ways that leadership is popularly understood in the Global North. As leadership scholars, we are also required to change the ways we engage in epistemic violence by enforcing white ways of seeing, knowing and profiting from marginalized communities. Abolishing whiteness presents a more fundamental dismantling of white supremacy through the dismantling of whiteness itself. It rallies white people to disidentify with being white and, by extension, reject the attendant culture of violence that is embedded in what it means to be white. While these practices may be conceptually exclusive, combined they offer a range of responses to white supremacy that can be applied and adapted by white allies in the ways most meaningful to the context of their allyship.

If leadership as we have come to recognize and romanticize it in the West is predicated on whiteness, then redoing whiteness and abolishing whiteness may indeed redeem leadership.

[64] Boler, 1999, p 200.

8

Restoration

Violence is engrained in the everyday life of societies and organizations. While far-right politicians and sexually abusive executives have garnered increased media attention of late, violence is not confined to overt incidences and events. Rather, violence is inherent in our cultures, where oppressions along the lines of gender, sexuality, race, class and dis/ability intersect in our everyday lives.

Leadership is a vehicle through which this violence becomes not only normalized but romanticized. Hegemonic masculinity, as defined by the qualities of individualism, control and conquest that served to justify centuries of patriarchy, white supremacy and European colonialism, is instilled into our ideas and ideals about leadership. Leaders and aspiring leaders in turn contort their identities in line with the fantasies of leadership to convince others and themselves that they are 'leaders'. As we saw with the media representations of Richard Branson, Steve Jobs, Sheryl Sandberg and Carolyn McCall, corporate executives are most readily recognized as 'leaders' when they conform to traditional white elite-class gender norms.

Anti-racist feminist thought and activism offer a wealth of knowledge in the resistance against interlocking oppressions in our organizations and society. Yet as leadership has been sculpted from the very ideologies of imperialism, white supremacy and patriarchy, we have historically failed to recognize it beyond narrow celebrations of heroic individualism. In our neoliberal era alongside the rise of capitalism, leadership has been further moulded in the image of professional success and material wealth. As such, the efforts of those from the margins who struggle towards social transformation are rarely permitted into the sacred definitional boundaries of leadership.

This book

Leadership, and its glorification in our cultures, is problematic. In the Global North, our ideas and ideals of leadership are set in the values of imperialism, white supremacy and patriarchy. From the mid-20th century, leadership began its eventual rise to its sacred status with the conceptualization of charisma. The charismatic leader was sculpted from Enlightenment fantasies, standing as an independent and autonomous subject who exerts his spirit on the world through his decisive thought and energetic action. He is governed only by his inner conviction and repudiates the communal concern for others as a trait of the 'weaker sex'. Such was the leader who sailed from Europe armed with weapons in the name of colonialism. His intellect, rationality and resolve not only made him the most suitable ruler of women, but his dominion was to extend around the world. Wielding his rules of scientific objectivity, the Enlightenment man installed his whiteness and masculinity as markers of his rightful role to rule.

In popular management handbooks, the rising prominence of executive women may ostensibly seem to challenge the legacy of the Enlightenment man. Often waving the banner of 'feminism', female business leaders have promoted the idea that gender equality is imminent as long as confident, resilient and ambitious women step up and lean in. This growing discourse is not so much feminist as it is postfeminist, where certain feminist values such as freedom of choice, equality of opportunity and self-determination are subsumed into patriarchal expectations around female sexuality, beauty and motherhood, so that feminism becomes tamed into something less threatening. Despite the celebratory and celebrated language around female empowerment, emerging ideals of female leadership bear a similar imperialist heritage to masculine leadership models. In particular, the persistent construction of white feminine innocence is used to constrain female leaders within traditional heteronormative elite-class norms, while denying the ways white women reproduce white supremacy in the past and present.

It seems then that while it has become politically correct to tout the importance of diversity in organizations and society, many of us can only tolerate tokenistic representations of visible differences as long as the imperialist, white supremacist, capitalist and patriarchal order of things remains in place. This context has given rise to racial capitalism, where people of colour come to be degraded into commodities to be 'pursued, captured, possessed and used' by white people and white institutions.[1] When people of colour attempt to enact leadership, leadership often becomes illegible on their bodies. The underlying distinction here is that diversity is not something that organizations or societies *are*, but something that they *have*.[2] The 'inclusion' that diversity promises is ultimately hollow and remains insufficient to undo white patriarchal violence.

The irony is that much of this violence is so naturalized and normalized that it can be exerted under the guise of benevolence. White male saviours live a 'sincere fiction'[3] in which they assume that because women and people of colour are 'inferior, incompetent, and generally useless',[4] they alone can ensure the greater good of organizations and societies. At the same time, the construct of leadership itself continues to be held out of the reach of critique. When leaders are exposed for ethical misconduct, we accuse the individual of not being a *real* leader, so that the inherent goodness of leadership may be maintained. We can no longer ignore the ways our enduring romances of leadership are steeped in myths of white strength, innocence and benevolence that have served to maintain gendered and racial hierarchies. Leadership, as we have come to know it, needs to be undone before there is hope of its redemption.

In this book, I looked towards anti-racist feminist movements to identify and challenge the interlocking systems of power that undergird leadership. Specifically, I explored how our theorizing and practice of leadership may embrace a recognition of interlocking oppressions, experiment with language and reach, and struggle towards solidarity, self-definition and love. Anti-racist feminisms comprise diverse interests, standpoints and intellectual traditions that speak with many voices. I reject a homogenizing reduction of these movements into any universal 'how-to' guide for leadership. Rather, I sought to draw out how some of its wisdoms may be adopted in our ongoing resistance against dominator culture in ways that make sense within our local contexts of struggle.

Perhaps leadership cannot be redeemed. Administration, coordination, collaboration, communication, supervision, teamwork, community building and decision making are all terms that can capture the activities that so-called 'leaders' do without filling the emptiness of leadership with fantasies of power. Yet, admittedly, leadership holds

[1]   Leong, 2012, p 2155.
[2]   Borrowing Hage's (1998) poignant remarks on Australian multiculturalism.
[3]   Vera and Gordon, 2002.
[4]   Shepherd et al, 2011, p 2.

firm to its sacred status. For those of us entangled with leadership and its violences, I suggest three interrelated paths for resistance, starting with decolonizing our minds, finding new ways to relate to one another and reimagining our social meanings of leadership. By rejecting the leadership norms around heroic individualism, control and conquest, we may come closer to developing forms of leadership built on the basis of love.

While such efforts follow in the steps of anti-racist feminist intellectuals and activists who have strived to do leadership differently from the margins, white allies play an important role in dismantling white supremacy. However, allyship is not easy and some white people may struggle to overcome white fragility in their attempts to build solidarity with people of colour. In particular, idealizations of whiteness and leadership overlap in the valorization of invulnerability. Anti-racist feminisms have highlighted white people's potential gains from racial equality, but this promise can only be met if white allies are willing to tarry with discomfort in their collective work with marginalized people and communities to undo and redeem leadership.

An anti-racist feminist future

As my country sees its fifth prime minister in five years,[5] I am reminded of the challenges we face in imagining a real alternative to what we currently know as leadership. Structural change can feel like a painful impossibility as we watch one self-proclaimed saviour after another pledge to deliver leadership. With this book, I have sought to rethink leadership, analysing how it is less a panacea for organizational and societal problems as part of the problem of dominator culture itself. To redeem leadership, as I argued, it is first necessary to critically interrogate this sacred construct, to strip away the myths of imperialism, white supremacy, capitalism and patriarchy that have shaped its sociopolitical meaning. Our hopes for a more just world are unlikely to be carried on the back of any one heroic individual, but rather will be brought about by a coalition of committed people struggling in small, quiet ways at the grassroots of organizations and societies.

---

[5]   On 24 August 2018, Scott Morrison was selected by the Liberal Party as its new leader, ousting the moderate incumbent, Malcolm Turnbull. Since 2007, no Australian prime minister has served their full four-year term through a series of four leadership 'spills'. Morrison is a social conservative who opposed the same-sex marriage bill and co-developed Australia's hardline immigration policy.

Such stories of leadership may not make for glamorous editorials in business magazines, how-to management handbooks or executive development programmes. Studies of such forms of leadership may also find it difficult to be accepted for publication in prestigious scientific journals. But for leadership theorizing and practice to move beyond the perpetuation of violent systems of power, we need to reimagine leadership as an anti-racist feminist practice.

Yet the anti-racist feminist path is marked with many hurdles and pitfalls. Our theorizing is continually at risk of being co-opted by hegemonic systems of power and our activism domesticated into tame organizational practices. We need to be deliberate in our choice of language. For example, when we explicitly designate the interlocking oppressions that characterize our cultures as the 'imperialist white supremacist capitalist patriarchy',[6] this makes it more difficult for users to impose their own wilful misinterpretations that dislocate our theorizing from its social justice roots. In contrast, terms like 'intersectionality' can become more readily folded into white supremacy. Despite Crenshaw's bold and unambiguous elucidation of intersectionality's application to challenging interlocking oppressions,[7] it has been evoked in organizational practice in some cases as an empty symbol of diversity and in others as an excuse to avoid 'doing' intersectionality altogether.

We also need to continue to identify and challenge false saviours. Anti-racist feminist movements have historically resisted white feminist agendas to collapse social oppressions into the single-axis issue of gender while prioritizing the needs and interests of (cis-gender, heterosexual, elite-class, able-bodied) white women. Similarly, there are those within anti-racist and socialist movements who profess that race or class respectively should trump all other concerns as an excuse to maintain

---

[6]   hooks, 2003, 2009b.

[7]   It is well worth reading Crenshaw's (1989, 1991) original texts on intersectionality. In the *Stanford Law Review* piece in particular, Crenshaw (1991, pp 1242–1243) states from the outset that her theorizing seeks to redress how in isolation, 'contemporary feminist and antiracist discourses have failed to consider intersectional identities such as women of color'. She then grounds her conceptualization of intersectionality in the concrete experiences of 'two dimensions of male violence against women — battering and rape' (Crenshaw, 1991, p1243) in order to explore 'how the experiences of women of color are frequently the product of intersecting patterns of racism and sexism, and how these experiences tend not to be represented within the discourses of either feminism or antiracism. Because of their intersectional identity as both women *and* of color within discourses that are shaped to respond to one *or* the other, women of color are marginalized within both' (Crenshaw, 1991, p 1244).

gender domination. As Audre Lorde attested, 'there is no such thing as a single-issue struggle because we do not live single-issue lives'.[8]

To be clear, this is not to say that the onus should be on anti-racist activists to somehow make their movements incorruptible. Instead, the depoliticization of our efforts, of which intersectionality is just one recent example, is a reminder that ours is an ongoing struggle. As we co-create our resistances against the imperialist white supremacist capitalist patriarchy, so we must continue to identify and challenge attempts to subsume and erase what we stand for.

We also need to continue decolonizing our minds, to detoxify the ideologies of domination implanted in all of us that seduce us back to violence. In *Racism Without Racists*, Eduardo Bonilla-Silva anticipates that the coordinates of racial stratification will shift in the 21st century in line with demographic trends. Specifically, he predicts a 'triracial' stratification system that resembles certain Latin American and Caribbean nations where the power hierarchy comprises "whites" at the top, an intermediary group of "honorary whites" ... and a nonwhite group or the "collective black" at the bottom'.[9] In the United States, Bonilla-Silva expects that light-skinned Latinos, East Asian Americans and Asian Indians, Middle Eastern Americans and most multiracial people will be likely to form this honorary white[10] stratum. Honorary whites not only enjoy a higher status under the white gaze and greater privileges in a white supremacist system, but they will also probably internalize this stratification and regard themselves as superior to the collective Black stratum.

Indeed, in Australia I have seen the ways that English-speaking East Asians like myself can trade on their class status to offset racial disadvantage. The privileges that I now hold as a member of the educated middle class are incomparable to my experiences growing up as a child of non-English-speaking migrant workers. This trading of class advantage with racial disadvantage can generate the illusion that racial injustice is eroding. During the year when I conducted the study of Asian Australian professionals, I encountered individuals who were fervently committed to acquiring material wealth with the belief that professional and economic success will propel them

---

[8] This quote is often attributed to Lorde's address, 'Learning from the 60s' delivered in February 1982 at Harvard University.

[9] Bonilla-Silva, 2006, p 179.

[10] Bonilla-Silva utilizes the term '*honorary* whites' to emphasize that members of this stratum will always remain secondary. They will still face discrimination and will not possess equal power and privileges to whites.

up the racial hierarchy. Appealing to colourist logic,[11] many East Asian professionals I met performed whiteness by attempting to build and then exert class power while distancing themselves from other people 'of colour'.

When society as it is today continues to progress like this, Bonilla-Silva believes that there will only be more racial inequality rather than less. In our anti-racist feminist resistance, it is imperative that we reject false salvations that trick lighter-skinned people of colour into class domination, working-class whites into racial domination or men of colour into gender domination. Such illusory forms of power and privilege have failed to liberate white women who were offered economic power in exchange for their complicity in white supremacy, yet who continued to be defined in subordination to white elite-class men. Instead of seeking safety with false saviours and false salvations, we need to build solidarity with all those who are marginalized in society, while convincing race and gender 'traitors' to join our struggles as allies.

The intersectional movements of anti-racist feminisms offer an understanding of 'leadership' that is worthy of our engagement. Rather than serve extant structures of domination, an anti-racist feminist practice is committed to social transformation and grounded in radical solidarity and love. This reimagination of leadership is not idealistic. It is necessary in an increasingly hostile world that has seen imperialist, white supremacist, capitalist and patriarchal violences exerted in both aggressive and subtle ways. It is necessary as society's elites amass an unprecedented concentration of power and wealth while the rest of us become more vulnerable in organizations and society. With inequality and injustice as the taken-for-granted nature of our everyday lives, anti-racist feminist resistance may be our most viable response.

---

[11] Colourism refers to a form of racial prejudice against individuals with dark skin tones. Colourism can often manifest within groups of colour who have internalized white supremacy so that the lighter-skinned members of the racial group might be considered more beautiful or moral (Lovell Banks, 2000; see also Burton et al, 2010). Colourism is closely interlinked with white supremacy and white racism (Gabriel, 2007).

References

Aal, W. (2001) 'Moving from guilt to action: Antiracist organizing and the concept of "whiteness" for activism and the academy', in Brander Rasmussen, B., Klinenberg, E., Nexica, I.J. and Wray, M. (eds) *The Making and Unmaking of Whiteness*. Durham, NC: Duke University Press, pp 294–310.

Adamson, M. (2017) 'Postfeminism, neoliberalism and a "successfully" balanced femininity in celebrity CEO autobiographies', *Gender, Work and Organization*, 24(3), pp 314–327.

Ahmed, S. (2007) '"You end up doing the document rather than doing the doing": Diversity, race equality and the politics of documentation', *Ethnic and Racial Studies*, 30(4), pp 590–609.

Ahmed, S. (2008) 'The politics of good feeling', *Australian Critical Race and Whiteness Studies Association*, 4(1), pp 1–18.

Ahmed, S. (2009) 'Embodying diversity: Problems and paradoxes for Black feminists', *Race Ethnicity and Education*, 12(1), pp 41–52.

Ahmed, S. (2012) *On Being Included: Racism and Diversity in Institutional Life*. Durham, NC: Duke University Press.

Ahmed, S. and Swan, E. (2006) 'Introduction: Doing diversity', *Policy Futures in Education*, 4(2), pp 96–100.

Ailon, G. (2008) 'Mirror, mirror on the wall: Culture's consequences in a value test of its own design', *Academy of Management Review*, 33(4), pp 885–904.

Ailon-Souday, G. and Kunda, G. (2003) 'The local selves of global workers: The social construction of national identity in the face of organizational globalization', *Organization Studies*, 24(7), pp 1073–1096.

Alarcón, N. (1983) 'Chicana's feminist literature: A re-vision through Malintzin or Malintzin: Putting flesh back on the object', in Moraga, C. and Anzaldúa, G. E. (eds) *This Bridge Called My Back: Writings by Radical Women of Color*. 2nd edn. New York: Kitchen Table: Women of Color Press, pp 182–190.

Alimahomed, S. (2010) 'Thinking outside the rainbow: Women of color redefining queer politics and identity', *Social Identities*, 16(2), pp 151–168.

Alvesson, M. and Kärreman, D. (2016) 'Intellectual failure and ideological success in organization studies: The case of transformational leadership', *Journal of Management Inquiry*, 25(2), pp 139–152.

Alvesson, M. and Sveningsson, S. (2003a) 'The great disappearing act: Difficulties in doing "leadership"', *The Leadership Quarterly*, 14(3), pp 359–381.

Alvesson, M. and Sveningsson, S. (2003b) 'Managers doing leadership: The extra-ordinarization of the mundane', *Human Relations*, 56(12), pp 1435–1459.

Alvesson, M. and Willmott, H. (2002) 'Identity regulation as organizational control: Producing the appropriate individual', *Journal of Management Studies*, 39(5), pp 619–644.

Ambedkar, B.R. (2014) *Annihilation of Caste*. Edited by Anand, S. London: Verso.

Ang, I. (2003) 'From White Australia to Fortress Australia: The anxious nation in the new century', in Jayasuriya, L., Walker, D. and Gothard, J. (eds) *Legacies of White Australia: Race, Culture and Nation*. Crawley: University of Western Australia Press, pp 51–69.

Ang, I. (2014) 'Beyond Chinese groupism: Chinese Australians between assimilation, multiculturalism and diaspora', *Ethnic and Racial Studies*, 37(7), pp 1184–1196.

Anon (2012) Supreme Court orders Halla-aho to pay for hate speech, 8 June. Available at: https://yle.fi/uutiset/osasto/news/supreme_court_orders_halla-aho_to_pay_for_hate_speech/6171739 (Accessed: 2 March 2018).

Anon (2016) Race issues: The safety pins puncturing post-Brexit racism, *The Guardian*, 29 June. Available at: www.theguardian.com/world/shortcuts/2016/jun/29/the-safety-pins-puncturing-post-brexit-racism (Accessed: 17 July 2018).

Anon (2017a) Anti-immigration Sweden Democrats overtake Moderates as Sweden's second-largest party: Poll, 1 June. Available at: www.thelocal.se/20170601/anti-immigration-sweden-democrats-overtake-moderates-as-swedens-second-largest-party-poll (Accessed: 1 March 2018).

Anon (2017b) ITV names EasyJet's Carolyn McCall as new chief executive, 17 July. Available at: www.bbc.com/news/business-40628869 (Accessed: 23 April 2018).

Applebaum, B. (2010) *Being White, Being Good: White Complicity, White Moral Responsibility, and Social Justice Pedagogy*. Lanham, MD: Lexington Books.

Applebaum, B. (2017) 'Comforting discomfort as complicity: White fragility and the pursuit of invulnerability', *Hypatia*, 32(4), pp 862–875.

Atewologun, D. and Sealy, R. (2014) 'Experiencing privilege at ethnic, gender and senior intersections', *Journal of Managerial Psychology*, 29(4), pp 423–439.

Australian Bureau of Statistics (2012) Reflecting a nation: Stories from the 2011 Census. Available at: www.abs.gov.au/ausstats/abs@.nsf/Lookup/2071.0main+features902012-2013 (Accessed: 12 March 2014).

Australian Industry Group (2012) Australia in the Asian Century, Australian Industry Group. Available at: http://cdn.aigroup.com.au/Submissions/General/2012/Ai_Group_Submission_March_2012.pdf (Accessed: 12 August 2019).

Avolio, B.J., Waldman, D.A. and Yammarino, F.J. (1991) 'Leading in the 1990s: The four I's of transformational leadership', *Journal of European Industrial Training*, 15(4), pp 9–16.

Baca Zinn, M. (2012) 'Patricia Hill Collins: Past and future innovations', *Gender & Society*, 26(1), pp 28–32.

Baca Zinn, M. and Thorton Dill, B. (1996) 'Theorizing difference from multiracial feminism', *Feminist Studies*, 22(2), pp 321–331.

Baird, C. and Dooey, P. (2014) 'Ensuring effective student support in higher education alleged plagiarism cases', *Innovative Higher Education*, 39(5), pp 387–400.

Baker, D.T. and Kelan, E.K. (2018) 'Splitting and blaming: The psychic life of neoliberal executive women', *Human Relations*, pp 1–29.

Baker, E. (2005) 'Loving Indianess: Native women's storytelling as survivance', *Atlantis*, 29(2), pp 111–121.

Baker, P. (2018) Dinesh D'Souza, pardoned by Trump, claims victory over Obama Administration, *The New York Times*, 1 June. Available at: www.nytimes.com/2018/06/01/us/politics/trump-pardon-dsouza.html (Accessed: 4 June 2018).

Baldwin, L. V. and Burrow, R. (eds) (2013) *The Domestication of Martin Luther King Jr.: Clarence B. Jones, Right-Wing Conservatism, and the Manipulation of the King Legacy*. Eugene, OR: Cascade Books.

Ball, M. (2016) Donald Trump and the politics of fear, *The Atlantic*. Available at: www.theatlantic.com/politics/archive/2016/09/donald-trump-and-the-politics-of-fear/498116/ (Accessed: 2 August 2018).

Ballinas, J. (2017) 'Where are you from and why are you here? Microaggressions, racialization, and Mexican college students in a new destination', *Sociological Inquiry*, 87(2), pp 385–410.

Banerjee, S.B. and Linstead, S. (2001) 'Globalization, multiculturalism and other fictions: Colonialism for the new millennium?', *Organization*, 8(4), pp 683–722.

Bass, B.M. (1998) *Transformational Leadership: Industry, Military, and Educational Impact*. Mahwah, NJ: Lawrence Erlbaum.

Bass, B.M. (2008) *Bass and Stogdill's Handbook of Leadership: Theory, Research, and Managerial Applications*. 4th edn. New York: Free Press.

Bass, B.M. and Avolio, B.J. (1994) 'Shatter the glass ceiling: Women may make better managers', *Human Resource Management*, 33(4), pp 549–560.

Bass, B.M., Avolio, B.J. and Atwater, L. (1996) 'The transformational and transactional leadership of men and women', *Applied Psychology*, 45(1), pp 5–34.

Bassel, L. and Emejulu, A. (2018) *Minority Women and Austerity: Survival and Resistance in France and Britain*. Bristol: Policy Press.

Bell, D.A. (1989) *And We Are Not Saved: The Elusive Quest for Racial Justice*. New York: Basic Books.

Bell, D.A. (1995) 'Who's afraid of critical race theory?', *University of Illinois Law Review*, pp 893–910.

Benschop, Y. (2001) 'Pride, prejudice and performance: Relations between HRM, diversity and performance', *International Journal of Human Resources Management*, 12(7), pp 1166–1181.

Berger, M.T. and Guidroz, K. (eds) (2009) *The Intersectional Approach: Transforming the Academy through Race, Class, and Gender*. Chapel Hill: University of North Carolina Press.

Berger, P.L. and Luckmann, T. (1966) *The Social Construction of Reality: A Treatise in the Sociology of Knowledge*. Garden City, NY: Doubleday.

Berzon, A., Kirkham, C., Bernstein, E. and O'Keeffe, K. (2018) Dozens of people recount pattern of sexual misconduct by Las Vegas mogul Steve Wynn, *The Wall Street Journal*, 27 January. Available at: www.wsj.com/articles/dozens-of-people-recount-pattern-of-sexual-misconduct-by-las-vegas-mogul-steve-wynn-1516985953 (Accessed: 1 March 2018).

Bilge, S. (2013) 'Intersectionality undone: Saving intersectionality from feminist intersectionality studies', *Du Bois Review*, 10(2), pp 405–424.

Bird, S.R. (1996) 'Welcome to the men's club: Homosociality and the maintenance of hegemonic masculinity', *Gender & Society*, 10(2), pp 120–132.

Blackmore, J. (2010) '"The Other Within": Race/gender disruptions to the professional learning of white educational leaders', *International Journal of Leadership in Education*, 13(1), pp 45–61.

Blee, K.M. (2009) *Women of the Klan: Racism and Gender in the 1920s.* Berkeley: University of California Press.

Bligh, M.C. and Schyns, B. (2007) 'The romance lives on: Contemporary issues surrounding the romance of leadership', *Leadership*, 3(3), pp 343–360.

Bligh, M.C., Kohles, J.C. and Pillai, R. (2011) 'Romancing leadership: Past, present, and future', *The Leadership Quarterly*, 22(6), pp 1058–1077.

Boddy, C.R. (2011) 'The Corporate Psychopaths theory of the Global Financial Crisis', *Journal of Business Ethics*, 102(2), pp 255–259.

Boje, D.M. and Rhodes, C. (2006) 'The leadership of Ronald McDonald: Double narration and stylistic lines of transformation', *The Leadership Quarterly*, 17(1), pp 94–103.

Boler, M. (1999) *Feeling Power: Emotions and Education.* New York: Routledge.

Bologh, R.W. (1990) *Love or Greatness: Max Weber and Masculine Thinking – A Feminist Inquiry.* London: Routledge.

Bonilla-Silva, E. (2006) *Racism Without Racists: Color-Blind Racism and the Persistence of Racial Inequality in the United States.* Lanham, MD: Rowman & Littlefield.

Bonilla-Silva, E. (2012) 'The invisible weight of whiteness: The racial grammar of everyday life in contemporary America', *Ethnic and Racial Studies*, 35(2), pp 173–194.

Bordo, S. (2000) *The Male Body: A New Look at Men in Public and in Private.* New York: Farrar Straus Giroux.

Bort, J. (2017) Yahoo's Marissa Mayer is the 'least likable' CEO in tech, survey finds, *Business Insider*, 26 May. Available at: www.businessinsider.com.au/marissa-mayer-yahoo-least-likable-tech-ceo-survey-2017-5 (Accessed: 18 April 2018).

Bourdieu, P. (1990) *The Logic of Practice.* Translated by Nice, Richard. Stanford, CA: Stanford University Press.

Bourdieu, P. (2004) 'Gender and symbolic violence', in Scheper-Hughes, N. and Bourgois, P.I. (eds) *Violence in War and Peace: An Anthology.* Malden, MA: Blackwell, pp 339–342.

Bourgault-Côté, G., Huss, C. and Pineda, A. (2018) Charles Dutoit, un homme et 'son' orchestre, *Le Devoir*, 27 January. Available at: www.ledevoir.com/culture/musique/518636/dutoit-quand-l-osm-niait-le-harcelement-psychologique (Accessed: 1 March 2018).

Bracey, C.A. (2008) *Saviors or Sellouts: The Promise and Peril of Black Conservatism, from Booker T. Washington to Condoleezza Rice*. Boston, MA: Beacon Press.

Brenner, O.C., Tomkiewicz, J. and Schein, V.E. (1989) 'The relationship between sex role stereotypes and requisite management characteristics revisited', *Academy of Management Journal*, 32(3), pp 662–669.

Brod, H. (1989) 'Work clothes and leisure suits: The class basis and bias of the men's movement', in Kimmel, M.S. and Messner, M.A. (eds) *Men's Lives*. New York: Macmillan.

Broman, G., Robèrt, K.-H., Basile, G., Larsson, T., Baumgartner, R., Collins, T. and Huisingh, D. (2014) 'Systematic leadership towards sustainability', *Journal of Cleaner Production*, 64, pp 1–2.

Brown, M.E. and Mitchell, M.S. (2010) 'Ethical and unethical leadership: Exploring new avenues for future research', *Business Ethics Quarterly*, 20(4), pp 583–616.

Brown, M.E. and Treviño, L.K. (2006) 'Ethical leadership: A review and future directions', *The Leadership Quarterly*, 17(6), pp 595–616.

Brown, M.E., Treviño, L.K. and Harrison, D.A. (2005) 'Ethical leadership: A social learning perspective for construct development and testing', *Organizational Behavior and Human Decision Processes*, 97(2), pp 117–134.

Buckley, C. (2018) Powerful Hollywood women unveil anti-harassment action, *The New York Times*, 1 January. Available at: www.nytimes.com/2018/01/01/movies/times-up-hollywood-women-sexual-harassment.html (Accessed: 6 March 2018).

Burnett, J. (2017) 'Racial violence and the Brexit state', *Race & Class*, 58(4), pp 85–97.

Burns, J.M. (1978) *Leadership*. New York: Harper & Row.

Burton, L.M., Bonilla-Silva, E., Ray, V., Buckelew, R. and Hordge Freeman, E. (2010) 'Critical race theories, colorism, and the decade's research on families of color', *Journal of Marriage and Family*, 72(3), pp 440–459.

Butler, J. (1993) *Bodies that Matter: On the Discursive Limits of 'Sex'*. New York: Routledge.

Butler, J. (1999) *Gender Trouble: Feminism and the Subversion of Identity*. New York: Routledge.

Butler, P. (2017) *Chokehold: Policing Black Men*. New York: The New Press.

Cabrera, N.L. (2014a) 'Exposing whiteness in higher education: White male college students minimizing racism, claiming victimization, and recreating white supremacy', *Race Ethnicity and Education*, 17(1), pp 30–55.

Cabrera, N.L. (2014b) '"But I'm oppressed too": White male college students framing racial emotions as facts and recreating racism', *International Journal of Qualitative Studies in Education*, 27(6), pp 768–784.

Camara, S.K. and Orbe, M.P. (2011) 'Understanding interpersonal manifestations of "reverse discrimination" through phenomenological inquiry', *Journal of Intercultural Communication Research*, 40(2), pp 111–134.

Campbell, D., Moore, G. and Metzger, M. (2002) 'Corporate philanthropy in the U.K. 1985–2000: Some empirical findings', *Journal of Business Ethics*, 39(1/2), pp 29–41.

Campbell, J. (1968) *The Hero with a Thousand Faces*. 2nd edn. Princeton, NJ: Princeton University Press.

Carissimo, J. (2016) Van Jones calls Trump's surprise victory a whitelash against a changing country, *The Independent*, 9 November. Available at: www.independent.co.uk/arts-entertainment/tv/news/van-jones-calls-trump-s-surprise-victory-a-whitelash-against-a-changing-country-a7406511.html (Accessed: 1 March 2018).

Carlson, N. (2013) Marissa Mayer, who just banned working from home, paid to have a nursery built at her office, *Business Insider*, 26 February. Available at: www.businessinsider.com.au/marissa-mayer-who-just-banned-working-from-home-paid-to-have-a-nursery-built-at-her-office-2013-2?r=US&IR=T (Accessed: 18 April 2018).

Carrillo Rowe, A. (2008) *Power Lines: On the Subject of Feminist Alliances*. Durham, NC: Duke University Press.

Carroll, H. (2011) *Affirmative Reaction: New Formations of White Masculinity*. Durham, NC: Duke University Press.

Chae, H.S. (2004) 'Talking back to the Asian model minority discourse: Korean-origin youth experiences in high school', *Journal of Intercultural Studies*, 25(1), pp 59–73.

Chakrabarty, D. (1992) 'Postcoloniality and the artifice of history: Who speaks for "Indian" pasts?', *Representations*, (37), pp 1–26.

Chambers, L., Drysdale, J. and Hughes, J. (2010) 'The future of leadership: A practitioner view', *European Management Journal*, 28(4), pp 260–268.

Chan, J.W. (2001) *Chinese American Masculinities: From Fu Manchu to Bruce Lee*. New York: Routledge.

Chan, R. (2017) My complicated relationship with a traditional Chinese garment, *Racked*. Available at: www.racked.com/2017/4/9/15022012/qipao-traditional-chinese-new-year (Accessed: 21 April 2018).

Chavez, L.R. (2003) *The Latino Threat: Constructing Immigrants, Citizens, and the Nation.* 2nd edn. Stanford, CA: Stanford University Press.

Chen, A.S. (1999) 'Lives at the center of the periphery, lives at the periphery of the center: Chinese American masculinities and bargaining with hegemony', *Gender and Society*, 13(5), pp 584–607.

Cherniavsky, E. (2006) *Incorporations: Race, Nation, and the Body Politics of Capital.* Minneapolis, MN: University of Minnesota Press.

Childs, P. and Williams, P. (2013) *An Introduction to Post-Colonial Theory.* 2nd edn. London: Routledge.

Cho, S.K. (1997) 'Converging stereotypes in racialized sexual harassment: Where the model minority meets Suzie Wong', *Journal of Gender, Race and Justice*, 1(1), pp 177–211.

Cho, S.K. (2013) 'Post-intersectionality: The curious reception of intersectionality in legal scholarship', *Du Bois Review*, 10(2), pp 385–404.

Chon-Smith, C. (2015) *East meets Black: Asian and Black Masculinities in the Post-Civil Rights Era.* Jackson, MS: University Press of Mississippi.

Chou, R.S. (2012) *Asian American Sexual Politics: The Construction of Race, Gender, and Sexuality.* Lanham, MD: Rowman & Littlefield Publishers.

Chuck, E. (2018) James Damore, Google engineer fired for writing manifesto on women's 'neuroticism,' sues company, *NBC News*, 9 January. Available at: www.nbcnews.com/news/us-news/google-engineer-fired-writing-manifesto-women-s-neuroticism-sues-company-n835836 (Accessed: 7 May 2018).

Chun, J.J., Lipsitz, G. and Shin, Y. (2013) 'Intersectionality as a social movement strategy: Asian immigrant women advocates', *Signs: Journal of Women in Culture and Society*, 38(4), pp 917–940.

Ciulla, J.B. (2004) *Ethics, the Heart of Leadership.* 2nd edn. Westport, CT: Praeger.

Ciulla, J.B. (2005) 'The state of leadership ethics and the work that lies before us', *Business Ethics: A European Review*, 14(4), pp 323–335.

Clough, P.T. (1994) *Feminist Thought: Desire, Power, and Academic Discourse.* Oxford: Blackwell.

Cohen, C. (2015) Women can be CEOs and mothers. But Marissa Mayer's maternity leave is a bum deal, *The Telegraph*, 5 September. Available at: www.telegraph.co.uk/women/womens-life/11844128/Yahoo-CEO-Marissa-Mayer-maternity-leave-a-bum-deal-for-women.html (Accessed: 18 April 2018).

Colebatch, T. (2012) Land of many cultures, ancestries and faiths, *The Sydney Morning Herald*, 22 June. Available at: www.smh.com.au/federal-politics/political-news/land-of-many-cultures-ancestries-and-faiths-20120621-20r3g.html (Accessed: 16 March 2015).

Coleman, L. and Pinder, S. (2010) 'What were they thinking? Reports from interviews with senior finance executives in the lead-up to the GFC', *Applied Financial Economics*, 20(1–2), pp 7–14.

Collins, P.H. (1986) 'Learning from the outsider within: The sociological significance of Black feminist thought', *Social Problems*, 33(6), pp S14–S32.

Collins, P.H. (1998) 'The tie that binds: Race, gender and US violence', *Ethnic and Racial Studies*, 21(5), pp 917–938.

Collins, P.H. (1999) 'Reflections on the outsider within', *Journal of Career Development*, 26(1), pp 85–88.

Collins, P.H. (2000) *Black Feminist Thought: Knowledge, Consciousness, and the Politics of Empowerment*. 2nd edn. Hoboken, NJ: Taylor & Francis.

Collins, P.H. (2004) *Black Sexual Politics: African Americans, Gender, and the New Racism*. New York: Routledge.

Collins, P.H. (2012) 'Social inequality, power, and politics: Intersectionality and American pragmatism in dialogue', *Journal of Speculative Philosophy*, 26(2), pp 442–457.

Collins, P.H. (2015) 'Intersectionality's definitional dilemmas', *Annual Review of Sociology*, 41, pp 1–20.

Collinson, D.L. (2005) 'Dialectics of leadership', *Human Relations*, 58(11), pp 1419–1442.

Collinson, D.L. (2011) 'Critical leadership studies', in Bryman, A., Collinson, D., Grint, K., Jackson, B. and Uhl-Bien, M. (eds) *The SAGE Handbook of Leadership*. Thousand Oaks, CA: Sage, pp 181–194.

Collinson, D.L. (2014) 'Dichotomies, dialectics and dilemmas: New directions for critical leadership studies?', *Leadership*, 10(1), pp 36–55.

Collinson, D.L. and Hearn, J. (eds) (1996) *Men as Managers, Managers as Men: Critical Perspectives on Men, Masculinities, and Managements*. London: Sage.

Combahee River Collective, The (1977) 'A Black feminist statement', in McCarthy, T.P. and McMillian, J. (eds) *Protest Nation: Words that Inspired a Century of American Radicalism*. New York: The New Press, pp 212–216.

Commonwealth of Australia (2012) *Australia in the Asian Century: White Paper*. Canberra: Department of the Prime Minister and Cabinet. Available at: www.defence.gov.au/whitepaper/2013/docs/australia_in_the_asian_century_white_paper.pdf (Accessed: 12 August 2019).

Connell, C. (2010) 'Doing, undoing, or redoing gender? Learning from the workplace experiences of transpeople', *Gender & Society*, 24(1), pp 31–55.

Connell, R.W. (1987) *Gender and Power: Society, the Person and Sexual Politics*. Cambridge: Polity Press.

Connell, R.W. (1995) *Masculinities*. Berkeley, CA: University of California Press.

Connell, R.W. (2014) 'Margin becoming centre: For a world-centred rethinking of masculinities', *NORMA: International Journal for Masculinity Studies*, 9(4), pp 217–231.

Connell, R.W. and Messerschmidt, J.W. (2005) 'Hegemonic masculinity: Rethinking the concept', *Gender and Society*, 19(6), pp 829–859.

Cox, T. and Blake, S. (1991) 'Managing cultural diversity: Implications for organizational effectiveness', *Academy of Management Executive*, 5(3), pp 45–56.

Creese, G. (2018) '"Where are you from?" Racialization, belonging and identity among second-generation African-Canadians', *Ethnic and Racial Studies*, pp 1–19.

Crenshaw, K. (1989) 'Demarginalizing the intersection of race and sex: A black feminist critique of antidiscrimination doctrine, feminist theory, and antiracist politics', *University of Chicago Legal Forum*, 1989(1), pp 139–167.

Crenshaw, K. (1991) 'Mapping the margins: Intersectionality, identity politics, and violence against women of color', *Stanford Law Review*, 43(6), pp 1241–1299.

Curnalia, R.M.L. and Mermer, D.L. (2014) 'The "Ice Queen" melted and it won her the primary: Evidence of gender stereotypes and the double bind in news frames of Hillary Clinton's "emotional moment"', *Qualitative Research Reports in Communication*, 15(1), pp 26–32.

Curthoys, A. (2003) 'Liberalism and exclusionism: A prehistory of the White Australia Policy', in Jayasuriya, L., Walker, D. and Gothard, J. (eds) *Legacies of White Australia: Race, Culture and Nation*. Crawley: University of Western Australia Press, pp 8–32.

D'Angelo Fisher, L. (2013) A gift out of giving, *Business Review Weekly*, 14 November, p 55.

Danius, S. and Jonsson, S. (1993) 'An interview with Gayatri Chakravorty Spivak', *Boundary 2*, 20(2), pp 24–50.

Dar, S. (2018) 'De-colonizing the boundary-object', *Organization Studies*, 39(4), pp 565–584.

Dar, S. (2019) 'The masque of blackness: Or, performing assimilation in the white academe', *Organization,* 26(3), pp. 432–446.

Dar, S. and Salmon, U. (2019) 'Book review: *Inside the Ivory Tower: Narratives of Women of Colour Surviving and Thriving in British Academia* edited by Deborah Gabriel and Shirley Anne Tate', *Gender, Work and Organization*, 26(1), pp 64–67.

Davidson, A. (2003) 'The politics of exclusion in an era of globalisation', in Jayasuriya, L., Walker, D. and Gothard, J. (eds) *Legacies of White Australia: Race, culture and nation*. Crawley: University of Western Australia Press, pp 129–144.

Davidson, D. and Langan, D. (2006) 'The breastfeeding incident: Teaching and learning through transgression', *Studies in Higher Education*, 31(4), pp 439–452.

Deal, J.J. and Stevenson, M.A. (1998) 'Perceptions of female and male managers in the 1990s: Plus ça change...', *Sex Roles*, 38(3–4), pp 287–300.

De Hoogh, A.H.B. and Den Hartog, D.N. (2008) 'Ethical and despotic leadership, relationships with leader's social responsibility, top management team effectiveness and subordinates' optimism: A multi-method study', *The Leadership Quarterly*, 19(3), pp 297–311.

Deitch, E.A., Barsky, A., Butz, R.M., Chan, S., Brief, A.P. and Bradley, J. (2003) 'Subtle yet significant: The existence and impact of everyday racial discrimination in the workplace', *Human Relations*, 56(11), pp 1299–1324.

Deliovsky, K. (2008) 'Normative white femininity: Race, gender and the politics of beauty', *Atlantis*, 33(1), pp 49–59.

Deliovsky, K. (2010) *White Femininity: Race, Gender & Power*. Halifax: Fernwood Publishing.

Denzin, N.K. (2009) *Qualitative Inquiry under Fire: Toward a New Paradigm Dialogue*. Walnut Creek, CA: Left Coast Press.

Devlin, M. and Gray, K. (2007) 'In their own words: A qualitative study of the reasons Australian university students plagiarise', *Higher Education Research & Development*, 26(2), pp 181–198.

DiAngelo, R. (2011) 'White fragility', *International Journal of Critical Pedagogy*, 3(3), pp 54–70.

DiAngelo, R. (2012) *What Does It Mean to Be White? Developing White Racial Literacy*. New York: Peter Lang.

DiAngelo, R. (2018) *White Fragility: Why It's So Hard for White People to Talk About Racism*. Boston, MA: Beacon Press.

Díaz García, M.-C. and Welter, F. (2011) 'Gender identities and practices: Interpreting women entrepreneurs' narratives', *International Small Business Journal*, 31(4), pp 384–404.

Díaz-Sáenz, H.R. (2011) 'Transformational leadership', in Bryman, A., Collinson, D., Grint, K., Jackson, B. and Uhl-Bien, M. (eds) *The SAGE Handbook of Leadership*. Thousand Oaks, CA: Sage, pp 299–310.

Donaldson, L.E. (1999) 'On medicine women and white shame-ans: New Age Native Americanism and commodity fetishism as pop culture feminism', *Signs: Journal of Women in Culture and Society*, 24(3), pp 677–696.

Donaldson, M. and Tomsen, S.A. (2003) *Male Trouble: Looking at Australian Masculinities*. Sydney: Pluto Press.

Doyle, S. (2017) What every boss can learn about leadership from Sheryl Sandberg at Facebook, Inc. Available at: www.inc.com/shawn-doyle/what-every-boss-can-learn-about-leadership-from-sh.html (Accessed: 20 April 2018).

Dreher, T. (2009) 'Eavesdropping with permission: The politics of listening for safer speaking spaces', *Borderlands E-Journal*, 8(1), pp 1–21.

Druskat, V.U. (1994) 'Gender and leadership style: Transformational and transactional leadership in the Roman Catholic Church', *The Leadership Quarterly*, 5(2), pp 99–119.

D'Souza, D. (1995) *The End of Racism*. New York: Simon and Schuster.

DuBois, W.E.B. (2005) *The Souls of Black Folk*. New York: Pocket Books.

Duehr, E.E. and Bono, J.E. (2006) 'Men, women, and managers: Are stereotypes finally changing?', *Personnel Psychology*, 59(4), pp 815–846.

Duong, L.P. (2009) 'Traitors and translators: Reframing Trinh T. Minh-ha's Surname Viet Given Name Nam', *Discourse*, 31(3), pp 195–219.

Duong, L.P. (2012) *Treacherous Subjects: Gender, Culture, and Trans-Vietnamese Feminism*. Philadelphia, PA: Temple University Press.

Dyer, R. (1997) *White*. London: Routledge.

Dyer, R. (2004) *Heavenly Bodies: Film Stars and Society*. 2nd edn. London: Routledge.

Eagly, A.H. (1987) *Sex Differences in Social Behavior: A Social Role Interpretation*. Hillsdale, NJ: Erlbaum.

Eagly, A.H. and Carli, L.L. (2007) 'Women and the labyrinth of leadership', *Harvard Business Review*, 85(9), pp 62–71.

Eagly, A.H. and Johnson, B.T. (1990) 'Gender and leadership style: A meta-analysis', *Psychological Bulletin*, 108(2), pp 233–256.

Eagly, A.H., Wood, W. and Diekman, A.B. (2000) 'Social role theory of sex differences and similarities: A current appraisal', in T. Eckes and H.M. Trautner (eds) *The Developmental Social Psychology of Gender*. Mahwah, NJ: Lawrence Erlbaum, pp 123–174.

Edwards, G., Elliott, C., Iszatt-White, M. and Schedlitzki, D. (2013) 'Critical and alternative approaches to leadership learning and development', *Management Learning*, 44(1), pp 3–10.

Eisenberg, N. (2000) 'Emotion, regulation, and moral development', *Annual Review of Psychology*, 51(1), pp 665–697.

Ellingson, T. (2001) *The Myth of the Noble Savage*. Berkeley, CA: University of California Press.

Espiritu, Y.L. (2008) *Asian American Women and Men: Labor, Laws, and Love*. 2nd edn. Lanham, MD: Rowman & Littlefield.

Esposito, L. and Romano, V. (2014) 'Benevolent racism: Upholding racial inequality in the name of Black empowerment', *Western Journal of Black Studies*, 38(2), pp 69–83.

Essed, P. (1991) *Understanding Everyday Racism: An Interdisciplinary Theory*. Newbury Park, CA: Sage.

Faifua, D. (2010) 'Reclaiming the outsider-within space: An auto-ethnography', *Tamara: Journal of Critical Postmodern Organization Science*, 8(3), pp 119–132.

Fairhurst, G.T. and Grant, D. (2010) 'The social construction of leadership: A sailing guide', *Management Communication Quarterly*, 24(2), pp 171–210.

Faludi, S. (1991) *Backlash: The Undeclared War Against Women*. London: Chatto and Windus.

Fanon, F. (1994) *Black Skin, White Masks*. New York: Grove Press.

Feagin, J.R. (2013) *The White Racial Frame: Centuries of Racial Framing and Counter-Framing*. New York: Routledge.

Federal Bureau of Investigation (2017) 2016 hate crime statistics, Uniform Crime Reporting. Available at: https://ucr.fbi.gov/hate-crime/2016/hate-crime (Accessed: 28 February 2018).

Ferdig, M.A. (2007) 'Sustainability leadership: Co-creating a sustainable future', *Journal of Change Management*, 7(1), pp 25–35.

Fiorina, C. (2006) *Tough Choices: A Memoir*. New York: Penguin.

Frankenberg, R. (1993) *White Women, Race Matters: The Social Construction of Whiteness*. Minneapolis: University of Minnesota Press.

Fredrickson, G.M. (1971) *The Black Image in the White Mind: The Debate on Afro-American Character and Destiny, 1817–1914*. New York: Harper & Row.

Freeman, R.E. and Auster, E.R. (2011) 'Values, authenticity, and responsible leadership', *Journal of Business Ethics*, 98(1), pp 15–23.

Fry, L.W. and Cohen, M.P. (2009) 'Spiritual leadership as a paradigm for organizational transformation and recovery from extended work hours cultures', *Journal of Business Ethics*, 84(2), pp 265–278.

Frye, M. (1992) *Willful Virgin: Essays in Feminism, 1976–1992.* Freedom, California: Crossing Press.

Gabriel, D. (2007) *Layers of Blackness: Colourism in the African Diaspora.* London: Imani Media.

Gabriel, D. (2016) Racial categorisation and terminology, Black British academics. Available at: http://blackbritishacademics.co.uk/focus/racial-categorisation-and-terminology/ (Accessed: 21 April 2018).

Gabriel, D. and Tate, S.A. (eds) (2017) *Inside the Ivory Tower: Narratives of Women of Colour Surviving and Thriving in British Academia.* London: Trentham Books.

Galpin, T. and Whittington, J.L. (2012) 'Sustainability leadership: From strategy to results', *Journal of Business Strategy*, 33(4), pp 40–48.

Gambino, L., Siddiqui, S., Owen, P. and Helmore, E. (2017) Thousands protest against Trump travel ban in cities and airports nationwide, *The Guardian*, 30 January. Available at: www.theguardian.com/us-news/2017/jan/29/protest-trump-travel-ban-muslims-airports (Accessed: 6 March 2018).

García, L. (2009) '"Now why do you want to know about that?" Heteronormativity, sexism, and racism in the sexual (mis)education of Latina youth', *Gender & Society*, 23(4), pp 520–541.

Gardner, W.L., Avolio, B.J., Luthans, F., May, D.R. and Walumbwa, F.O. (2005) '"Can you see the real me?" A self-based model of authentic leader and follower development', *The Leadership Quarterly*, 16(3), pp 343–372.

Gardner, W.L., Cogliser, C.C., Davis, K.M. and Dickens, M.P. (2011) 'Authentic leadership: A review of the literature and research agenda', *The Leadership Quarterly*, 22(6), pp 1120–1145.

Garner, S. (2007) *Whiteness: An Introduction.* London: Routledge.

Gautier, A. and Pache, A.-C. (2013) 'Research on corporate philanthropy: A review and assessment', *Journal of Business Ethics*, 126(3), pp 343–369.

Gecker, J. (2017) Famed conductor accused of sexual misconduct, *Associated Press*, 22 December. Available at: https://apnews.com/278275ccc09442d98a794487a78a67d4 (Accessed: 1 March 2018).

Gemmill, G. and Oakley, J. (1992) 'Leadership: An alienating social myth', *Human Relations*, 45(2), pp 113–129.

George-Parkin, H. (2017) Thinx promised a feminist utopia to everyone but its employees, *Racked*. Available at: www.racked.com/2017/3/14/14911228/thinx-miki-agrawal-health-care-branding (Accessed: 18 June 2018).

Gherardi, S. and Poggio, B. (2001) 'Creating and recreating gender order in organizations', *Journal of World Business*, 36(3), pp 245–259.

Gill, R. (2014) 'Unspeakable inequalities: Post feminism, entrepreneurial subjectivity, and the repudiation of sexism among cultural workers', *Social Politics*, 21(4), pp 509–528.

Gill, R. and Orgad, S. (2015) 'The confidence cult(ure)', *Australian Feminist Studies*, 30(86), pp 324–344.

Gill, R., Kelan, E.K. and Scharff, C.M. (2017) 'A postfeminist sensibility at work', *Gender, Work and Organization*, 24(3), pp 226–244.

Gilson, E. (2014) *The Ethics of Vulnerability: A Feminist Analysis of Social Life and Practice*. New York: Routledge.

Giroux, H.A. (2003) 'Spectacles of race and pedagogies of denial: Anti-Black racist pedagogy under the reign of neoliberalism', *Communication Education*, 52(3/4), pp 191–211.

Glick, P. and Fiske, S.T. (1996) 'The Ambivalent Sexism Inventory: Differentiating hostile and benevolent sexism', *Journal of Personality and Social Psychology*, 70(3), pp 491–512.

Goffman, E. (1959) *The Presentation of Self in Everyday Life*. Garden City, NY: Doubleday.

Göpffarth, J. (2017) How Alternative für Deutschland is trying to resurrect German nationalism, *New Statesman*. Available at: www.newstatesman.com/world/europe/2017/09/how-alternative-f-r-deutschland-trying-resurrect-german-nationalism (Accessed: 2 March 2018).

Gorman-Murray, A. (2013) 'Urban homebodies: Embodiment, masculinity, and domesticity in inner Sydney', *Geographical Research*, 51(2), pp 137–144.

Greenleaf, R.K. (1970) *The Servant as Leader*. Indianapolis, IN: The Robert K. Greenleaf Centre.

Grewal, I. (1996) *Home and Harem: Nation, Gender, Empire and the Cultures of Travel*. Durham, NC: Duke University Press.

Grimes, D.S. (2001) 'Putting our own house in order: Whiteness, change and organization studies', *Journal of Organizational Change Management*, 14(2), pp 132–149.

Grimes, D.S. (2002) 'Challenging the status quo? Whiteness in the diversity management literature', *Management Communication Quarterly*, 15(3), pp 381–409.

Grint, K. (2010a) 'The sacred in leadership: Separation, sacrifice and silence', *Organization Studies*, 31(1), pp 89–107.

Grint, K. (2010b) 'The cuckoo clock syndrome: Addicted to command, allergic to leadership', *European Management Journal*, 28(4), pp 306–313.

Gronn, P. (2003) 'Leadership: Who needs it?', *School Leadership & Management*, 23(3), pp 267–290.

Guerrier, Y. and Wilson, C. (2011) 'Representing diversity on UK company web sites', *Equality, Diversity and Inclusion: An International Journal*, 30(3), pp 183–195.

Guthey, E., Clark, T. and Jackson, B. (2009) *Demystifying Business Celebrity*. Oxford: Routledge.

Gutiérrez, E.R. (2008) *Fertile Matters: The Politics of Mexican-Origin Women's Reproduction*. Austin, TX: University of Texas Press.

Hage, G. (1998) *White Nation: Fantasies of White Supremacy in a Multicultural Society*. Hoboken, NJ: Taylor and Francis.

Haggis, J. and Schech, S. (2000) 'Meaning well and global good manners: Reflections on white women feminist cross cultural praxis', *Australian Feminist Studies*, 15(3), pp 387–399.

Hall, L.J. and Donaghue, N. (2012) '"Nice girls don't carry knives": Constructions of ambition in media coverage of Australia's first female prime minister', *British Journal of Social Psychology*, 52(4), pp 631–647.

Hall, S. (1997) *Representation: Cultural Representations and Signifying Practices*. London: Sage.

Hammonds, E.M. (1999) 'Toward a genealogy of black female sexuality: The problematic of silence', in Price, J. and Shildrick, M. (eds) *Feminist Theory and the Body: A Reader*. New York: Routledge, pp 93–104.

Hannah-Jones, N. (2016) What Abigail Fisher's affirmative action case was really about, *ProPublica*, 23 June. Available at: www.propublica.org/article/a-colorblind-constitution-what-abigail-fishers-affirmative-action-case-is-r (Accessed: 7 May 2018).

Hartocollis, A. and Alcindor, Y. (2017) Women's March highlights as huge crowds protest Trump: 'We're not going away', *The New York Times*, 21 January. Available at: www.nytimes.com/2017/01/21/us/womens-march.html (Accessed: 6 March 2018).

Harvey, J. (2007) *Whiteness and Morality: Pursuing Racial Justice Through Reparations and Sovereignty*. Basingstoke: Palgrave Macmillan.

Hassan, S., Mahsud, R., Yukl, G. and Prussia, G.E. (2013) 'Ethical and empowering leadership and leader effectiveness', *Journal of Managerial Psychology*, 28(2), pp 133–146.

Hearn, J. (1994) 'The organization(s) of violence: Men, gender relations, organizations and violences', *Human Relations*, 47(6), pp 731–754.

Hearn, J. (2003) 'Organization violations in practice: A case study in a university setting', *Culture and Organization*, 9(4), pp 253–273.

Heilman, M.E., Block, C.J. and Martell, R.F. (1995) 'Sex stereotypes: Do they influence perceptions of managers?', *Journal of Social Behavior & Personality*, 10(6), pp 237–252.

Heizmann, H. and Liu, H. (2018) 'Becoming green, becoming leaders: Identity narratives in sustainability leadership development', *Management Learning*, 49(1), pp 40–58.

Hempel, J. (2017) Sheryl Sandberg's accidental revolution, *Wired*. Available at: www.wired.com/2017/04/sheryl-sandbergs-accidental-revolution/ (Accessed: 21 April 2018).

Hewett, J. (2013) Forrests' $65m giveaway to University of Western Australia, *The Australian Financial Review*, 15 October, p.1.

Hill, J.H. (2009) *The Everyday Language of White Racism*. Chichester: John Wiley.

Hirose, A. and Pih, K.K. (2010) 'Men who strike and men who submit: Hegemonic and marginalized masculinities in mixed martial arts', *Men and Masculinities*, 13(2), pp 190–209.

Hodes, M.E. (1997) *White Women, Black Men: Illicit Sex in the Nineteenth-Century South*. New Haven, CT: Yale University Press.

Hofstede, G. (1980) 'Motivation, leadership, and organization: Do American theories apply abroad?', *Organizational Dynamics*, 9(1), pp 42–63.

Hofstede, G. (2001) *Culture's Consequences: Comparing Values, Behaviors, Institutions and Organizations across Nations*. 2nd edn. Thousand Oaks, CA: Sage.

Holland-Muter, S. (1995) 'Opening Pandora's Box: Reflections on "whiteness" in the South African women's movement', *Agenda*, 11(25), pp 55–62.

Hollinger, P. (2014) Carolyn McCall: Flying high at easyJet, *Financial Times*, 22 November. Available at: www.ft.com/content/8e57d15e-70ac-11e4-8113-00144feabdc0 (Accessed: 23 April 2018).

Hollinger, P. (2017) Carolyn McCall wins over critics in 7 years at easyJet, *Financial Times*, 18 July. Available at: www.ft.com/content/985b8a82-6b05-11e7-bfeb-33fe0c5b7eaa (Accessed: 23 April 2018).

hooks, b. (1981) *Ain't I A Woman: Black Women and Feminism*. Boston, MA: South End Press.

hooks, b. (1984) *Feminist Theory: From Margin to Center*. Boston, MA: South End Press.

hooks, b. (1989) *Talking Back: Thinking Feminist, Thinking Black*. Boston, MA: South End Press.

hooks, b. (1992a) 'Eating the Other', in *Black Looks: Race and Representation*. Boston, MA: South End Press, pp 21–39.

hooks, b. (1992b) *Black Looks: Race and Representation*. Boston, MA: South End Press.

hooks, b. (1994) *Outlaw Culture: Resisting Representations*. New York: Routledge.

hooks, b. (2000a) *All About Love: New Visions*. New York: William Morrow.

hooks, b. (2000b) *Feminism Is for Everybody: Passionate Politics*. London: Pluto Press.

hooks, b. (2000c) 'To love again: The heart of feminism', in *Feminism Is for Everybody: Passionate Politics*. London: Pluto Press, pp 100–104.

hooks, b. (2003) *We Real Cool: Black Men and Masculinity*. Hoboken, NJ: Taylor and Francis.

hooks, b. (2004) *The Will to Change: Men, Masculinity, and Love*. New York: Atria Books.

hooks, b. (2009a) *Teaching Critical Thinking: Practical Wisdom*. Hoboken, NJ: Taylor and Francis.

hooks, b. (2009b) *Belonging: A Culture of Place*. New York: Routledge.

Ifekwunigwe, J.O. (1998) 'Borderland feminisms: Towards the transgression of unitary transnational feminisms', *Gender & History*, 10(3), pp 553–557.

Ignatiev, N. (1995) *How the Irish Became White*. New York: Routledge.

Ignatiev, N. (1997) The point is not to interpret Whiteness but to abolish it, Race Traitor. Available at: https://web.archive.org/web/20190420020605/http://racetraitor.org/abolishthepoint.pdf (Accessed: 12 August 2019).

Ingram, D. (2005) 'Toward a cleaner white(ness): New racial identities', *The Philosophical Forum*, 36(3), pp 243–277.

Isaacson, W. (2012) 'The real leadership lessons of Steve Jobs', *Harvard Business Review*, 90(4), pp 92–102.

Jack, G. and Westwood, R. (2009) *International and Cross-Cultural Management Studies: A Postcolonial Reading*. Basingstoke: Palgrave Macmillan.

Jamieson, K.H. (1995) *Beyond the Double Bind: Women and Leadership*. New York: Oxford University Press.

Jaya, P.S. (2001) 'Do we really "know" and "profess"? Decolonizing management knowledge', *Organization*, 8(2), pp 227–233.

Jayasuriya, L., Walker, D. and Gothard, J. (eds) (2003) *Legacies of White Australia: Race, Culture and Nation*. Crawley: University of Western Australia Press.

Jean-Marie, G., Williams, V.A. and Sherman, S.L. (2009) 'Black women's leadership experiences: Examining the intersectionality of race and gender', *Advances in Developing Human Resources*, 11(5), pp 562–581.

Jepson, D. (2010) 'The importance of national language as a level of discourse within individuals' theorising of leadership – A qualitative study of German and English employees', *Leadership*, 6(4), pp 425–445.

Jhally, S. (2006) *Reel Bad Arabs: How Hollywood Vilifies a People*. Media Education Foundation.

Jibrin, R. and Salem, S. (2015) 'Revisiting intersectionality: Reflections on theory and praxis', *Trans-Scripts*, 5, pp 7–24.

John, S. (2015) 'Idle no more: Indigenous activism and feminism', *Theory in Action*, 8(4), pp 38–54.

Johnson, J.M. (2015) Thinking about the 'X', *Black Perspectives*. Available at: www.aaihs.org/thinking-about-an-x/ (Accessed: 6 June 2018).

Johnson, K. (2018) Starbucks CEO: Reprehensible outcome in Philadelphia incident, Starbucks Newsroom. Available at: https://news.starbucks.com/views/starbucks-ceo-reprehensible-outcome-in-philadelphia-incident (Accessed: 30 April 2018).

Johnston, W. and Packer, A. (1987) *Workforce 2000: Work and Workers for the 21st Century*. Indianapolis, IN: Hudson Institute.

Jordan-Zachery, J.S. (2007) 'Am I a black woman or a woman who is black? A few thoughts on the meaning of intersectionality', *Politics & Gender*, 3(2), pp 254–263.

Josephson, M. (2010) *The Robber Barons: The Great American Capitalists, 1861–1901*. New York: Harcourt, Brace & Company.

Kantor, J. and Twohey, M. (2017) Harvey Weinstein paid off sexual harassment accusers for decades, *The New York Times*, 5 October. Available at: www.nytimes.com/2017/10/05/us/harvey-weinstein-harassment-allegations.html (Accessed: 6 March 2018).

Kanungo, R.N. (2001) 'Ethical values of transactional and transformational leaders', *Canadian Journal of Administrative Sciences*, 18(4), pp 257–265.

Kark, R., Waismel-Manor, R. and Shamir, B. (2012) 'Does valuing androgyny and femininity lead to a female advantage? The relationship between gender-role, transformational leadership and identification', *The Leadership Quarterly*, 23(3), pp 620–640.

Keating, A. (2013) *Transformation Now! Toward a Post-Oppositional Politics of Change*. Urbana, IL: University of Illinois Press.

Keating, F. (2017) Facebook's Sheryl Sandberg says we should 'teach girls to lead at a very young age', *The Independent*, 30 July. Available at: www.independent.co.uk/news/world/sheryl-sandberg-facebook-desert-island-discs-beyonce-queen-dave-goldberg-girls-leadership-a7867271.html (Accessed: 20 April 2018).

Kelly, S. (2014) 'Towards a negative ontology of leadership', *Human Relations*, 67(8), pp 905–922.

Kerfoot, D. and Knights, D. (1993) 'Management, masculinity and manipulation: From paternalism to corporate strategy in financial services in Britain', *Journal of Management Studies*, 30(4), pp 659–677.

Kets de Vries, M. (1996) 'Leaders who make a difference', *European Management Journal*, 14(5), pp 486–493.

Kets de Vries, M. (1998) 'Charisma in action: The transformational abilities of Virgin's Richard Branson and ABB's Percy Barnevik', *Organizational Dynamics*, 26(3), pp 7–21.

Kets de Vries, M. and Balazs, K. (2011) 'The shadow side of leadership', in Bryman, A., Collinson, D., Grint, K., Jackson, B. and Uhl-Bien, M. (eds) *The SAGE Handbook of Leadership*. Thousand Oaks, CA: Sage, pp 380–391.

Khurana, R. (2011) *Searching for a Corporate Savior*. Princeton, NJ: Princeton University Press.

Kincheloe, J.L., Steinberg, S.R., Rodriguez, N.M. and Chennault, R.E. (eds) (1998) *White Reign: Deploying Whiteness in America*. New York: Palgrave Macmillan.

Kirchgaessner, S. and Ellis-Petersen, H. (2017) 'The cult of Harvey': Weinstein's staff at Miramax describe bullying and abuse, *The Guardian*, 26 October. Available at: www.theguardian.com/film/2017/oct/25/the-cult-of-harvey-weinsteins-staff-at-miramax-describe-bullying-and-abuse (Accessed: 6 March 2018).

Kirton, G. and Greene, A.-M. (2011) *The Dynamics of Managing Diversity: A Critical Approach*. 3rd edn. Oxford: Elsevier.

Knights, D. and O'Leary, M. (2006) 'Leadership, ethics and responsibility to the Other', *Journal of Business Ethics*, 67(2), pp 125–137.

Knights, D. and Tullberg, M. (2011) 'Managing masculinity/mismanaging the corporation', *Organization*, 19(4), pp 385–404.

Kong, T.S.K. (2006) 'Sexualizing Asian male bodies', in Seidman, S., Fischer, N. and Meeks, C. (eds) *Handbook of the New Sexuality Studies*. Abingdon: Routledge, pp 90–95.

Koyama, E. (2003) 'The transfeminist manifesto', in Dicker, R. and Piepmeier, A. (eds) *Catching a Wave: Reclaiming Feminism for the 21st Century*. Boston, MA: Northeastern University Press, pp 244–260.

Kuo, M. (2013) 'Confucian heritage, public narratives and community politics of Chinese Australians at the beginning of the twentieth century', *Journal of Chinese Overseas*, 9(2), pp 212–244.

Kwek, D. (2003) 'Decolonizing and re-presenting culture's consequences: A postcolonial critique of cross-cultural studies in management', in Prasad, A. (ed) *Postcolonial Theory and Organizational Analysis: A Critical Engagement*. New York: Palgrave Macmillan, pp 121–146.

Lawler, J. and Ashman, I. (2012) 'Theorizing leadership authenticity: A Sartrean perspective', *Leadership*, 8(4), pp 327–344.

Lawrence, B. and Anderson, K. (2005) 'Introduction to "Indigenous Women: The State of Our Nations"', *Atlantis*, 29(2), pp 1–10.

LeBlanc, L. (1999) *Pretty in Punk: Girls' Gender Resistance in a Boys' Subculture*. New Brunswick, NJ: Rutgers University Press.

Lentin, A. and Titley, G. (2011) *The Crises of Multiculturalism: Racism in a Neoliberal Age*. London: Zed Books.

Leonardo, Z. (2009) *Race, Whiteness, and Education*. New York: Routledge.

Leong, N. (2012) 'Racial capitalism', *Harvard Law Review*, 126(8), pp 2151–2224.

Lerner, G. (1986) *The Creation of Patriarchy*. Oxford: Oxford University Press.

Levine-Rasky, C. (2013) *Whiteness Fractured*. Farnham: Ashgate.

Lewis, P., Benschop, Y. and Simpson, R. (2017) 'Postfeminism, gender and organization', *Gender, Work and Organization*, 24(3), pp 213–225.

Liden, R.C., Wayne, S.J., Zhao, H. and Henderson, D. (2008) 'Servant leadership: Development of a multidimensional measure and multi-level assessment', *The Leadership Quarterly*, 19(2), pp 161–177.

Lindsay, K. (2016) Maybe don't buy a solidarity pin necklace for this much money, *Refinery29*. Available at: www.refinery29.com/2016/11/129862/safety-pin-solidarity-necklace (Accessed: 17 July 2018).

Linstead, S. (1997) 'Abjection and organization: Men, violence, and management', *Human Relations*, 50(9), pp 1115–1145.

Liu, H. (2015) 'Constructing the GFC: Australian banking leaders during the financial "crisis"', *Leadership*, 11(4), pp 424–450.

Liu, H. (2017a) 'Redeeming difference in CMS through anti-racist feminisms', in Pullen, A., Harding, N. and Phillips, M. (eds) *Feminists and Queer Theorists Debate the Future of Critical Management Studies*. Dialogues in Critical Management Studies. Bingley: Emerald Group, pp 39–56.

Liu, H. (2017b) 'Beneath the white gaze: Strategic self-Orientalism among Chinese Australians', *Human Relations*, 70(7), pp 781–804.

Liu, H. (2017c) 'Undoing whiteness: The Dao of anti-racist diversity practice', *Gender, Work and Organization*, 24(5), pp 457–471.

Liu, H. (2017d) 'Sensuality as subversion: Doing masculinity with Chinese Australian professionals', *Gender, Work & Organization*, 24(2), pp 194–212.

Liu, H. (2017e) 'Reimagining ethical leadership as a relational, contextual and political practice', *Leadership*, 13(3), pp 343–367.

Liu, H. (2018) 'Leadership from the margins: Practising inclusivity with "outsiders within"', in Adapa, S. and Sheridan, A. (eds) *Inclusive Leadership: Negotiating Gendered Spaces*. Basingstoke: Palgrave Macmillan, pp 1–20.

Liu, H. (2019a) 'An embarrassment of riches: The seduction of postfeminism in the academy', *Organization*, 26(1), pp 20–37.

Liu, H. (2019b) 'Just the servant: An intersectional critique of servant leadership', *Journal of Business Ethics*, 156(4), pp 1099–1112.

Liu, H. (2019c) 'Decolonising organisations with bell hooks', in McMurray, R. and Pullen, A. (eds) *Routledge Focus on Women Writers in Organization Studies: Power, Politics & Exclusion in Organization and Management*. London: Routledge, pp 110–128.

Liu, H. and Baker, C. (2016) 'White Knights: Leadership as the heroicisation of whiteness', *Leadership*, 12(4), pp 420–448.

Liu, H. and Pechenkina, E. (2016) 'Staying quiet or rocking the boat? An autoethnography of organisational visual white supremacy', *Equality, Diversity and Inclusion: An International Journal*, 35(3), pp 186–204.

Liu, H., Cutcher, L. and Grant, D. (2015) 'Doing authenticity: The gendered construction of authentic leadership', *Gender, Work & Organization*, 22(3), pp 237–255.

Lo, J. (2006) 'Disciplining Asian Australian studies: Projections and introjections', *Journal of Intercultural Studies*, 27(1–2), pp 11–27.

Lord, R.G., De Vader, C.L. and Alliger, G.M. (1986) 'A meta analysis of the relationship between personality traits and leadership perceptions: An application of validity generalization procedures', *Journal of Applied Psychology*, 71(3), pp 402–410.

Lorde, A. (1984) *Sister Outsider: Essays and Speeches*. Trumansburg, NY: Crossing Press.

Lorde, A. (2009) *I Am Your Sister: Collected and Unpublished Writings of Audre Lorde*. Edited by Byrd, R.P., Betsch Cole, J. and Guy-Sheftall, B. Oxford: Oxford University Press.

Louie, K. (2002) *Theorising Chinese Masculinity: Society and Gender in China*. New York: Cambridge University Press.

Lovell Banks, T. (2000) 'Colorism: A darker shade of pale', *UCLA Law Review*, 47(6), pp 1705–1746.

Lugones, M. (2006) 'On complex communication', *Hypatia*, 21(3), pp 75–85.

Lugones, M. (2010) 'Toward a decolonial feminism', *Hypatia*, 25(4), pp 742–759.

Lugones, M. (2014) 'Radical multiculturalism and women of color feminisms', *Journal for Cultural and Religious Theory*, 13(1), pp 68–80.

MacMullan, T. (2009) *Habits of Whiteness: A Pragmatist Reconstruction*. Bloomington: Indiana University Press.

Mak, A. (2003) 'Negotiating identity: Ethnicity, tourism and Chinatown', *Journal of Australian Studies*, 27(77), pp 93–100.

Mallenbaum, C. and Jones, J.M. (2016) Here's why #BeckyWithTheBadGrades is trending, *USA Today*, 23 June.

Mann, F.C. (1965) 'Toward an understanding of the leadership role in formal organization', in Dublin, R., Homans, G.C., Mann, F.C. and Miller, D.C. (eds) *Leadership and Productivity: Some Facts of Industrial Life*. San Francisco, CA: Chandler, pp 68–103.

Mann, R.D. (1959) 'A review of the relationships between personality and performance in small groups', *Psychological Bulletin*, 56(4), pp 241–270.

Markowitz, S. (2001) 'Pelvic politics: Sexual dimorphism and racial difference', *Signs*, 26(2), pp 389–414.

Martinez Dy, A., Marlow, S. and Martin, L. (2017) 'A web of opportunity or the same old story? Women digital entrepreneurs and intersectionality theory', *Human Relations*, 70(3), pp 286–311.

Martino, M. (2016) Pauline Hanson's maiden speech: Has Australia been 'swamped by Asians'?, *ABC News*, 14 September. Available at: www.abc.net.au/news/2016-09-14/pauline-hanson-maiden-speech-asian-immigration/7645578 (Accessed: 1 March 2018).

Matthews, J. (2002) 'An ambiguous juncture: Racism and the formation of Asian femininity', *Australian Feminist Studies*, 17(38), pp 207–219.

Mauss, M. (1966) *The Gift: Forms and Functions of Exchange in Archaic Societies*. London: Routledge & Kegan Paul.

Mayer, R.C., Davis, J.H. and Schoorman, F.D. (1995) 'An integrative model of organizational trust', *The Academy of Management Review*, 20(3), pp 709–734.

McDowell, L. (2009) *Working Bodies: Interactive Service Employment and Workplace Identities*. Chichester: John Wiley & Sons.

McGregor, J. (2016) To improve diversity, don't make people go to diversity training. Really, *The Washington Post*, 1 July. Available at: www.washingtonpost.com/news/on-leadership/wp/2016/07/01/to-improve-diversity-dont-make-people-go-to-diversity-training-really-2/ (Accessed: 1 May 2018).

McIntosh, P. (1988) White privilege: Unpacking the invisible knapsack, Racial Equity Tools. Available at: www.racialequitytools.org/resourcefiles/mcintosh.pdf (Accessed: 22 March 2018).

McKenna, B., Rooney, D. and Boal, K.B. (2009) 'Wisdom principles as a meta-theoretical basis for evaluating leadership', *The Leadership Quarterly*, 20(2), pp 177–190.

McLaren, P. (2000) 'Unthinking whiteness: Rearticulating diasporic practice', in Trifonas, P.P. (ed) *Revolutionary Pedagogies.* New York: Routledge, pp 140–173.

McNay, L. (2009) 'Self as enterprise: Dilemmas of control and resistance in Foucault's *The Birth of Biopolitics*', *Theory, Culture and Society*, 26(6), pp 55–77.

McSweeney, B. (2002) 'Hofstede's model of national cultural differences and their consequences: A triumph of faith – a failure of analysis', *Human Relations*, 55(1), pp 89–118.

Meacham, S. (2008) The retiring philanthropist, *Sydney Morning Herald*, 1 March, p 31.

Medland, D. (2017) easyJet CEO Dame Carolyn McCall on transformative leadership, *Chartered Management Institute*. Available at: www.managers.org.uk/insights/news/2017/april/easyjet-ceo-dame-carolyn-mccall-on-transformative-leadership (Accessed: 23 April 2018).

Meindl, J.R., Ehrlich, S.B. and Dukerich, J.M. (1985) 'The romance of leadership', *Administrative Science Quarterly*, 30(1), pp 78–102.

Merica, D. (2017) Trump condemns 'hatred, bigotry and violence on many sides' in Charlottesville, *CNN*, 13 August. Available at: https://edition.cnn.com/2017/08/12/politics/trump-statement-alt-right-protests/index.html (Accessed: 1 March 2018).

Merleau-Ponty, M. (1962) *Phenomenology of Perception*. London: Routledge.

Messner, M.A. (2007) 'The masculinity of the governator: Muscle and compassion in American politics', *Gender & Society*, 21(4), pp 461–480.

Metcalf, L. and Benn, S. (2013) 'Leadership for sustainability: An evolution of leadership ability', *Journal of Business Ethics*, 112(3), pp 369–384.

Mies, M. and Shiva, V. (1993) *Ecofeminism*. London: Zed Books.

Mignolo, W. (2009) 'Epistemic disobedience: Independent thought and decolonial freedom', *Theory, Culture and Society*, 26(7–8), pp 159–181.

Mills, C.W. (2000) *The Sociological Imagination*. Oxford: Oxford University Press.

Milne, R. (2017) True Finns split holds lesson for Europe's populists, *Financial Times*, 16 June. Available at: www.ft.com/content/fe376512-51b8-11e7-bfb8-997009366969 (Accessed: 2 March 2018).

Mirchandani, K. and Butler, A. (2006) 'Beyond inclusion and equity: Contributions from transnational anti-racist feminism', in Konrad, A.M., Prasad, P. and Pringle, J. (eds) *Dimensions of Workplace Diversity*. London: Sage, pp 475–488.

Mirza, H.S. (2009) 'Plotting a history: Black and postcolonial feminisms in "new times"', *Race Ethnicity and Education*, 12(1), pp 1–10.

Mohanty, C.T. (2003) *Feminism without Borders: Decolonizing Theory, Practicing Solidarity*. 2nd edn. Durham, NC: Duke University Press.

Mohanty, C.T. (2013) 'Transnational feminist crossings: On neoliberalism and radical critique', *Signs: Journal of Women in Culture and Society*, 38(4), pp 967–991.

Moraga, C. and Anzaldúa, G. E. (eds) (1983) *This Bridge Called My Back: Writings by Radical Women of Color*. 2nd edn. New York: Kitchen Table; Women of Color Press.

Morales, R. (1983) 'We're all in the same boat', in Moraga, C. and Anzaldúa, G.E. (eds) *This Bridge Called My Back: Writings by Radical Women of Color*. 2nd edn. New York: Kitchen Table; Women of Color Press, pp 91–93.

Moreton-Robinson, A. (2000) 'Troubling business: Difference and whiteness within feminism', *Australian Feminist Studies*, 15(33), pp 343–352.

Moreton-Robinson, A. (2004) 'Whiteness, epistemology and Indigenous representation', in Moreton-Robinson, A. (ed) *Whitening Race: Essays in Social and Cultural Criticism*. Canberra: Aboriginal Studies Press, pp 75–88.

Moreton-Robinson, A. (2015) *White Possessive: Property, Power, and Indigenous Sovereignty*. Minneapolis, MN: University of Minnesota Press.

Mortimer, C. (2016) Donald Trump's national security adviser meets with Austrian far-right leader, *The Independent*, 21 December. Available at: www.independent.co.uk/news/world/americas/donald-trump-national-security-adviser-general-michael-flynn-austrian-far-right-leader-heinz-a7488326.html (Accessed: 2 March 2018).

Murphy, K. (2016) Pauline Hanson calls for immigration ban: 'Go back to where you came from', *The Guardian*, 14 September. Available at: www.theguardian.com/australia-news/2016/sep/14/pauline-hanson-first-speech-senate-calls-for-immigration-ban (Accessed: 1 March 2018).

Murphy, M.K. and Harris, T.M. (2018) 'White innocence and black subservience: The rhetoric of white heroism in *The Help*', *Howard Journal of Communications*, 29(1), pp 49–62.

Nanus, B. (1995) *Visionary Leadership*. San Francisco: Jossey-Bass.

Narayan, U. (2000) 'Undoing the "package picture" of cultures', *Signs*, 25(4), pp 1083–1086.

Nath Chakraborty, M. (2004) 'Wa(i)ving it all away: Producing subject and knowledge in feminisms of colour', in Gillis, S., Howie, G. and Munford, R. (eds) *Third Wave Feminism: A Critical Exploration.* Basingstoke: Palgrave Macmillan, pp 205–215.

Negra, D. (2009) *What a Girl Wants? Fantasizing the Reclamation of Self in Postfeminism.* London: Routledge.

Nkomo, S.M. (1992) 'The emperor has no clothes: Rewriting "race in organizations"', *The Academy of Management Review*, 17(3), pp 487–513.

Nkomo, S.M. (2011) 'A postcolonial and anti-colonial reading of "African" leadership and management in organization studies: Tensions, contradictions and possibilities', *Organization*, 18(3), pp 365–386.

Nkomo, S.M. and Al Ariss, A. (2014) 'The historical origins of ethnic (white) privilege in US organizations', *Journal of Managerial Psychology*, 29(4), pp 389–404.

Noon, M. (2007) 'The fatal flaws of diversity and the business case for ethnic minorities', *Work, Employment and Society*, 21(4), pp 773–784.

Noon, M. (2018) 'Pointless diversity training: Unconscious bias, new racism and agency', *Work, Employment and Society*, 32(1), pp 198–209.

Oakley, J. (2000) 'Gender-based barriers to senior management positions: Understanding the scarcity of female CEOs', *Journal of Business Ethics*, 27(4), pp 321–334.

Offermann, L.R., Kennedy, J.K. and Wirtz, P.W. (1994) 'Implicit leadership theories: Content, structure, and generalizability', *The Leadership Quarterly*, 5(1), pp 43–58.

Office of Multicultural Affairs (1989) *National Agenda for a Multicultural Australia: Sharing Our Future.* Canberra: Department of the Prime Minister and Cabinet, Office of Multicultural Affairs.

O'Leary, J. and Tilly, J. (2014) *Cracking the Cultural Ceiling: Future Proofing Your Business in the Asian Century.* Sydney: Diversity Council Australia.

Omi, M. and Winant, H. (1994) *Racial Formation in the United States: From the 1960s to the 1990s.* 2nd edn. New York: Routledge.

Ospina, S. and Su, C. (2009) 'Weaving color lines: Race, ethnicity, and the work of leadership in social change organizations', *Leadership*, 5(2), pp 131–170.

Pacholok, S. (2009) 'Gendered strategies of self: Navigating hierarchy and contesting masculinities', *Gender, Work and Organization*, 16(4), pp 471–500.

Parker, D. (2000) 'The Chinese takeaway and the diasporic habitus: Space, time and power geometries', in Hesse, B. (ed) *Un/Settled Multiculturalisms: Diasporas, Entanglements, Transruptions.* London: Zed Books, pp 73–95.

Parker, P.S. (2005) *Race, Gender, and Leadership: Re-envisioning Organizational Leadership from the Perspectives of African American Women Executives*. Mahwah, NJ: Lawrence Erlbaum.

Parker, P.S. and ogilvie, d.t. (1996) 'Gender, culture, and leadership: Toward a culturally distinct model of African-American women executives' leadership strategies', *The Leadership Quarterly*, 7(2), pp 189–214.

Pearce, C.L., Manz, C.C. and Akanno, S. (2013) 'Searching for the holy grail of management development and sustainability: Is shared leadership development the answer?', *Journal of Management Development*, 32(3), pp 247–257.

Pells, R. (2018) Cardiff plans review after suicide of 'overworked' lecturer, *Times Higher Education*, 8 June. Available at: www.timeshighereducation.com/news/cardiff-plans-review-after-suicide-overworked-lecturer (Accessed: 13 June 2018).

Pérez Huber, L. and Solórzano, D.G. (2015) 'Visualizing everyday racism: Critical Race Theory, visual microaggressions, and the historical image of Mexican banditry', *Qualitative Inquiry*, 21(3), pp 223–238.

Perriton, L. (2009) '"We don't want complaining women!" A critical analysis of the business case for diversity', *Management Communication Quarterly*, 23(2), pp 218–243.

Perry, I. (2011) *More Beautiful and More Terrible: The Embrace and Transcendence of Racial Inequality in the United States*. New York: New York University Press.

Peus, C., Wesche, J.S., Streicher, B., Braun, S. and Frey, D. (2012) 'Authentic leadership: An empirical test of its antecedents, consequences, and mediating mechanisms', *Journal of Business Ethics*, 107(3), pp 331–348.

Pincus, F.L. (2003) *Reverse Discrimination: Dismantling the Myth*. Boulder, CO: Lynne Rienner.

Pitts, D.W. (2005) 'Leadership, empowerment, and public organizations', *Review of Public Personnel Administration*, 25(5), pp 5–28.

Powell, G.N., Butterfield, D.A. and Parent, J.D. (2002) 'Gender and managerial stereotypes: Have the times changed?', *Journal of Management*, 28(2), pp 177–193.

Prasad, A. (ed) (2003) *Postcolonial Theory and Organizational Analysis: A Critical Engagement*. New York: Palgrave Macmillan.

Prasad, P. and Mills, A.J. (1997) 'From showcase to shadow: Understanding the dilemmas of managing workplace diversity', in Prasad, P., Mills, A.J., Elmes, M. and Prasad, A. (eds) *Managing the Organizational Melting Pot: Dilemmas of Workplace Diversity*. Thousand Oaks, CA: Sage, pp 3–30.

Price, T.L. (2000) 'Explaining ethical failures of leadership', *Leadership & Organization Development Journal*, 21(4), pp 177–184.

Price, T.L. (2003) 'The ethics of authentic transformational leadership', *The Leadership Quarterly*, 14(1), pp 67–81.

Price, T.L. (2008) 'Kant's advice for leaders: "No, you aren't special"', *The Leadership Quarterly*, 19(4), pp 478–487.

Puar, J. (2011) '"I would rather be a cyborg than a goddess": Intersectionality, assemblage, and affective politics', *Transversal*. Available at: http://eipcp.net/transversal/0811/puar/en (Accessed: 28 May 2018).

Puwar, N. (2004) *Space Invaders: Race, Gender and Bodies Out of Place*. Oxford: Berg.

Pyke, K.D. and Johnson, D.L. (2003) 'Asian American women and racialized femininities: "Doing" gender across cultural worlds', *Gender & Society*, 17(1), pp 33–53.

Radford Ruether, R. (2007) *America, Amerikkka: Elect Nation and Imperial Violence*. London: Equinox.

Rafael, V.L. (2000) *White Love and Other Events in Filipino History*. Durham, NC: Duke University Press.

Ray, K. (2003) 'Constituting "Asian women": Political representation, identity politics and local discourses of participation', *Ethnic and Racial Studies*, 26(5), pp 854–878.

Reave, L. (2005) 'Spiritual values and practices related to leadership effectiveness', *The Leadership Quarterly*, 16(5), pp 655–687.

Redmond, S. and Holmes, S. (2007) 'Introduction', in Redmond, S. and Holmes, S. (eds) *Stardom and Celebrity: A Reader*. London: Sage, pp 1–12.

Reed, L.L., Vidaver-Cohen, D. and Colwell, S.R. (2011) 'A new scale to measure executive servant leadership: Development, analysis, and implications for research', *Journal of Business Ethics*, 101(3), pp 415–434.

Rich, A. (1979) *On Lies, Secrets and Silence*. New York: Norton.

Richards, S.A. and Jaffee, C.L. (1972) 'Blacks supervising whites: A study of interracial difficulties in working together in a simulated organization', *Journal of Applied Psychology*, 56(3), pp 234–240.

Richardson, A. and Loubier, C. (2008) 'Intersectionality and leadership', *International Journal of Leadership Studies*, 3(2), pp 142–161.

Riley, B.F. (1910) *The White Man's Burden, a Discussion of the Interracial Question with Special Reference to the Responsibility of the White Race to the Negro Problem*. Birmingham, AL: B.F. Riley.

Rodríguez, C.E. (ed) (1997) *Latin Looks: Images of Latinas and Latinos in the U.S. Media*. Boulder, CO: Westview Press.

Rodríguez, C.E. (2004) *Heroes, Lovers, and Others: The Story of Latinos in Hollywood*. Washington, DC: Smithsonian Books.

Rodriguez, A. (2017) 'A new rhetoric for a decolonial world', *Postcolonial Studies*, 20(2), pp 176–186.

Rodriguez, J. and Freeman, K.J. (2016) '"Your focus on race is narrow and exclusive:" The derailment of anti-racist work through discourses of intersectionality and diversity', *Whiteness and Education*, 1(1), pp 69–82.

Roediger, D. (1994) *Towards the Abolition of Whiteness*. London: Verso.

Róisín, F. (2017) Why Hollywood's white savior obsession is an extension of colonialism, *Teen Vogue*. Available at: www.teenvogue.com/story/hollywoods-white-savior-obsession-colonialism (Accessed: 26 April 2018).

Rose, H. (1994) *Love, Power, and Knowledge: Towards a Feminist Transformation of the Sciences*. Bloomington, IN: Indiana University Press.

Rosener, J.B. (1990) 'Ways women lead', *Harvard Business Review*, 68(6), p 119.

Rosette, A.S., Leonardelli, G.J. and Phillips, K.W. (2008) 'The White standard: Racial bias in leader categorization', *Journal of Applied Psychology*, 93(4), pp 758–777.

Roy, A. (2014) 'The doctor and the saint', in Anand, S. (ed) *Annihilation of Caste*. London: Verso, pp 11–117.

Russell, R.F. and Stone, A.G. (2002) 'A review of servant leadership attributes: Developing a practical model', *Leadership & Organization Development Journal*, 23(3), pp 145–157.

Ruth, D. (2014) 'Leader as priest: Plucking the fruit of a flawed metaphor', *Leadership*, 10(2), pp 174–190.

Safronova, V. (2016) Safety pins show support for the vulnerable, *The New York Times*, 14 November. Available at: www.nytimes.com/2016/11/14/fashion/safety-pin-ally-activism.html (Accessed: 29 June 2018).

Said, E.W. (1978) *Orientalism*. London: Penguin.

Said, E.W. (1994) *Culture and Imperialism*. New York: Vintage Books.

Salamon, L.M. (1992) *America's Nonprofit Sector: A Primer*. New York: Foundation Center.

Sanchez-Hucles, J.V. and Davis, D.D. (2010) 'Women and women of color in leadership: Complexity, identity, and intersectionality', *American Psychologist*, 65(3), pp 171–181.

Sankaran, C. and Chng, H.H. (2004) '"We women aren't free to die": Transacting Asian sexualities in a feminism classroom in Singapore', *Critical Asian Studies*, 36(2), pp 285–301.

Saul, H. (2014) Richard Branson profile: The billionaire entrepreneur behind the Virgin Group empire, *The Independent*, 1 November. Available at: www.independent.co.uk/news/people/richard-branson-profile-the-billionaire-entrepreneur-behind-the-virgin-group-empire-9832952.html (Accessed: 20 March 2018).

Sayers, J.G. (2017) 'Feminist CMS writing as difficult joy: Via birds and bitches', in Pullen, A., Harding, N. and Phillips, M. (eds) *Feminists and Queer Theorists Debate the Future of Critical Management Studies*. Dialogues in Critical Management Studies. Bingley: Emerald Group, pp 155–169.

Scharff, C.M. (2016) 'The psychic life of neoliberalism: Mapping the contours of neoliberal subjectivity', *Gender, Work and Organization*, 33(6), pp 107–122.

Schein, V.E. (1973) 'The relationship between sex role stereotypes and requisite management characteristics', *Journal of Applied Psychology*, 57, pp 95–100.

Schein, V.E. (1975) 'The relationship between sex role stereotypes and requisite management characteristics among female managers', *Journal of Applied Psychology*, 60, pp 340–344.

Schein, V.E. (2001) 'A global look at psychological barriers to women's progress in management', *Journal of Social Issues*, 57(4), pp 675–688.

Schminke, M., Wells, D., Peyrefitte, J. and Sebora, T.C. (2002) 'Leadership and ethics in work groups: A longitudinal assessment', *Group & Organization Management*, 27(2), pp 272–293.

Schnurr, S. (2008) 'Surviving in a man's world with a sense of humour: An analysis of women leaders' use of humour at work', *Leadership*, 4(3), pp 299–319.

Schultheis, E. (2017) Marine Le Pen's real victory, *The Atlantic*. Available at: www.theatlantic.com/international/archive/2017/05/le-pen-national-front-macron-france-election/525759/ (Accessed: 2 March 2018).

Sczesny, S. (2003) 'A closer look beneath the surface: Various facets of the think-manager–think-male stereotype', *Sex Roles*, 49(7–8), pp 353–363.

Secomb, L. (2007) 'Colonial love in Fanon and Moffatt', in *Philosophy and Love: From Plato to Popular Culture*. Edinburgh: Edinburgh University Press, pp 75–92.

Sharma, A. and Grant, D. (2011) 'Narrative, drama and charismatic leadership: The case of Apple's Steve Jobs', *Leadership*, 7(1), pp 3–26.

Shepherd, M., Erchull, M.J., Rosner, A., Taubenberger, L., Forsyth Queen, E. and McKee, J. (2011) '"I'll get that for you": The relationship between benevolent sexism and body self-perceptions', *Sex Roles*, 64(1), pp 1–8.

Shome, R. (2001) 'White femininity and the discourse of the nation: Re/membering Princess Diana', *Feminist Media Studies*, 1(3), pp 323–342.

Shome, R. (2011) '"Global motherhood": The transnational intimacies of white femininity', *Critical Studies in Media Communication*, 28(5), pp 388–406.

Shome, R. (2014) *Diana and Beyond: White Femininity, National Identity, and Contemporary Media Culture*. Urbana: University of Illinois Press.

Sinclair, A. (2007) *Leadership for the disillusioned: Beyond myths and heroes to leading that liberates*. Sydney: Allen & Unwin.

Sinclair, A. (2006) 'Critical diversity management practice in Australia: Romanced or co-opted?', in Konrad, A.M., Prasad, P. and Pringle, J. (eds) *Dimensions of workplace diversity*. London: Sage, pp 511–530.

Sisters of Resistance (2019) Solidarity with @GoldAntiRacism #goldoccupy #myracistcampus, Sisters of Resistance. Available at: https://sistersofresistance.wordpress.com/2019/04/23/solidarity-with-goldantiracism-goldoccupy-myracistcampus/ (Accessed: 27 May 2019).

Sleeter, C.E. (1996) 'White silence, white solidarity', in Ignatiev, N. and Garvey, J. (eds) *Race Traitor*. New York: Routledge, pp 257–265.

Śliwa, M., Spoelstra, S., Sørensen, B.M. and Land, C. (2012) 'Profaning the sacred in leadership studies: A reading of Murakami's *A Wild Sheep Chase*', *Organization*, 20(6), pp 860–880.

Smithers, G.D. (2009) 'The "pursuits of the Civilized Man": Race and the meaning of civilization in the United States and Australia, 1790s–1850s', *Journal of World History*, 20(2), pp 245–272.

Solórzano, D.G. and Yosso, T.J. (2001) 'From racial stereotyping and deficit discourse toward a critical race theory in teacher education', *Multicultural Education*, 9(1), pp 2–8.

Spangler, W.D., Gupta, A., Kim, D.H. and Nazarian, S. (2012) 'Developing and validating historiometric measures of leader individual differences by computerized content analysis of documents', *The Leadership Quarterly*, 23(6), pp 1152–1172.

Spoelstra, S. and Ten Bos, R. (2011) 'Leadership', in Painter-Morland, M. and Ten Bos, R. (eds) *Business Ethics and Continental Philosophy*. Cambridge: Cambridge University Press, pp 181–198.

Srivastava, S. (2006) 'Tears, fears and careers: Antiracism and emotion in social movement organizations', *Canadian Journal of Sociology*, 31(1), pp 55–90.

Steyaert, C. (2015) 'Three women. A kiss. A life. On the queer writing of time in organization', *Gender, Work and Organization*, 22(2), pp 163–178.

Stoler, A.L. (1995) *Race and the Education of Desire: Foucault's History of Sexuality and the Colonial Order of Things*. Durham, NC: Duke University Press.

Stratton, J. and Ang, I. (2013) 'Multicultural imagined communities: Cultural difference and national identity in the USA and Australia', in Bennett, D. (ed) *Multicultural States: Rethinking Difference and Identity*. London: Routledge, pp 135–162.

Sullivan, S. (2006) *Revealing Whiteness: The Unconscious Habits of Racial Privilege*. Bloomington: Indiana University Press.

Sullivan, S. (2014) *Good White People: The Problem with Middle-Class White Anti-Racism*. Albany, NY: SUNY.

Sunderland, R. (2017) How new ITV chief Dame Carolyn McCall became Britain's most wanted boss: From taking jobs she loved, to shunning an office, and transforming easyJet, *Mail Online*, 18 July. Available at: www.thisismoney.co.uk/money/news/article-4704610/Dame-Carolyn-McCall-wanted-boss-Britain.html (Accessed: 23 April 2018).

Sung, K.K. (2015) '"Hella ghetto!": (Dis)locating race and class consciousness in youth discourses of ghetto spaces, subjects and schools', *Race Ethnicity and Education*, 18(3), pp 363–395.

Sveningsson, S. and Larsson, M. (2006) 'Fantasies of leadership: Identity work', *Leadership*, 2(2), pp 203–224.

Swan, E. (2017) 'What are white people to do? Listening, challenging ignorance, generous encounters and the "not yet" as diversity research praxis', *Gender, Work and Organization*, 24(5), pp 547–563.

Tajima, R.E. (1989) 'Lotus blossoms don't bleed: Images of Asian women', in Asian Women United (ed) *Making Waves: An Anthology of Writings by and about Asian American Women*. Boston: Beacon Press, pp 308–317.

Taliaferro Baszile, D. (2015) 'Rhetorical revolution: Critical race counterstorytelling and the abolition of white democracy', *Qualitative Inquiry*, 21(3), pp 239–249.

Tan, C. (2003) 'Living with "difference": Growing up "Chinese" in white Australia', *Journal of Australian Studies*, 27(77), pp 101–112.

Tan, C. (2006) '"The tyranny of appearance": Chinese Australian identities and the politics of difference', *Journal of Intercultural Studies*, 27(1–2), pp 65–82.

Tariq, M. and Syed, J. (2017) 'Intersectionality at work: South Asian Muslim women's experiences of employment and leadership in the United Kingdom', *Sex Roles*, 77(7–8), pp 510–522.

Tasker, Y. and Negra, D. (2007) *Interrogating Postfeminism: Gender and the Politics of Popular Culture*. Durham, NC: Duke University Press.

Tate, S.A. and Page, D. (2018) 'Whiteliness and institutional racism: Hiding behind (un)conscious bias', *Ethics and Education*, 13(1), pp 141–155.

Tett, G. (2009) *Fool's gold: How Unrestrained Greed Corrupted a Dream, Shattered Global Markets and Unleashed a Catastrophe*. London: Little, Brown.

Theriault, A. (2014) The white feminist savior complex, *Huffington Post*, 23 January. Available at: www.huffingtonpost.com/anne-theriault-/the-white-feminist-savior_b_4629470.html (Accessed: 26 April 2018).

Thomas, D.A. and Ely, R.J. (2001) *Making Differences Matter: A New Paradigm for Managing Diversity*. Boston, MA: Harvard Business School Press.

Thomas, R.R. (1992) *Beyond Race and Gender: Unleashing the Power of Your Total Workforce by Managing Diversity*. New York: AMACOM.

Tourish, D. (2013) *The Dark Side of Transformational Leadership*. Hoboken, NJ: Taylor and Francis.

Treviño, L.K., Brown, M.E. and Hartman, L.P. (2003) 'A qualitative investigation of perceived executive ethical leadership: Perceptions from inside and outside the executive suite', *Human Relations*, 56(1), pp 5–37.

Treviño, L.K., Butterfield, K.D. and McCabe, D.L. (1998) 'The ethical context in organizations: Influences on employee attitudes and behaviors', *Business Ethics Quarterly*, 8(3), pp 447–476.

Treviño, L.K., Hartman, L.P. and Brown, M.E. (2000) 'Moral person and moral manager: How executives develop a reputation for ethical leadership', *California Management Review*, 42(4), p 128–142.

Trinh, T.M. (1989) *Woman, Native, Other: Writing Postcoloniality and Feminism*. Bloomington, IN: Indiana University Press.

Tuman, J.S. (2010) *Communicating Terror: The Rhetorical Dimensions of Terrorism*. Thousand Oaks, CA: Sage.

Tyson, T.B. (2017) *The Blood of Emmett Till*. New York: Simon & Schuster.

Uchida, A. (1998) 'The Orientalization of Asian women in America', *Women's Studies International Forum*, 21(2), pp 161–174.

Vachhani, S. (2015) 'Organizing love – Thoughts on the transformative and activist potential of feminine writing', *Gender, Work and Organization*, 22(2), pp 148–162.

Van den Brink, M. and Benschop, Y. (2012) 'Slaying the seven-headed dragon: The quest for gender change in academia', *Gender, Work and Organization*, 19(1), pp 71–92.

Van Dierendonck, D. (2011) 'Servant leadership: A review and synthesis', *Journal of Management*, 37(4), pp 1228–1261.

Van Engen, M.L. and Willemsen, T.M. (2004) 'Sex and leadership styles: A meta-analysis of research published in the 1990s', *Psychological Reports*, 94(1), pp 3–18.

Van Knippenberg, D. and Sitkin, S.B. (2013) 'A critical assessment of charismatic-transformational leadership research: Back to the drawing board?', *The Academy of Management Annals*, 7(1), pp 1–60.

Van Laer, K. and Janssens, M. (2011) 'Ethnic minority professionals' experiences with subtle discrimination in the workplace', *Human Relations*, 64(9), pp 1203–1227.

Vásquez, M.A. (2014) 'From colonialism to neo-liberal capitalism: Latino/a immigrants in the US and the new biopolitics', *Journal for Cultural and Religious Theory*, 13(1), pp 81–100.

Vecchio, R.P. (2002) 'Leadership and the gender advantage', *The Leadership Quarterly*, 13(6), pp 643–671.

Vera, H. and Gordon, A. (2002) *Screen Saviors: Hollywood Fictions of Whiteness*. Lanham, MD: Rowman & Littlefield Publishers.

Vinkenburg, C.J., van Engen, M.L., Eagly, A.H. and Johannesen-Schmidt, M.C. (2011) 'An exploration of stereotypical beliefs about leadership styles: Is transformational leadership a route to women's promotion?', *The Leadership Quarterly*, 22(1), pp 10–21.

Von Wahl, A. (2011) 'A "women's revolution from above"? Female leadership, intersectionality, and public policy under the Merkel government', *German Politics*, 20(3), pp 392–409.

Wadiwel, D.J. (2009) 'Solidarity, authenticity and anti racism', *Cosmopolitan Civil Societies: An Interdisciplinary Journal*, 1(2), pp 77–85.

Walsh, J.P. (2012) 'The marketization of multiculturalism: Neoliberal restructuring and cultural difference in Australia', *Ethnic and Racial Studies*, 37(2), pp 280–301.

Walumbwa, F.O. and Schaubroeck, J. (2009) 'Leader personality traits and employee voice behavior: Mediating roles of ethical leadership and work group psychological safety', *Journal of Applied Psychology*, 94, pp 1275–1286.

Wang, G. (2009) 'Chinese history paradigms', *Asian Ethnicity*, 10(3), pp 201–216.

Ware, V. (2015) *Beyond the Pale: White Women, Racism, and History*. London: Verso.

Wasserman, J.A., Clair, J.M. and Platt, C. (2012) 'The "homeless problem" and the double consciousness', *Sociological Inquiry*, 82(3), pp 331–355.

Weaver, G.R., Treviño, L.K. and Cochran, P.L. (1999) 'Corporate ethics programs as control systems: Influences of executive commitment and environmental factors', *Academy of Management Journal*, 42(1), pp 41–57.

Weber, M. (1922) *Economy and Society*. Edited by Roth, G. and Wittich, C. Berkeley: University of California Press.

Weitzner, D. and Darroch, J. (2009) 'Why moral failures precede financial crises', *Critical Perspectives on International Business*, 5(1/2), pp 6–13.

West, C. and Zimmerman, D.H. (1987) 'Doing gender', *Gender & Society*, 1(2), pp 125–151.

West, C. and Zimmerman, D.H. (2009) 'Accounting for doing gender', *Gender & Society*, 23(1), pp 112–122.

West, C.M. (2012) 'Mammy, Jezebel, Sapphire, and their homegirls: Developing an "oppositional gaze" toward the images of Black women', in Chrisler, J.C., Golden, C. and Rozee, P.D. (eds) *Lectures on the Psychology of Women*. 4th edn. Long Grove, IL: Waveland Press, pp 286–299.

Westen, D. (2007) *The Political Brain: The Role of Emotion in Deciding the Fate of the Nation*. New York: PublicAffairs.

Western, S. (2012) *Leadership: A Critical Text*. 2nd edn. London: Sage.

Westwood, R. (2001) 'Appropriating the Other in the discourses of comparative management', in Westwood, R. and Linstead, S. (eds) *The Language of Organization*. London: Sage, pp 242–283.

Westwood, R. (2003) 'Economies of violence: An autobiographical account', *Culture and Organization*, 9(4), pp 275–293.

Williams, J. (2017) White American men are a bigger domestic terrorist threat than Muslim foreigners, *Vox*, 2 October. Available at: www.vox.com/world/2017/10/2/16396612/las-vegas-mass-shooting-terrorism-islam (Accessed: 5 June 2018).

Williams, J.E. and Best, D.L. (1990) *Measuring Sex Stereotypes: A Multination Study*. Newbury Park, CA: Sage.

Wilson, S. (2016) *Thinking Differently about Leadership: A Critical History of Leadership Studies*. Cheltenham: Edward Elgar.

Woo, D. (2000) *Glass Ceiling and Asian Americans: New Face of Workforce Barriers.* Walnut Creek, CA: Alta Mira Press.

Woo, M. (1983) 'Letter to Ma', in Moraga, C. and Anzaldúa, G.E. (eds) *This Bridge Called My Back: Writings by Radical Women of Color.* 2nd edn. New York: Kitchen Table; Women of Color Press, pp 140–147.

Yanco, J.J. (2014) *Misremembering Dr. King: Revisiting the Legacy of Martin Luther King Jr.* Bloomington, IN: Indiana University Press.

Yancy, G. (2012) *Look, a White! Philosophical Essays on Whiteness.* Philadelphia, PA: Temple University Press.

Yancy, G. (2018) *Backlash: What Happens When We Talk Honestly about Racism in America.* Lanham, MD: Rowman & Littlefield.

Yang, S. (2008) 'A process view of wisdom', *Journal of Adult Development,* 15(2), pp 62–75.

Yang, S. (2011) 'Wisdom displayed through leadership: Exploring leadership-related wisdom', *The Leadership Quarterly,* 22(4), pp 616–632.

Ybema, S. and Byun, H. (2009) 'Cultivating cultural differences in asymmetric power relations', *International Journal of Cross Cultural Management,* 9(3), pp 339–358.

Yeh, D. (2014) 'Contesting the "model minority": Racialization, youth culture and "British Chinese"/"Oriental" nights', *Ethnic and Racial Studies,* 37(7), pp 1197–1210.

Yosso, T.J. and García, D.G. (2010) 'From Ms. J. to Ms. G.: Analyzing racial microaggressions in Hollywood's urban school genre', in Frymer, B., Kashani, T., Nocella, A.J. and Van Heertum, R. (eds) *Hollywood's Exploited: Public Pedagogy, Corporate Movies, and Cultural Crisis.* New York: Palgrave Macmillan, pp 85–103.

Yuval-Davis, N. (2006) 'Intersectionality and feminist politics', *European Journal of Women's Studies,* 13(3), pp 193–209.

Zacharek, S., Dockterman, E. and Sweetland Edwards, H. (2017) The silence breakers, *TIME.* Available at: http://time.com/time-person-of-the-year-2017-silence-breakers/ (Accessed: 2 March 2018).

Zanoni, P., Janssens, M., Benschop, Y. and Nkomo, S. (2010) 'Unpacking diversity, grasping inequality: Rethinking difference through critical perspectives', *Organization,* 17(1), pp 9–29.

Index